A Pathway to God's Presence

Published by Christian Art Publishers
PO Box 1599, Vereeniging, 1930, RSA

First edition 2018

Devotions written by Solly Ozrovech

Cover designed by Christian Art Gifts

Images used under license from Shutterstock.com

Set in 12 on 15 pt Palatino LT Std
by Christian Art Publishers

Printed in China

ISBN 978-1-4321-2659-9

18 19 20 21 22 23 24 25 26 27 – 10 9 8 7 6 5 4 3 2 1

Dedicated, in loving appreciation, to
Glen and Esta Harvey with whom
we have shared an exciting part of
our earthly journey.

Before you begin …

Your word is a lamp to guide my feet
and a light for my path.

~ Psalm 119:105

It is of utmost importance with whom you share your pathway of life. Experience has taught me that there is no better traveling companion than Jesus Christ. He guides, and we follow in the light of His kindness and grace.

Every aspect of our lives is enriched and purified by His presence – and we walk in His light for all eternity.

God's grace knows no boundaries.

Soli Deo Gloria.

Contents

January

His light on my path lights up the truth of the Word.

Your Word is a lamp to guide my feet and a light for my path.
~ Ps. 119:105 ~

Where truth goes I will go, and where truth is I will be, and nothing but death shall divide me and the truth.
~ Thomas Brooks ~

Holy God and in Jesus Christ, our Heavenly Father:
We thank You that You made Your will and person known
to us through Your Word and through Your Spirit.
Help us to get to know You better and love You more as
we spend time in Your Word. Jesus, our Savior, we
worship You as the Word Incarnate, sent by the Father
to deliver us from our burden of sin. You came to us as a
reflection of God so that we may love Him and serve Him.
Holy Spirit of God, we praise You as the One who
inspired people to make the Word available to us.
Thank You that You open up and interpret the
Word for us so that we can discover God's purpose with it.
Triune God, we worship You as the God of the Word
and we confess with joy and thankfulness:
Word of God, Word of Life, Word forever firm and true.
Through the unfailing Word of God,
He shows Himself to me and you!
Word we can trust, Word firm and true,
through misjudgment, peril, strife.
What could ever let us tremble?
For in His Word we all have life!

Amen.

To God the Glory and Praise

May you always be filled with the fruit of your salvation – the righteous character produced in your life by Jesus Christ – for this will bring much glory and praise to God (Phil. 1:11).

Most of us have a childlike need to be acknowledged, accepted and even hugged now and then. Sometimes it becomes a *childish* yearning for prominence and fame. Someone said on occasion, "Even the greatest long for a gentle touch."

When writing to the people of Philippi, Paul showered them with praise and appreciation. They made him happy and were his partners in the gospel. God started a good work in them and they had a special place in his heart. His deepest desire was that they would grow to maturity. Everything they had already achieved and everything that was still to happen through their faith and good works dare not make them proud of their spiritual achievements. Their good qualities could be solely attributed to Christ and the Holy Spirit working in them.

A man can no more diminish God's glory by refusing to worship Him than a lunatic can put out the sun by scribbling the word "darkness" on the walls of his cell.
~ C. S. Lewis ~

Don't pursue honor and glory for yourself. Don't strive to see your name prominently displayed when you have done something worthwhile for God. Give God the credit and glory. Be prepared to stand aside and let other people praise God for what He did in and through you. Don't destroy Christ's work by your efforts to turn the spotlight on yourself. Thank the Lord that you were able to be involved and give Him all the honor and glory.

Lord my God, let the glory always go where it is due: to You.

Amen.

Good Can Come from Bad?

I want you to know, my dear brothers and sisters, that everything that has happened to me here has helped to spread the Good News (Phil. 1:12).

When things go wrong in your life, try to remember that often, in some way or another, it happens to all people. The important question is how you react to misfortune, disappointment and frustration. You can become panic-stricken and complain, "This is it; I've had it!" You can wallow in self-pity and say, "Just look what happened to me. Why?" Or you could say, "This is a bit of a problem; let me find a way to turn it into something I can use to my advantage, and to the glory of God."

> If you are not busy lighting candles, don't complain about the darkness.
> ~ Anonymous ~

Paul used his exceptional gifts and intelligence to advance the spread of the gospel of Jesus Christ. He traveled far and wide to preach and establish congregations. It was in fact while he was planning more journeys to spread the Good News that disaster struck. He was arrested and locked up. Did this mean it was the end of his mission? Not at all – he started working from prison. He used his time in jail to evangelize the guards and other prisoners and to write letters that help and guide us to this day. What some people saw as a disaster, Paul changed into an opportunity.

Do not allow misfortune to ruin you. Find a way to use it to your own advantage. Give it some serious thought and ask God in prayer what He is telling you through your misfortune. It isn't just a technique of looking for the silver lining to the dark cloud, but must be seen as something God wants you to grab hold of and use to His honor and glory.

Holy God, open my eyes to spot the opportunities that You hide in my disappointment. Amen.

Forgive and Forget

"I will forgive their wickedness and will never again remember their sins" (Jer. 31:34).

A group of high-spirited students once played a prank on the principal of their college. The principal overreacted and the whole business caused quite an upheaval. Lectures were canceled, there was an emergency staff meeting and punishment was meted out. During the course of the day, the students in question decided to apologize, and asked for a meeting with the principal. After listening to their story and apology, the principal answered, "Gentlemen, I accept your apology and there will be no punishment. The incident will be removed from the record books."

We human beings sometimes find it possible to forgive, but we seldom forget. God both forgives and forgets. God made it possible for the people of Israel to start over by forgiving and forgetting their unfaithfulness and disobedience.

We are certain there is forgiveness, because there is a gospel, and the very essence of the gospel lies in the proclamation of the forgiveness of sin.
~ Charles H. Spurgeon ~

Jesus offers you the same forgiveness. He is ready and waiting to let you start over with no record of past wrongs. If you turn back to Him, repent, confess and decide to break with your wicked ways, He accepts your confession and says, "I will never even give this another thought." The record is blank and He puts your sins behind you forever so that you can move on with a clear conscience. You don't need to feel guilty about anything anymore because you are now in the right relationship with God. You are now free to be a new, mature person "in Christ."

Father God, enable me to follow Your example and to forgive and forget. Amen.

The Lord, the Almighty

The LORD appoints the sun to shine by day, He decrees the moon and stars to shine by night, He stirs up the sea so that its waves roar – the LORD Almighty is His name (Jer. 31:35 NIV).

The most amazing fact in the world is not that God saves, loves and redeems. It is the fact that He *is*. Compared to this small world of space, time, matter and human beings, He is a God of greatness and majesty, of glory and grace.

It was necessary for the Israelites to be reminded of this. They had been conquered by a stronger army and exiled to a miserable existence in a faraway land. There they were forced to serve new masters. It would have been easier for them to give up their faith in God and worship the gods of their Babylonian oppressors; to go with the flow. But Jeremiah confronted them with the fact that their God had always been the Lord, the Almighty; sovereign ruler of the nations and Lord of His entire creation.

Before I begin to think and consider the love of God and the mercy and compassion of God, I must start with the holiness of God.
~ Martyn Lloyd-Jones ~

To this day He is still the Lord, the Almighty. In spite of the increasing confidence of humanity to solve their own problems; in spite of the pressure to be independent of God, they still need God and need to be reminded that He *is*. There is One who is more important, and rises above the daily realities of money, sex, power and human striving, and He rules as the Almighty – superior and mystic. In Christ He saved the human race from their worst misery and misdeeds. He bends down to gain access to your small heart and claim you for Himself. He is the Lord, the Almighty.

Lord, the Almighty, I acknowledge You in Your omnipotence and glory. Amen.

God's Constant Faithfulness

"Just as the heavens cannot be measured and the foundations of the earth cannot be explored, so I will not consider casting them [Israel] away for the evil they have done. I, the LORD, have spoken!" (Jer. 31:37).

Every human has a breaking point. Under a certain amount of pressure you will crack, although the threshold varies from person to person. The interrogation of criminals is meant to "break" people so that they will confess or betray their colleagues. Sometimes it works – then people go back on their loyalties.

God didn't and wouldn't go back on His covenant to love and care for the people of Israel. No human being can measure the heavens, or fathom the depths of the seas, or tear the cloak of mystery from the universe. Since Jeremiah's day, science has expanded the limits of human knowledge immensely, but there are still unexplained mysteries and undetermined borders, which God will reveal to us when we get to heaven.

> God did not call us to be successful but to be faithful.
> ~ Mother Teresa ~

Jesus is constant in His commitment to you, no matter how flawed your commitment to Him might be. He will not disappoint you or let you down. You can fully trust Him. He will be the same tomorrow as He was yesterday and He will stand by you today, whatever happens. No matter to what extent the mysteries of creation might elude human understanding, God's constant faithfulness is no secret and this will never change. Can you say the same about your faithfulness to Him?

Faithful God, make me just as constantly faithful to You as You are to me. Amen.

When God Speaks

"I, the LORD, have spoken!" (Jer. 31:37).

The act of speaking has a variety of qualities and authority, depending on who is doing the talking. Some people talk a lot and say nothing – they simply can't stand keeping quiet. Then there are others who say little, but what they say is regarded as wise and worthwhile. They can make the most profound things seem simple because they are such accomplished communicators.

The Bible creates a deep awareness that God is speaking and that when He speaks He has something very important to say. He spoke during the Creation. He spoke to Moses at the burning bush; to Isaiah in the temple; to Samuel in the sanctuary. He spoke forcefully at the birth of Christ when His Word became flesh.

The Word is the face, the countenance, the representation of God, in whom He is brought to light and made known.
~ Clement of Alexandria ~

In our Scripture passage for today God speaks through the prophet Jeremiah about a covenant of eternal constancy, trustworthiness and grace. It is as if God is saying, "Listen! This is what I want to say to you. This is My promise and when I make a promise I keep it. You can take My word for it."

Jesus is God's Word to us and the entire human race. But sometimes He speaks to you as an individual. He may give an order; or a word of caution and correction. It may be a word of encouragement or comfort, even forgiveness or healing. You cannot force God to speak, but you can be ready to listen when He speaks and then obey Him. Are you ready?

Holy God, make me willing and eager to listen when You speak.
Amen.

Freed from the Ropes of Death

The ropes of death entangled me; floods of destruction swept over me ... But in my distress I cried out to the LORD; yes, I prayed to my God for help. He heard me from His sanctuary; my cry to Him reached His ears (Ps. 18:4, 6).

Many people have near-death experiences. Once they recover, they often forget how close they were to dying. People are attacked by thugs; others are involved in car accidents; sometimes health problems lead to emergency operations that bring patients close to death's door. Even natural disasters can be life-threatening. There are people who manage to survive time after time.

> Men fear death as children fear to go in the dark.
> ~ Francis Bacon ~

David, the writer of Psalm 18, knew what it meant to rub shoulders with death. But he was saved and gave God's love all the credit for his survival. He is saying, "Human existence is an uncertain affair. I survived – but only just! Without God's help I wouldn't have stood a chance. He heard my desperate cry and responded."

Of course we know about many who cried out to God for help in times of tragedy and distress, and died in spite of this. We don't know why God hears the anguished cries of some and not of others. Cry out to Him in your anxiety, and plead with Him to help you. Follow the example of the disciples in the storm on the Sea of Galilee when they thought they were going to die. Then, if you make it and get through the ordeal alive, remember to give the honor and glory to God for His amazing grace.

Thank You, Father God, that You have often heard my anxious cries and saved me from death. Amen.

Majestic and Almighty

Then the earth quaked and trembled. The foundations of the mountains shook; they quaked because of His anger. He opened the heavens and came down (Ps. 18:7, 9).

There are people who say the God they believe in mustn't be a "watered-down" God. A watered-down God is a weak and timid God, and all He expects is that everyone must be friendly and understanding. This is not enough to sustain faith in the face of unbearable suffering in the world today.

David worshiped a revered, majestic and omnipotent God. What David describes in today's Scripture could have been a volcanic eruption or a mighty thunderstorm. One thing that he was certain of was that God was there – controlling it, using it, talking to humankind through it and destroying his enemies in this way. The great truth here is that God will act in order to save His servants.

Even in the church we seem to have lost the vision of the majesty of God.
~ John Stott ~

The same God appears in the New Testament. He is a strong, and at the same time a loving God. He performed mighty miracles and cast evil spirits out. He commanded the wind and the waves. He raised the dead. He came at Pentecost in the form of fire and wind, and forced open the tomb on Easter Sunday. He offers life and salvation to all who believe in Him. He sent His messengers to proclaim the Good News of His kingdom. His followers are so convinced of His glory and omnipotence that they are willing to die for their faith.

Make Him your God, too. He is the true, sovereign and Almighty God.

Lord, my God, I worship You forever in Your majesty and glory.
Amen.

Sometimes Things Go Wrong

If the LORD of Heaven's Armies had not spared a few of us, we would have been wiped out like Sodom, destroyed like Gomorrah (Isa. 1:9).

It is so easy for people of faith to think that everything will always be all right. Except for a few problems, nothing can really go wrong in our lives, because God will not allow it. We can soothe ourselves into a state of false security with this attitude. In our modern day and age we trust scientific wonders to solve our problems. This makes us believe even more strongly that nothing can go wrong. But it can and it does.

In the ancient world, the twin cities, Sodom and Gomorrah, were destroyed – according to the Bible, by God Himself. Isaiah believed that Jerusalem was in just as much danger, but that it was spared by the grace of God. Later on, 85% of the Israelites were sent into exile by the Assyrians. The rest were later taken captive by the Babylonians.

> God created everything out of nothing. Therefore, until man is nothing, God can make nothing out of him.
>
> ~ Martin Luther ~

Certainly, disasters do take place. Millions die in wars; just as many die of poverty-related diseases. Humankind's future is threatened by massive destruction because of climate change and global warming. International tension could easily lead to another world war.

Pray for people in authority. Support organizations that work for peace and the upliftment of the poor. See the necessity of conserving our earth and do your part to make it a reality. Pray to God and plead that He will save us from disaster, and look forward to His kingdom to come.

Creator God, keep me from being complacent and self-assured about Your world. Amen.

What Is God Saying to You?

Hear the word of the LORD, you rulers of Sodom; listen to the instruction of our God, you people of Gomorrah! (Isa.1:10 NIV).

When strange things happen to us, we sometimes say, "Somewhere in this there must be a lesson for me." Indeed, the wise find that life teaches them lessons throughout their lives. Whether they take notice of this or learn from it is quite a different matter.

It is perhaps not strange that the ancient Hebrews thought of God as a Teacher. They even knew the Ten Commandments He gave them to obey as "The Teachings." Obeying these commandments was learning to be obedient.

The teaching of Christ is more excellent than all the advice of the saints, and he who has Christ's spirit within will find in it a hidden strength.
~ Thomas à Kempis~

God's Son, Jesus Christ, was often referred to as Rabbi or Teacher. His ministry on earth was teaching people about the Kingdom of God. Jesus' teachings, many of them in the form of stories and parables, are some of the most unforgettable things we will ever hear or learn.

What is God's message for you? You should make it a lifelong task to learn more and more about God. Ask yourself: What is God doing through me by means of this incident? What does the Bible say about this? How is He using these circumstances to show me a better way? You will discover so many interesting, life-changing things that will magnify and deepen your faith and wisdom. Don't ever stop learning from the Great Teacher.

Teacher of life, teach me more and more every day. Amen.

Holy! Holy! Holy!

They were calling out to each other, "Holy, holy, holy is the LORD of Heaven's Armies!" (Isa. 6:3).

The word *holy* is a word that many people find difficult to accommodate. We speak of the Pope as the Holy Father. In a moment of great astonishment we sometimes say, "Holy mackerel!" We snidely refer to someone who parades his virtues as a "Holy Joe" or we say he has a "holier than thou" attitude.

Isaiah emphasized more than anyone else that only God is holy. He detested the corruption, sin, unrighteousness and faithlessness. When Isaiah referred to God's holiness he meant that God was "different." He rose above weakness and impurity. Habakkuk said to God, "Your eyes are too pure to look on evil; You cannot tolerate wrong. Why then do You tolerate the treacherous? Why are You silent while the wicked swallow up those more righteous than themselves?" (Hab. 1:13 NIV). It is because of His holiness that God hates sin. When Isaiah chronicled that the seraphs called out "Holy" three times, it was to emphasize and underline God's holiness. It was to bring home to those who listened to him preach that God does not tolerate the wickedness of the people.

True love to God must begin with a delight in His holiness, and not with a delight in any other attribute; for no other attribute is truly lovely without this.
~ Jonathan Edwards ~

We see holy love in Christ, not just goodness and ordinary love, but the holy love of the Holy God. It is an exceptional kind of love that comes *from* God and creates love *for* God. This is why it is godly love instead of human warmth and kindness. Jesus calls on us to love in the holy or godly way that He loved.

Holy Spirit of God, enable me to respect God's holiness. Amen.

Where Is God's Glory?

The whole earth is filled with His glory (Isa. 6:3).

At first it may seem strange to think that God is majestic, mystical and "completely different." After all, doesn't He reveal Himself in Jesus Christ? Isn't He revealing Himself all the time in the beauty of nature, and the miracle of human life that is filled with grace and empowerment through His Spirit?

In Isaiah's vision the angels surrounding the throne sang about two things: Some called out, "Holy, holy, holy!" Others called out, "The whole earth is filled with His glory!" This response sings the praises of a God that emerges from His sanctuary – if we might put it this way – and makes very clear what, and who, and wherever He is. This is the aspect of God that we can see, know, appreciate and respond to. We may ask, "Where is God?" One answer is, "He is a hidden mystery whom we will never fully know." But another is, "He is in a rose in all its splendor and glory; in a breathtaking sunset; in the overwhelming grandeur of majestic mountains."

> The radiance of the divine beauty is wholly inexpressible: words cannot describe it, nor the ear grasp it.
> ~ Philimon ~

You sense the glory of God and catch hold of it when you gaze in awe at His presence in nature and the work of His hands in a life totally devoted to love and service. Therefore, admire God's beauty around you – not just for a fleeting moment – absorb it and allow it to fill you with wonderment. Join in with the universal chorus that praises Him, and in which nature, humans and angels all take part.

Creator God, the whole earth is filled with Your glory! Amen.

Spiritual Qualifications

Yet I have seen the King, the LORD of Heaven's Armies (Isa. 6:5).

Endless discussions take place in Christian circles on the qualities and qualifications necessary for people who have to take leadership positions in groups or congregations. Various systems are used to train people in providing effective spiritual guidance to Christian communities.

Isaiah's vision and calling show us the three fundamental qualifications. First, he had a vision of God. He could say, "Yet I have seen the King, the Lord of Heaven's Armies." Direct knowledge of God in which the person involved knows without a doubt that he met with God, is decisive.

Secondly, Isaiah saw himself exposed in all his human weakness, fallibility and sinfulness. A crucial part of spiritual leadership is realistic self-conviction and the consciousness of human weakness.

Thirdly, Isaiah knew that he had been forgiven and accepted by God. He could go to the people with self-confidence that was not born of his own achievements and competence, but of humility that came from the knowledge that he was dependent on God's grace. He would serve, knowing that he was nothing in himself and that God was everything.

Don't ask for an easier life; ask to be a stronger person. Sometimes you just have to take a leap, and build your wins on the way down.
~ Kobi Yamada ~

Whoever is a servant of the Lord, or wishes to be His servant, needs this inner equipment. You must meet God face to face, and know that God has accepted you in spite of all your weaknesses. These are the qualities every Christian believer should work on.

Father, allow me to see You often and to know that You hold me close and want to use me. Amen.

Touched and Purified

> Then one of the seraphim flew to me with a burning coal he had taken from the altar with a pair of tongs. He touched my lips with it and said, "See, this coal has touched your lips. Now your guilt is removed, and your sins are forgiven" (Isa. 6:6-7).

It is no secret that human beings have disappointed God since the beginning of time with their sinful weaknesses. On top of it, their sin causes a tremendous abyss between God and them. The desire to have our sins removed is an exercise that all religions share. The big question is: How should it be done and who must do it? Many people agonize about their guilt and go to extremes to get rid of it.

> The glory of Christianity is to conquer by forgiveness.
> ~ William Blake ~

Isaiah was overwhelmed by his feeling of guilt. But he would soon discover the solution. There was no profound ritual that had to be performed or fine that had to be paid, no formula or words to be chanted. The confession of his sin was as far as he could take the matter. Then God took over and forgave him. In the temple, where sensational offerings were normally sacrificed to atone for sin, no offering was required. God used one of the seraphs who simply touched his impure lips and he was purified. All Isaiah had to do was to be aware of this and accept God's act of love.

If feelings of guilt happen to be your problem, come to Jesus and let Him touch you. You can't cleanse or forgive yourself – only Jesus Christ can do that. If you want to be healed and need to be spiritually equipped to serve Him better, surrender yourself to His purifying and healing action.

Merciful Father, through Jesus Christ purify me, heal and forgive me so that I may serve You better. Amen.

The Source of Praise

From You comes the theme of my praise in the great assembly (Ps. 22:25 NIV).

What do you praise the Lord for and how do you do it? When someone has performed a heroic deed, or created an astonishing work of art or a magnificent woodcarving, we praise them by telling them how exceptional they are.

Some people can't tell the difference between thanking God and praising Him. We *thank* Him for what He has done for us: for the fact that He gave us life; for the beauty of the world around us; for specific things He gives us, like the rain, for healing, for a safe journey; or for obtaining a job. We *praise* Him for who and what He is. We praise Him because He created the universe; because He rules in glory; because He is the Savior and Helper of those who look up to Him; because He empowers us through His Spirit.

My highest purpose is to glorify God!
~ St. Augustine ~

In Psalm 22, something very important comes to the fore. David is so happy that God carried him through his trials that he states that God is the one who gives him the theme for his praise: "From You comes the theme of my praise." In other words, when David praises God, it is God who gives him the gift of praise.

God lifts him out of his own foolish and inadequate words and gives him the ideas, words and theme to praise Him. Even the praise we bring the Lord is a gift from Him. If you find it difficult to praise God, pray that He will give you this gift.

I want to praise You, Lord; praise You with all my heart! Amen.

Do You Keep Your Promises?

I will fulfill my vows in the presence of those who worship You (Ps. 22:25).

Years ago there was a politician who became known as "Piet Promises." He was given this nickname because he always promised to solve the country's problems, but never delivered. Many people are like this. It's easy enough to say what you will do something, but much more difficult to put your words into action.

God set David, the psalmist, free from suffering and misery and David wanted to do something big to celebrate his healing. He would go to the temple and bring an offering to God to thank Him for His grace and mercy. Words alone were not enough for the Israelites. You had to praise and thank God with a gift worthy of Him; a gift that cost you something. When everybody saw David doing this, they would be satisfied that he gave God the honor and that he fulfilled the vows he made to God.

Every promise God has ever made finds its fulfillment in Jesus.
~ Joni Eareckson Tada ~

At some time or another, all of us make promises to God. Perhaps you made a vow to love Him dearly, to serve Him devotedly, to worship Him only, to always put Him first in your life, to give up your previous sinful life. It is likely that you made these vows while you were riding the wave of enthusiasm and emotion. How successful were you in keeping your promises? It is all very well to promise God these things, but it is much better to make sure all your plans, vows and dreams lead to positive action.

Lord Jesus, I promised to serve You to the end. Enable me to do this through Your Spirit. Amen.

A Lack of Love

Everyone who sees me mocks me. They sneer and shake their heads saying, "Is this the one who relies on the LORD? Then let the LORD save him! If the LORD loves him so much, let the LORD rescue him!" (Ps. 22:7-8).

When someone is seriously ill, we think of it as a terrible trial. But emotional and spiritual suffering is worse. We experience emotional suffering when someone betrays or rejects us. We may feel that God has deserted us.

This is just what happened to the writer of today's Scripture. It was bad enough coping with sickness. It was a terrible feeling that God had forsaken him. But when his so-called friends mocked him because he trusted God, it was too much. In their opinion, the only reason why people believed in God was to have someone to help them when they were in trouble. So they ridiculed him and this made his suffering even harder to bear. The words and attitude of his friends showed a total lack of love.

> I have held many things in my hands, and I have lost them all; but whatever I have placed in God's hands, that I still possess.
> ~ Corrie ten Boom ~

When you are seriously ill, some of your "Christian" friends will probably tell you that your condition is caused by a lack of faith. Jesus suffered – and He definitely didn't lack faith in His Father. Others might say that you must have done something terrible to suffer God's wrath in this way. Both wicked and good people suffer. Don't allow anyone to add spiritual suffering to your physical pain by planting seeds of doubt in your mind that your faith is not strong enough. Ignore them and hold on to Jesus through good times and bad.

Lord Jesus, hold me through my dark days and help me to trust You at all times. Amen.

Back to the Start

You brought me safely from my mother's womb and led me to trust You at my mother's breast. I was thrust into Your arms at my birth. You have been my God from the moment I was born (Ps. 22:9-10).

As human beings, we don't live in the present only. With the help of our memories we can recall the past, and sometimes adapt it to remember things the way we would have wanted them to be. We can also look at the future and dream about things we hope will happen – or fear what lies ahead. We carry our past along with us and sometimes also our future.

The God of the Christians is a God of love and consolation; a God who fills the soul and the heart which He possesses.
~ Blaise Pascal ~

We sometimes get a better perspective on the present by going back to the past. This is what David did in this Scripture. He went as far back as his birth. His life had not always been as hard. When he reflected on it, he remembered how God had helped him since birth. In truth, the very fact that he existed was God's will. Looking back, he knew that his whole existence was God's work. There was more to life than his suffering at the time.

If you are going through a difficult time, do what David did. Look back to the very beginning, to God who created everything and who brought you into this world in His own good time. He was even with you in your mother's womb and has journeyed with you through all the years. When you were in the depths of despair, He gave you the strength to carry on. When you fell, He picked you up – and He will do it again and again! Praise the Lord because He is good!

Thank You, Creator Father, that You are always there for me, all the years of my life. Amen.

Set Apart by God

"I knew you before I formed you in your mother's womb. Before you were born I set you apart and appointed you as My prophet to the nations" (Jer. 1:5).

Do you know any prophets? Some people see things so distinctly, analyze them so correctly and wisely that they speak with authority to those listening to them. Some secular writers, poets and playwrights speak prophetically to the people of their generation. Sometimes God might speak through them, as well as through people He calls to be His servants.

Jeremiah was set apart by God as His "prophet to the nations". His message was not mainly for individuals, but for Israel as a nation. This reminds us that God sometimes uses individuals to address an entire nation, and sometimes even all of humanity, or the world. Jeremiah watched the course of great empires of his time and saw the hand of God in all that happened.

Not everyone speaking in the Spirit is a prophet, but only if he should have a lifestyle of the Lord's character.
~ The Didache ~

God still rules over the nations of the world and He works in the wide-ranging activities of humanity, no matter how inconspicuous He sometimes chooses to be. If we want to know where He is at work and in which direction He is leading humanity, we need prophets to explain this to us. Without them we would probably stay just where we are. And we might not notice what God is doing, like the people in Jeremiah's time. Listen to God's prophets. Hear what God is saying through them and determine how and where He is at work among the nations of the world.

Raise up Your prophets, O God, so that they may tell us Your will for us. Amen.

The Sovereign Lord!

"O Sovereign LORD," I said, "I can't speak for You! I'm too young!" (Jer. 1:6).

During the Second World War, a campaign was launched to recruit people for the U. S. Army. The image of a well-known military chief was displayed on posters all over the country, pointing his index finger straight at you. The words at the bottom read, "Your country needs you!" It addressed everyone reading the poster. Every citizen knew that his country needed him.

This was the case with Jeremiah. He served the king of Israel but responded to God's command by addressing Him as "Sovereign Lord"! He knew that he was a subject of a much mightier king than the one who was king over Israel. The earthly king had the power to recruit people for military service or demand that people pay taxes.

The Higher Authority calls on Jeremiah to take up a prophetic ministry. He does so because He is much more than just a friend, a shepherd or someone to help in need. He is more than a rock and a refuge. He is the Sovereign Lord who calls, equips and sends out His servants. If you respond to this call, you join a royal service. It is giving up your right to rule and surrendering to the highest authority in the universe. Jeremiah did it and you are called to follow suit.

The Lord doesn't ask about your ability, only your availability; and, if you prove your dependability, the Lord will increase your capability.
~ Anonymous ~

Lord, today we pray that You will empower those You call and who hear Your voice, to say, "Here I am Lord. I will go!" Amen.

The Second Coming

I want you to understand what really matters, so that you may live pure and blameless lives until the day of Christ's return (Phil. 1:10).

When we talk about the distant past, we say, "In days gone by." When we talk about an indefinite future, we say, "Till kingdom come."

The early Christians lived in an up-to-the-minute consciousness and strong conviction that Christ would come again any day. As a result, all planning was short-term. We might have lost much of that urgency as time passed, but we still believe that Christ will come again – we just don't know when. This means that it could even be today or tomorrow. Christians live with the conviction that the end of all things is in God's omniscient hands and that we have limited time ahead of us.

Paul pleaded with his Christian friends to be ready for Christ's second coming. Because God could call them to account for their lives, they had to live "pure and blameless" lives. One of the qualities they would need to make sure of this was not only to keep themselves pure, but also that they wouldn't cause anyone to stumble. This meant that they would be pure, but not in such a self-righteous way that they would frighten others off with their "goodness." Their pure lives were to be acceptable and not hypocritical.

> We must never speak to simple, excitable people about "the Day" without emphasizing again and again the utter impossibility of prediction.
> ~ C. S. Lewis ~

Whenever you are tempted to do something wrong, always look ahead. "What would happen if Christ would find me involved in this?" Remember that God always brings the future to the present and we must be ready.

Lord Jesus, grant that I will be ready for Your second coming and that I will look forward to it. Amen.

Use Time Wisely

I want you to understand what really matters, so that you may live pure and blameless lives until the day of Christ's return. May you always be filled with the fruit of your salvation (Phil. 1:10-11).

There is an old saying, "The devil makes work for idle hands." This is so true. Spiritually, you are most vulnerable when you have nothing or little to do.

Paul reminded the Christians of Philippi of this and made use of their willingness to be his partners. He encouraged them to spread the gospel. The fact that Paul was in prison when he wrote this letter doesn't mean that they could be less zealous, or that they should do nothing until he was set free.

> Temptation usually comes in through a door that has deliberately been left open.
> ~ Anonymous ~

Christians often think they are helpless when the leader of their group is not present. Nothing is further from the truth. Idle time is dangerous. If they would occupy themselves with good deeds, there wouldn't be any time left for mischief and wickedness.

Paul's advice is just as valid today. If you forge ahead, helping others, you will have no time to get involved in sinful things. You won't moan and complain either – something we tend to get better at the older we get and the more prosperous we are! Christ expects you to be busy. He wants you to work together in building the Christian community; passing on the faith to others; ministering to those who struggle; walking alongside those who mourn.

Holy Spirit of God, fill me with usefulness so that I will have no time for evil. Amen.

Just a Man

You, a mere man, claim to be God (John 10:33).

In the Andrew Lloyd Webber show *Jesus Christ Superstar,* Mary Magdalene sings, referring to Jesus, "He is but a man. And I have had so many men before." Obviously this is what the world thinks of Jesus: He is only human after all; a good man, but we have had good men before and we will have them again.

When Jesus came, the people divided into two groups. There were those who thought He was just an ordinary human being, and those who saw much more in Him.

This second group saw God in Jesus. They saw Him in things Jesus did, the truths that He taught, the love that He shared and the way in which He died. They also noticed this in the impact He had on their lives. There was depth and height, hope and joy that they never knew before. God was visiting with them in the form of Jesus.

> If ever a man was God,
> or God was a man,
> Jesus was both.
> ~ Lord Byron ~

Thus Jesus comes to you through the ages, there in your own small private world. He asks if He is merely human, an ordinary mortal, or the Lord God in human form. If you decide on the first choice you will stay "only human," an ordinary mortal forever. But find God in Him, your Redeemer and your Savior, and your life will be raised to a level that will make others wonder about the astounding things God can do in the lives of ordinary people.

Lord Jesus, I worship You as my Redeemer and Savior; the God of my life. Amen.

Set Apart by the Father

"Why do you call it blasphemy when I say, 'I am the Son of God?' After all, the Father set Me apart and sent Me into the world" (John 10:36).

Some countries concluded that sport was of crucial importance to their national image. In order to develop the best sportsmen and -women, to reach the highest standards they target athletes at an early age. Then they send them to academies to be trained by the best coaches. Such potential stars are "set apart" and prepared for great things.

God did something similar – especially in the Bible. He chose, and set apart, certain people to be His chosen instruments; He would use them to help achieve His goal of bringing hope, healing and wholeness to all of humanity. This "setting apart" is called "sanctification" (to make holy). Jesus knew that God the Father set Him apart and sanctified Him as Savior and to be His Son. Jesus was not set apart *from* the world. He was set apart *in* the world, to be God's special envoy *for* the world.

I have a great need for Christ, I have a great Christ for my need.
~ Charles H. Spurgeon ~

He has always been God's representative for you. His ministry is for the whole world, but He also has a special ministry to you. You are His follower and friend and He is with you through whatever problems or victories you may have. He is the person that God set apart to be there for you; to help you as you wrestle with faith; in your suffering and successes. Because He lived in the world of labor, strife and pain Himself, it is possible for Him to instruct you to stay on the right path.

I praise and thank You, Lord Jesus, that You were set apart by God for my benefit and that of the whole world. Amen.

The King of Israel

Praise God! Blessings on the one who comes in the name of the LORD! Hail to the King of Israel! (John 12:13).

In some countries, people idolize their heads of state. This is encouraged by the media and sometimes even becomes a kind of cult. There are leaders who have their photos displayed all over and this contributes to the atmosphere of glory that surrounds them.

The Israelites also idolized some of their leaders. In Jesus' time, the Roman Emperor was considered a god, like the other gods they worshiped. After all the miracles Jesus performed, the people of His day thought that He would become the new king of Israel. They hoped that He would help them cast off the Roman yoke and replace Caesar. For this reason, they made use of His visit to Jerusalem to honor Him as king in public.

Christ is not valued at all, unless He is valued above all.
~ St. Augustine ~

He was King indeed, but another kind of king. Don't make the mistake of idolizing your king or president. Human rulers come, have their day, and then disappear from the scene. Some of them even do good things. All of them make mistakes. Jesus, however, is forever. He reigns over an extended kingdom of people all over the world and from all nations. They have complete trust in Him and to them He gives meaning to life.

To them His Word is law and His method is love. He is the Light in their darkness, the Truth in their confusion, their Hope in desperate times, their Joy in sorrow. He brings peace in their turbulent lives and order in their chaos. No human ruler is honored to this extent. This is the Jesus that you owe your loyalty and love to.

Heavenly King, lead the rulers of countries where there is unrest and confusion. Amen.

Pomp and Ceremony

Don't be afraid, people of Jerusalem. Look, your King is coming, riding on a donkey's colt (John 12:15).

When high society is involved in public pomp and ceremony, money is no object in making sure the most expensive vehicle is used to transport them. A large number of VIPs accompany them, and as protection for these prominent people, those in charge of security make sure that their presence is clearly visible. Then there is still the publicity and media to cover the event. The more prestigious the person, the greater the spectacle.

When Jesus decided to enter Jerusalem, however, He chose a donkey's colt to ride on. Normally, when kings or emperors made a triumphal entrance, they used horses. It was a sign of nobility, authority and victory. A donkey, being a somewhat humble creature, was the symbol of peace. Later, when the disciples thought about this, they recalled verses in the Old Testament that predicted such an event.

Christ's character was more wonderful than the greatest miracle.
~ Alfred Tennyson ~

Jesus changed the normal manner of human conduct. He was not interested in prestige, publicity or pomp and ceremony. It wasn't necessary for Him to impress anybody.

Think about the way you do things. Are you concerned with the impression you create in the minds of those who see you? If so, remember that the only One who really needs to know you and see what you do, is God. He sees deep into your inner being and is not impressed by show and publicity. Jesus did everything in a simple and humble manner. We would do well to take a leaf out of His book.

Lord Jesus, enable me through Your Spirit to do things in Your perfect way. Amen.

A Home for the Sun

God has made a home in the heavens for the sun. It bursts forth like a radiant bridegroom after his wedding. It rejoices like a great athlete eager to run the race (Ps. 19:4-5).

Every evening, thousands of people wait for the weather forecast on TV, to see what influence the sun will have on their plans for the following day. It's not surprising that people worshiped the sun in days gone by, because it dominated such a great part of their lives. Now that we are more knowledgeable, we are aware of the extent of our dependence on the energy, warmth, light and rays that the sun provides.

The people of the Bible knew better. It was not the sun behind the meaning of life – it was the Creator of the sun. Beyond the sun there was – and still is – a Creator God. No physical part of the universe is God; neither are all the parts of the physical universe put together a manifestation of God. (This religion is known as Pantheism). No. God is totally different from creation. Everything in creation was put into place by God. It functions on His command and in accordance with His wisdom and plan. "God has made a home in the heavens for the sun" is David's way of saying that even the sun is inferior to God. Appreciate God's creation. Rejoice in it. Honor and love God who created it all.

No philosophical theory which I have yet come across is a radical improvement on the words of Genesis that, "in the beginning God made heaven and earth."
~ C. S. Lewis ~

Lord, my God, how great is Your name over the entire earth!

Amen.

Wholesome Thinking

This is my second letter to you, dear friends, and in both of them I have tried to stimulate your wholesome thinking and refresh your memory (2 Pet. 3:1).

Not all thinking that takes place in Christian circles today is altogether clear or wholesome. Sometimes people choose a specific kind of spiritual experience because many believe in it. At other times, irrational fear mounts because of this experience. Some of the current religions do not have a truly biblical origin. Superstition sometimes sneaks into our thinking.

The early Christians were convinced that Jesus would return in their lifetime. When some died and it still hadn't happened, it posed a problem for those who remained. Would Jesus ever come? Peter wanted to bring about calm and wisdom in these circumstances. His task was to lead people to green pastures and give them wholesome spiritual nourishment.

> The greatest vicissitude of things amongst men is the vicissitudes of sects and religions.
> ~ Francis Bacon ~

Make sure that you attend healthy teaching regularly, as it will stimulate wholesome thinking and good practices. Always ask if the teachings are in line with the comprehensive message of the Bible.

Do the congregants understand what they are being taught? Were the instructors delegated to do the job by a recognized Christian church or religious body? Does their teaching spur you on to spiritual growth or does it leave you more confused? Does it give Jesus all the glory or does it lead you into a dead-end street? If a new movement proclaims new ideas, are they truly Christian or is the main aim to make money?

Lord, lead me through the Spirit to the right teachings that are wholesome and clear. Amen.

God's Covenant

"I will make a covenant with you, by which I will guarantee to give you countless descendants" (Gen. 17:2).

In today's world, a covenant takes on many forms. Marriage is one and so is a legal contract; employment is another; the buying and selling of goods or services also involve a covenant. Some friendships have become so strong that it could be said that they are a covenant of mutual help and support.

There are three types of covenants or commitments in the Bible. The first is a one-sided covenant in which one party makes a covenant with another. The second is where one party demands a commitment from the other. In the third, both parties agree to a commitment. When God made His covenant with Abraham, it was the first type of covenant. It was not a matter of "I will, if you agree." God presented His covenant to Abraham. God made it, and by making it He called on Abraham to respond to it and submit to it in obedience.

Walk so close to God that nothing can come between you.
~ Joseph Addison ~

When Christ called you to be His disciple, He called you to become part of His covenant. Just as God promised Abraham many descendants, Jesus offers you His salvation, His love, His consolation and His hope. You may also make *your* covenant with Him by obeying Him, loving Him, glorifying Him and serving Him. Thus you hand complete control over to Him and you promise to serve Him through thick and thin, no matter what it takes and how difficult that task might be.

Lord Jesus, I promised to serve You until the end. Give me the grace to follow You as my Master and my Friend until the very end. Amen.

God's Presence

At this, Abram fell face down in the dust. Then God said to him, "This is My covenant with you" (Gen. 17:3-4).

There are people who speak with familiarity about God, as if their relationship with Him is one of friendship: "I didn't know if I should give my wife a book or a voucher, so I said, 'Lord, what do You think she'll like?'" One could be forgiven for thinking that these people see God as a voice on the other side of a spiritual cell phone.

Abraham didn't respond to God's declaration by saying, "That's fine with me, Lord. From now on we walk together, hand in hand." He knew that he was in the presence of the Almighty, Sovereign, Holy God. Abraham didn't jump up and down with joy; he didn't shout it from the rooftops; he didn't burst into song. He fell on his face in reverence for God, in speechless worship; in this way acknowledging that God is the Sovereign Authority in the universe. This response was also an indication that he submitted himself to God and to God's covenant; that he accepted God's will without question.

The perfect church service would be one we were almost unaware of; our attention would have been focused on God.
~ C. S. Lewis ~

The Almighty God is not a pocket-god – something you keep in your pocket and take out when you have no one else to talk to. He is the Creator God, our Heavenly Father; King of kings; Savior of humanity. Be humble and respectful and react to His commands with worship and submission.

The Lord is in His Holy temple. Let all the earth be silent before Him (Hab. 2:20). Amen.

You Are the Message

Here am I, and the children the LORD has given me. We are signs and symbols in Israel from the LORD Almighty (Isa. 8:18 NIV).

Some years ago, one of the great Christian preachers died at a relatively young age: Dr Will Sangster. He inspired large crowds with his preaching and many of his sermons appeared in book form. Thousands of people flocked to his meetings to hear the Word of God. After his death, his son wrote his life story. One of the remarkable things that impressed his son was that close to 1, 400 people wrote to his widow after his death. A thousand of them did not mention the major sermons that had inspired them, but some insignificant act of love and compassion that had touched them. Brilliant as his sermons were, the person himself was a resounding message of God to others.

It is better to live for God than to be perpetually talking about Him.
~ Anonymous ~

Isaiah means "The Lord will save." Sear-Jasub means "A remnant will return." Maher-Shalal-Hash-Bas means "Swift to plunder and quick to spoil." These were the names of Isaiah and his children, and Isaiah knew that he *and* his children were messengers of God. Irrespective of whether the king or the people wanted to listen to what they had to say, God spoke in any case through His presence in their midst. The prophet knew this and he also knew that it was even more important for him to live close to God so that the mission of his life – to direct people to God – would be effective.

You and I are also messengers of God. If you believe in Jesus and follow Him, you convey a message. It is not necessary to speak about religion all the time. However, make sure you pass on the message that God entrusted you with.

Lord Jesus, grant that I will be Your trustworthy messenger.

Amen.

February

His light on my path gives me confidence.

Because of His grace He declares us righteous and gave us confidence.
~ Titus 3:7 ~

Confidence in God's grace and knowledge of it makes men glad and bold and happy.
~ Martin Luther ~

Gracious God and in Jesus Christ,
our heavenly Father: You are the Source
of every precious moment we are given in life.
Already one month of the new year has
passed like a fleeting thought,
and I must confess in shame as I stand before You,
that I am guilty of allowing the chances
and opportunities You offered me to pass by.
So much that I wanted to do,
and so many noble resolutions fell by the wayside:
prayer time in conversation with You to strengthen my faith;
Bible study to know Your will for my life;
reflecting on Your greatness and omnipotence
and the wonder of Your creation;
fellowship with You and Your other children;
meaningful churchgoing for spiritual depth and growth;
willingness to freely give my love to others.
Thank You that You are a patient and merciful Gardener;
that You forgive time and time again,
and give me the strength to stay
on the road of victory.
Help me to make optimal use of this month,
and the rest of my life;
that I will love You more;
follow where You lead;
serve You with more faithfulness!
O God, who creates and restores, renew me and lead me through
Your Holy Spirit on the path that Jesus prepared for me.
I thankfully pray this in Jesus' name.

Amen.

Where God Reigns

Even the hotheads will be full of sense and understanding. Those who stammer will speak out plainly (Isa. 32:4).

The issue of poor rulers is not the only thing that affects our sense of right or wrong. There are people around us with disabilities and inabilities. Some are blind, others stammer and yet others have mental impairments. When we meet such a person, or know one, we might feel that life is unfair and even wonder why God allows it.

The writers of the Bible clearly thought this was an abnormality that was not in keeping with God's plan for complete perfection. The prophets refused to despair. They argued that if things were not like they were supposed to be, God would intervene in His time and put everything right. That's why they dreamt of a golden age in the future where there would be peace, a good government, prosperity rather than poverty on earth, and that physically, all people would be perfect. God would make all these things happen when He came to rule over the universe as the one sovereign, unquestionable King.

God can give only according to His might; therefore He always gives more than we ask for.
~ Martin Luther ~

It might sound like wishful thinking to talk about a perfect world. Don't be too quick to brush aside this thought. Jesus Christ taught us to pray for it: "Let Your Kingdom come! Let Your will be done on earth as it is in heaven." Dreaming and praying about it awakens hope in our hearts. And when we hope for it, we declare that God will make these things happen on earth one day. We hope and pray that He will.

Lord Jesus, we pray for all people with disabilities. Speed up the discovery of the means to make life more bearable for them.

Amen.

Prosperity and Abundance

Until at last the Spirit is poured out on us from heaven. Then the wilderness will become a fertile field, and the fertile field will yield bountiful crops (Isa. 32:15).

Most people dream about riches and luxury. They enter competitions with fabulous prizes, they buy lottery tickets, they purchase shares that they hope will rise sky-high, or they bet on the horses. They think their problems will be something of the past if they could only make more money. Some people are stuck with the consequences of these empty dreams for the rest of their lives – even if they possess enough to live comfortably.

> There is nothing wrong with people possessing riches. The wrong comes when riches possess people.
> ~ Billy Graham ~

In the Bible there is also a dream of wealth and luxury. It is the same as the dream of righteousness, peace and healed bodies. We read that it will happen when God pours out His Spirit over us. God's dream of prosperity is not that of incredible wealth in the hands of a privileged few, but an abundance of food so that everyone is nourished. God rejoices in human undertakings that flourish, especially if everyone benefits from it.

In the south of Israel, the desert is thriving where the abundant waters of the Galilean hills are canalized to the Negev desert. Farming is flourishing there, and in many parts of the world where relevant engineering is used, the sources of nature are being developed to the advantage of humankind.

Christians will hope, pray and work for a world in which there is enough for everybody. For this reason, they pray that the Spirit of God will act and bring about abundance as well as spiritual enrichment for all.

Lord of creation, let the time come when all people will have enough to eat and there won't be famine anymore. Amen.

Oversensitive

"Remain in Me, and I will remain in you. For a branch cannot produce fruit if it is severed from the vine, and you cannot be fruitful apart from Me" (John 15:4).

Perhaps you are one of those unfortunate people who go through life and are very easily hurt. Perhaps you are so sensitive about what others say and think about you that your whole life has become nothing but continuous misery. If you allow this condition to continue, it could seriously affect your mental and spiritual health. What a challenging thought that this is your own responsibility.

God gave you the responsibility of choice. You choose your thoughts and attitudes yourself, and you determine whether you will live on the mountain peaks of hope or in the valleys of despair. You might think these conditions are created by circumstances or your specific situation, but on a much deeper level it is the power of your own thoughts that shape you into what you are.

Good and evil both increase at compound interest. That is why the little decisions you and I make every day are of such infinite importance.
~ C. S. Lewis ~

This thought can be overwhelming if it isn't colored by the awareness of a Higher Authority. As it is possible for your thoughts to control your actions, it is also possible for the Spirit of Christ to control your thoughts. When you welcome the Spirit into every part of your life, He takes control of your thinking and you discover that the petty things that hurt you, don't have the power to harm you anymore. Christ's Spirit inside you is bigger than any influence or insult.

Dear Savior, because You are in me, I am able to meet and overcome all negative and evil forces. Amen.

Temptation

If you think you are standing strong, be careful not to fall (1 Cor. 10:12).

Nobody is safe against temptation. As you grow in the Christian faith, your confidence also grows, and eventually you think nothing can disturb your spiritual balance. This is an extremely dangerous way of thinking. If you think the fact that you are a devoted Christian exempts you from temptation, watch out, because that is the forerunner of being caught in the snare of pride.

The way to feel secure in the Christian life, and live it triumphantly, is to focus your thoughts and spirit on the Living Christ. There are subtle temptations you cannot overcome in your own strength. If you are more self-confident than Christ-confident, you are certainly heading for a fall.

Little by little, with patience and fortitude and with the help of God, you will sooner overcome temptations than with your own strength and persistence.
~ Thomas à Kempis ~

The Spirit of Christ reveals the subtlety of temptation. When you come face to face with temptation, you might become weak and find a good reason to give in to it. Don't try to resist temptation in your own strength, but appeal to the Living Christ to stand by you and guide you. Temptation will back away from His truth and protective love.

The Holy Spirit of God will reveal the destructive power and foulness of sin to you and enable you to discern between truth and lies. He will give you the wisdom and ability to avoid and resist it.

Through the guidance of Your Holy Spirit, Holy Master, I am able to resist temptation. Amen.

To Whom Do You Belong?

When I discovered Your words, I devoured them. They are my joy and my heart's delight, for I bear Your name, O LORD God of Heaven's Armies (Jer. 15:16).

Many military commanding officers enjoyed widespread recognition for their ability to command their troops. Just think of Pompey, Alexander, Napoleon, Wellington and Eisenhower, to name only a few. The infantrymen were proud to be called "Wellington-men" or "Napoleon-men," and so forth.

Jeremiah admitted that God was superior to all the gods and he often used the name "Lord, God Almighty." The name is of military origin and is often translated as "Lord of Hosts," the hosts being the soldiers. When a war is waged today, a general is appointed over all the others. He is known as the commander in chief. To Jeremiah, the God of Israel was the commander in chief and he was extremely proud to be on the Lord's side. He belonged to the Lord, the Commander in Chief not only of Israel, but the Almighty over all people.

A man with God is always in the majority.
~ Inscription on Reformation Monument, Geneva ~

You have a choice who you want to belong to. You can be satisfied with a lesser god, but if you are, you will be on the losing side. It would be better to join the army of the greatest Commander in Chief of all time. He has a perfect strategy, a master plan and the hosts He commands are always victorious. Only He knows exactly how strong the enemy is, but He is not impressed by it. He knows that He can appeal to faithful soldiers – not only all over the world, but also to a host of invisible spiritual warriors who serve Him. His cause is just, His weapons are love and sacrifice and His final victory is certain.

Thank You, Jesus, that I may belong to You, now and forever.

Amen.

When the Spring Goes Dry

Why then does my suffering continue? Why is my wound so incurable? Your help seems as uncertain as a seasonal brook, like a spring that has gone dry (Jer. 15:18).

When a water supply pipe in a big city breaks, it causes chaos and panic. For a few short hours the taps are dry and all the activities in the city are disrupted. Telephone lines are overloaded by anxious and furious people. When the wells in rural areas dry up, life is made very difficult.

Jeremiah was in the grip of problems and he started doubting God. He taught us earlier on that God is "the fountain of living water" (Jer. 2:13). Now he wondered if he was right. He was spiritually thirsty. Deep inside he started fearing that the message he brought to others was now backfiring on him. Some of the watercourses and brooks streamed with water in Israel during the rainy season. But many of them were deceptive streams. They dried up quickly and when the scorching summer heat came and the people were desperate for water, they had nothing to offer. He feared that God was acting like one of those unreliable brooks.

He lets me rest in green meadows; He leads me beside peaceful streams. He renews my strength.
~ Psalm 23:2-3 ~

Are you afraid that God is like a stream running dry in your life? God's answer to Jeremiah was, "No, Jeremiah, I never run dry." No matter how scorching the heat might be, some rivers are permanent and steady and never dry up. God is one of them. He is an endless supply of goodness, grace and strength. He will renew you and provide for you and sustain you. He flows like an everlasting stream.

Everlasting God and Father, flow strongly again for all who fear that You might disappoint them. Amen.

Respected!

Greet Andronicus and Junia, my fellow Jews, who were in prison with me. They are highly respected among the apostles and became followers of Christ before I did (Rom. 16:7).

Not all gifted people make the headlines or covers of magazines. Some of them remain unknown. J. S. Bach was the organist in a small village congregation. Every week he composed a new music piece for that Sunday's service. As soon as the service was over, the composition was set aside and forgotten. After his death, all the compositions were discovered and made available to the public. Bach lived and died a poor man – an unrecognized genius.

Our true worth does not consist in what human beings think of us. What we really are consists in what God knows us to be.
~ John Berchmans ~

When you serve Christ, you don't do it to become famous. You do it in obedience to Christ, in pure love for Him. Your greatest joy is to see Jesus' name glorified.

Today there are respected and outstanding people all over the world who spread the gospel, and don't give reward or recognition a thought. Some deliver impressive sermons, others compose outstanding music. Some teach little children about Jesus, and others care for the elderly. Some feel called to live in underdeveloped countries and pour their energy into uplifting the poor. Some nurse people in remote mission hospitals and others do the bookkeeping for Christian organizations. There are people who feel called to do pioneer mission work in dangerous places. Never stop thanking God for these "outstanding" people in His service and pray for those you know.

Loving Master, help me to serve You to the best of my ability without ever thinking of what I will gain by it. Amen.

Tested Christian

Greet Apelles, whose fidelity to Christ has stood the test (Rom. 16:10 NIV).

You have probably taken many tests in your life. At school, tests are necessary for you to improve and make progress. Passing the test for a driver's license qualifies you to drive a car on a public road. It is necessary that you have an eye test, to determine the quality of your vision. We find some tests easy and others difficult.

We know that many of the first Christians were slaves, and Apelles was probably one of them. It was not always easy when a slave converted to Christianity, because his master was often not sympathetic toward this faith. It was also difficult if his master was a Christian himself, because the master-slave relationship was maintained in Christian communities. Or it could happen that the slave held an important position in the church while the master was just an ordinary believer.

Afflictions are but the shadows of God's wings.
~ George MacDonald ~

We don't know exactly what tests and trials Apelles was put through. Whatever it was, Apelles endured it; and he endured it "in Christ." The strength, courage and dignity that he found in Jesus carried him through.

You and I are also put to the test. Some tests can break you. Whatever your trials and tribulations, it would be good if you meet them "in Christ." He can and wants to give you sources of strength far beyond your abilities, and they will enable you to pass every test.

Lord, my God, never let me flinch from facing the trials on my path, but let me take them on in the strength of Jesus Christ and the Holy Spirit. Amen.

Dry Fountains and Mists

These people are as useless as dried-up springs or as mist blown away by the wind (2 Pet. 2:17).

It is wonderful to start life with great expectations. Then nothing seems impossible and you meet each challenge with confidence, joy and an air of expectancy. Unfortunately, in the case of most people, it seems as if their hope fades and they become entangled in trivialities. Eventually they become satisfied with the mediocre, and disappointment and failure follow.

When this unfortunate condition develops, it should never be accepted as something unavoidable. It is necessary that you re-evaluate your values. Maybe the goals you strived for in the past are unreachable and the time has come that, in the light of what you have learnt, you must set yourself new goals that are inspiring, yet reachable.

If you have not succeeded in meeting the high expectations you once had, don't give in to self-pity, or blame other people for your difficult circumstances. Create goals that are within your reach and abilities, and work hard at reaching them. If you don't work towards a worthy purpose, your life will stay average and disappointing. No matter what happened in the past, you can meet the future with renewed energy, enthusiasm and expectation.

Ideals are like tuning forks: sound them often to bring your life up to standard pitch.
~ S. D. Gordon ~

By putting my faith in You completely, Holy Master, I strive to achieve Your purpose with my life. Amen.

Peace through Prayer

All of them are hot as an oven; they devour their rulers. All their kings fall, and none of them calls on me (Hosea 7:7 NIV).

Throughout the ages, the world we live in has known violence and war. Millions have suffered terribly and died as a result. If you analyze the reasons for this, you will find that they include greed, hunger for authority, jealousy, a thirst for revenge and blind aggression – to mention but a few.

While we are not for one moment trying to defend this conduct, it is, however, also true that the victims often react with counter revenge that leads to more bloodshed. The international battlefield proves the destructive results of war. It was like this in Old Testament history and it is still the case today.

Peace reigns where our Lord reigns.
~ Julian of Norwich ~

There is an essential urgency for all people in positions of authority to seek God's help – not only when danger is imminent, but at all times. The Lord undertook to listen to us and to answer our prayers. Therefore, we must be praying people, seeking God's guidance right through life in an effort to put an end to the atrocities born of violence and war.

Jesus instructed us to love. Do precisely this and see the amazing results. "Submit to God and be at peace with Him; in this way prosperity will come to you" (Job 22:21 NIV).

Prince of Peace, let the day come quickly then war will end and our hearts are filled with love. Amen.

Hope for World Peace

The LORD will settle international disputes. They will hammer their swords into plowshares and their spears into pruning hooks (Isa. 2:4).

Throughout the ages, many people have dreamt of a time when wars would end. Some of the wars were said to be "the war to end all wars." Greed, national pride, intolerance, fear, personal ambition and malicious troublemaking are all factors that make sure this dream does not come true. There is always war somewhere, and rumors of war.

Isaiah lived in a very small country that was often attacked by mighty armies on their way to do battle with other powerful armies. Yet he dreamt of peace, not because he sat down and calculated the relative power of any of the armies of his time, but because of his faith in God.

Who except God can give you peace? Has the world ever been able to satisfy the heart?
~ Gerard Majella ~

Approximately 700 years later (and a number of wars in between), Jesus was born as the "Prince of Peace." At His birth, the angels sang, "Peace on earth to all whom God favors." It is of the utmost importance that Christians are not cynical, fearful and doubtful. They need to hold on to the hope that people will turn their spears into pruning hooks. Hope is not wishful thinking. It admits that there are problems, troubles and disasters, but also dares to believe that on the other side of the chaos there will be order; on the other side of conflict there will be peace. Hope believes this because God is God and in the end, He is in charge and in control. Christians must also work for peace and pray for those who negotiate for international peace and understanding.

God of grace, in addition to all the blessings You shower on us, bless us with peace. Amen.

The Gift of God

Nation will no longer fight against nation, nor train for war anymore (Isa. 2:4).

There is a place in Jerusalem that is at the same time beautiful and hopeful, but also dismal and tragic. It is the Western Wall, also referred to as the Wailing Wall. It is the only remaining part of the big temple that was built by Herod the Great, in Jesus' time. Massive rocks were chiseled and piled up to form a wall. As time passed, deep, narrow crevices formed between these rocks. Dedicated Jews visit this wall, touch it and pray. Thousands of non-Jewish visitors do the same. Many of those who go there write messages or prayers on pieces of paper and push these in between the cracks in the rock wall. Most people who do this pray either for peace in Jerusalem or for world peace.

> The world would have peace if only men of politics would follow the Gospels.
> ~ Bridget of Sweden ~

It is right that people turn to God for peace in the world. Human structures and strategies may avoid certain conflicts, but they are by no means successful. The prophet Isaiah looked far into the future, not to when things would be "sorted out," but when God would bring the final chapter of history to fulfillment, and His kingdom of righteousness and peace came into existence. Ultimately, God is the only one who can bring perfect peace in the strife, conflict and chaos of the world. Only He can judge people and forgive their sins. If inner peace is the fruit of the Holy Spirit, intended peace is also a gift from God. We look forward to the time that He will give it – at His appointed time.

Lord Jesus, let there be peace on earth and let it start with me.

Amen.

Comforting Love

Keep yourselves in God's love as you wait for the mercy of our Lord Jesus Christ to bring you to eternal life (Jude 21 NIV).

Despite the fact that Christians receive eternal life from the hand of God and that it is our final aim and objective, the death of a loved one leaves us in a shocked state when we have to experience the reality of separation. In spite of the fact that we rejoice in the knowledge that the loved one, if a believer, has left us to enjoy the glory of God's kingdom, we don't really know how to fill this void in our hearts.

In Christ the heart of the Father is revealed and higher comfort there cannot be than to rest in the Father's heart.
~ Andrew Murray ~

When our Savior prepared His disciples for His farewell and return to His Father, He proclaimed His peace over them. Then He poured His Holy Spirit out over them so that the enveloping love of God would fill their lives on earth with the kind of love that would raise them up to the kingdom of God.

That same love and peace is Christ's gift to you. Trust Him and open your heart and life to Him; let Him lead you on paths of service in His name. Make your love and mercy available to others so that the Living Christ may work in and through you to the advantage of His people. In this manner, you will be embraced by Jesus' love. He will carry you through the disappointments in this life, until you see the glory of God in eternity.

O Love, deeply concerned about me, I rest my tired soul in You.
Amen.

The Irritations of Life

How long will you torture me? How long will you try to crush me with your words? (Job 19:2).

All of us experience irritations at some time in our lives. If you tend to be irritable, then you are easily offended; you might use strong language, and you are difficult to live with.

It is foolish to allow people, things or circumstances to annoy you and in this way gain control of your life. To free yourself from this danger, you must work on controlling your reaction to the things that irritate you. The irritations won't simply go away if you say you won't allow them to get the better of you. Rather tune in to God and become aware of all the beautiful, pleasant things in life. Then a feeling of harmony and peace will fill your heart and thoughts.

One sees great things from the valley; only small things from the peak.
~ G. K. Chesterton ~

In order to overcome the petty irritations of life, it is of the utmost importance to cling to the concept of God. If your idea of God is petty and insufficient, almost every human relationship and set of circumstances will carry the seed of irritation. When your concept of God is worthy of Him, you will be able to overcome every obstacle that comes your way.

Look at your life in the light of God's eternity and greatness. You will find that nothing is so important that it will irritate you up to the point where you lose your positive concept of God and the balance in your life.

Loving Father God, when I realize how great You are, it keeps me from allowing irritations to influence me. Amen.

The Human Savior

The Good News is about His Son. In His earthly life He was born into King David's family line (Rom. 1:3).

There have been many great and famous men and women of God through the ages. Some were prophets, some devout believers; many of them were very holy; others worked their fingers to the bone in serving their fellow men; yet others were famous teachers. Which one of these people describes Jesus best?

All these people were sent by God, yet they were ordinary people who God used in an exceptional way. Jesus was also a human being in the full sense of the word. He had the same physical appearance as anybody else. He ate and drank, worked and slept. He got tired and sometimes yearned for refreshing solitude. He prayed and was given the power of God to perform miracles. In biblical times a person's identity was not determined by an entry in a central register or a number, but by mentioning the person's parents. This could be extended by referring to the person's grandparents and their parents. Jesus is described as "born into King David's family line."

If ever the Divine has appeared on earth, it was in the person of Christ.
~ Johann Wolfgang von Goethe ~

Only a person who is fully human can be your Savior. He needs to experience your fears; battle with your temptations; and understand your sorrow and heartache to enable Him to give you life in all its abundance. Because Jesus became totally human, He raised the standard of humankind because He was a perfect human being. He added a new quality or dimension to human life and made it what God intended it to be. Have you experienced this miracle yet? Has Jesus turned you into what God intended you to be?

Holy Father, make me more and more like Jesus. Amen.

Son of God

He [Jesus Christ] was shown to be the Son of God when He was raised from the dead by the power of the Holy Spirit (Rom. 1:4).

You might sometimes reflect on the wonder that the life of a Galilean carpenter, dating back 2,000 years, has been admired and worshiped by millions of His followers ever since. What was it about Jesus that made so many people love Him so intensely? Why are so many lives radically changed by His impact on them?

Jesus was more than human. He was also totally and completely God. Jesus was the Son of God and He came from God. When He rose from the grave on Easter Sunday, it was the final declaration that He was God who had come to earth. This confirmed His sovereignty over the forces of evil and proved that He had triumphed over death.

Although Christ was God, He took flesh; and having been made man, He remained what He was, God.
~ Origen ~

The gospel of God is always the good news of Jesus' resurrection. Because He was raised from the dead, we can rule over temptation. This gives us the hope that life is always stronger than death. Because He lives forever, we can experience joy instead of sorrow; hope instead of despair; inner peace instead of confusion. We don't achieve or earn these blessings by becoming involved in spiritual gymnastics. They come as God's gift to us through faith in His resurrected Son, Jesus, the Living Christ.

Risen Savior, may my whole life be filled with the power of Your resurrection. Amen.

The Discipline of Service

"We will serve the LORD" (Josh. 24:21).

Your conversion is a special occasion in your life. Whether you experience emotional ecstasy or quiet reassurance, you are filled with an indescribably wonderful peace. There is no doubt that it could come only from Christ, the Lord you gave your life to. In the holy mystery of the moment, it is the most natural thing to devote yourself to God, and at that moment nothing and nobody can keep you from making that decision.

You must be ready for the after-effects. In the wake of your sublime joy of conversion, moments of uncertainty and doubt will follow. As you become more and more involved in the activities of His church, there will be times that you don't agree with other believers; you will most probably experience disillusionment and disappointment. Your faith will be tested in many different ways and you will experience hurt.

Trust Jesus, and you are saved. Trust self, and you are lost.
~ Charles H. Spurgeon ~

All these tough times form part of Satan's armory that constantly bombards Christians in the hope that their faith will fade and their testimonies about God will lose power. To resist this, cling to Jesus' promise that His grace is enough for you. Discipline yourself to look up to Jesus all the time and to trust Him. He will lead you away from temptation on to the path of dedication and service to this God who you surrendered your life to.

Savior and Redeemer, help me, comfort me, strengthen me, hold me and carry me through. Amen.

Spiritual Discipline

Teach me Your ways, O LORD, that I may live according to Your truth! (Ps. 86:11).

It is an uncontrollable human tendency to go your own way, do your own thing and then to ask God for His blessing on what you are doing. And then when things go wrong, you wonder why God allowed it and you become rebellious. After all, you did ask for godly blessing on your efforts, so why is everything falling apart?

As a child of God, you must learn to accept His discipline. Just like students need to be corrected if they want to make progress at school, Christians also need their heavenly Father's discipline. Without it, there cannot be spiritual growth.

However, God's discipline is never prejudiced. He does not punish some and let others get off scot-free. The discipline you undergo is mostly self-imposed. When you have disobeyed what you know is God's will, you have to pay the price. If you deliberately disobey His rules and thought in your foolishness that you could side-step the consequences, don't rebel against God when it seems that circumstances are turning against you. What you sow, you will definitely reap.

You will never be the person you can be if pressure, tension, and discipline are taken out of your life.
~ James G. Bilkey ~

When God disciplines you, it always has a constructive purpose. His love for you is constant and His aim is to bring you into a deeper and richer relationship with Him. The discipline you experience is part of your spiritual development and should be experienced with joy – even with thanksgiving!

Merciful Master, grant me the wisdom to learn the lessons You want to teach me through Your holy discipline. Amen.

What God Expects

His government and its peace will never end. He will rule with fairness and justice from the throne of His ancestor David for all eternity. The passionate commitment of the LORD of Heaven's Armies will guarantee this! (Isa. 9:7).

When Christians speak about God and His will they normally think of it in terms of what He expects of them personally: "Would it be God's will if I give up this job and look for another?" or "What does God expect me to do or give for His work?" God does have a will for the individual, but He also has a will for the whole world.

In this verse, Isaiah sets out his wish for the tiny Judah and what God expects from His world as a whole. Omnipotence is part of God's royal rule. There cannot be a power vacuum, but what God expects is responsible use of power and integrity from those who exercise it. He wants them to acknowledge that their power and authority are from Him, and they will account for the way they exercise it.

The God of the Bible is the God who reveals Himself in all the glory and the wonder of His miraculous, eternal power.
~ Martyn Lloyd-Jones ~

The fact is that many people are after power for their own selfish purposes. God wants peace on earth and He expects that it will not only be in the form of a short break between one war and the next, but forever. Too often peace is sacrificed by rulers driven by a need for more power.

The bottom line is: Everything God expects from His world boils down to justness and righteousness; the healthy warm-hearted, sincere moral order of those things that allow people to live creatively and peacefully under Christ's dominium.

Almighty God, let righteousness and peace flourish all over Your world. Amen.

The Necessity of Conversion

For after all this punishment, the people will still not repent. They will not seek the LORD of Heaven's Armies (Isa. 9:13).

Never assume that it is more difficult in our times to live life close to God than what it was a thousand years ago. In the olden days, people who battled to steer their lives in accordance with God's will often failed. This applies to people throughout the biblical period that spans about two thousand years.

The prophets called on the nations to be converted. They saw people worshiping false gods, doing immoral things and failing to walk close to God. In particular, they ignored His commandments. Even when they returned, only a brief period of spiritual dedication followed. In spite of the wonderful work of the Holy Spirit in the New Testament, there were many indications that these people lived a crumbling Christian life at most.

> One of the most fundamental marks of true repentance is a disposition to see our sins as God sees them.
> ~ Charles Simeon ~

We must also repent, confess and turn back to God. If you gave your life to Jesus years ago and are trying to live a Christian life, it is essential that you are regularly filled with remorse for the mistakes you have made, and start over again.

To be remorseful is to admit that you had the wrong attitudes, that you were quick to judge, and that you sought your own will above that of God. It is to admit that you lacked love and were selfish in your relationships. Take another look at the way you spend your money and to find ways of being more charitable. Re-commit your life to God, and become more and more like Jesus.

Holy Father, help me to regularly rethink my walk with You.

Amen.

The God of Fire

The LORD, the Light of Israel, will be a fire; the Holy One will be a flame. He will devour the thorns and briers with fire, burning up the enemy in a single night (Isa. 10:17).

It is said that God is many things and that there is nothing He cannot do: He is a Rock and a Refuge; He is the Good Shepherd who looks after His sheep; He is a Wind that blows, bringing life; He is a King who rules; and He is a Warrior who defends. Fire is an image often used to represent God.

While a fire provides warmth, it can also destroy. In the Scripture above, Isaiah prophesies the fate of the boastful king of Assyria, who was too big for his boots and didn't realize that He was no more than a servant of God. God would appear like a fire and destroy everything in His way; in the process Assyria would also be destroyed.

The Holy Spirit is not a blessing from God, He is God.
~ Colin Urquhart ~

The fire image is seen again on Pentecost when "tongues of fire" appeared and settled on the disciples who were gathered together to receive the Holy Spirit (Acts 2:3). It is symbolic of the presence of God and also of His judgment.

Ironically, some of the Christians who were filled with the Holy Spirit were later burnt at the stake because of their loyalty to Christ. Through the ages, believers understood that they needed the purifying fire of God to purge them spiritually.

Holy Spirit, purifying fire, come and purge my life of all that is dirty and impure. Amen.

The Faithful Remnant

A remnant will return to the Mighty God (Isa. 10:21).

It is amazing what a small group of people can achieve when their hearts are invested in a matter and they set about it with dedication and enthusiasm. Mighty political parties have come into being because of the dedication of a few "fanatics." Christianity has become a world religion as a result of twelve disciples who carried out Jesus' command to go into the world and spread His message.

Throughout the Scriptures, God carried out His salvation plan by means of small groups of people. When Noah and his family built the ark, God made the truth of His existence known to only one family. When Jacob sent his sons to Egypt in search of grain, God again used one small community. Then God called a few believers to maintain faith in Him. After the judgment over Assyria was carried out, there was a small "remnant" that would return to God in remorse.

When men cease to be faithful to their God, he who expects them to be faithful to each other will be much disappointed.
~ George Horne ~

The Christian community is usually a "faithful remnant." They remain true to their faith and in spite of opposition, the body of Christian believers lives on. At times it seems to be on the brink of extinction. In some groups it is brought back to life, and revival brings new hope and trust. Sometimes the community itself is guilty of confusing the faith with other forms and systems. Then God sends a prophet or evangelist to call them back to their true calling.

Are you one of the faithful remnants? Don't be discouraged by mass-unbelief, failure or godlessness around you. Persevere with your faith in Jesus. You will find your reward in heaven.

Lord Jesus, strengthen the faith of the remnant. Amen.

Fill the World with Love

Supplement brotherly affection with love for everyone. The more you grow like this, the more productive and useful you will be in your knowledge of our Lord Jesus Christ (2 Pet. 1:7-8).

Kind-heartedness and love are very much the same, yet there is a difference between the two. Kind-heartedness has to do with small acts of kindness in your everyday contact with people. Love is a deep and ongoing concern involving the spiritual and physical welfare of other people. It is not only ongoing, it is also outgoing.

To love is the highest and noblest activity a person is capable of, besides praising God. When Christ became human, He was the embodiment of God's love for humankind. And He did love! It was His love – His ongoing and outgoing love – that pressed Him to endure the sorrow of the cross.

Love is an act of faith, and whoever is of little faith is also of little love.
~ Erich Fromm ~

To become a believer is to be caught up in the love of Christ in your own heart, and to be urged on by that love to care for others. To love is to place other people first and yourself last. To love with Christian love is seeking to lead those you love to God's love. To love is to go on loving, even if the person you love shows no interest in responding to your love.

Become a loving disciple of Christ. Let the love of God fill you so abundantly that it will spill over onto others. Become part of God's healing of a world swamped with hatred, fear and greed.

Loving Father God, make me an instrument of Your love. Amen.

The Mighty Arm of God

By Your mighty power You rescue those who seek refuge from their enemies (Ps. 17:7).

All of us have enemies, even those who think they have none. Thieves who make it their business to rob us are our enemies. So are dishonest business people. People who drive cars when they are under the influence of alcohol or drugs are our enemies. Don't think because you're friendly you have no enemies. The world is evil. Don't bluff yourself.

But God is on your side, and He is a God with a mighty arm. He will sometimes intervene directly to protect you from the enemy, but not always. If you trust Him, however, it will make you wiser and more sensible so that you are able to protect yourself. Because you know the world is evil, you will be better prepared for the possibility of an onslaught and you'll be ready when it comes. You will be more careful about doing things that expose you to attacks from unknown enemies.

> There are three things that only God knows: the beginning of things, the cause of things and the end of things.
> ~ Welsh Proverb ~

Remember how Jesus approached the cross: fearlessly. Call to mind how, through the ages, Christian martyrs courageously faced tyrants, opponents, oppressors and hostile crowds in the power of Christ. Remember above all, that it is a battle and He who is mightier than all the enemies is fighting on your side if you are fighting on His.

Almighty God, save me, protect me and keep me. Amen.

What to Teach People

The purpose of my instruction is that all believers would be filled with love that comes from a pure heart, a clear conscience, and genuine faith (1 Tim. 1:5).

In their teachings, different Christian churches emphasize different aspects of their members' faith. One emphasizes giving. Another concentrates on evangelization. Yet another propagates appropriate behavior. Others promote involvement in social issues at the expense of everything else.

In his advice to Timothy on what he should emphasize in Ephesus to contradict the false teachings that were doing the rounds, Paul says they must learn to love sincerely. The love he is talking about is more than mere compassion. It is "agape" love, or God's kind of self-sacrificing love.

Love is the greatest thing that God can give us, for Himself is love: and it is the greatest thing we can give to God.
~ Jeremy Taylor ~

It is more than kindness. It is placing the other person's spiritual well-being first and forgetting about yourself. Paul knew that no matter how perfect or imperfect a Christian disciple's religious convictions may be, the quality of love revealed by the disciple was the true test of sincere faith.

Your Christian community presents God's love to the world inasmuch as it manifests Christian love, both within the Christian circle and toward those outside the group. The same goes for you as an individual. Love must always be the distinguishing mark of your faith. As your capacity to love increases, you also develop openness toward Christ to sense when wrong teachings are proclaimed. If you want the ability to love, you will need to open yourself up to the working of the Holy Spirit.

Triune God of love, fill my entire being with sincere, godly love.
Amen.

A Pure Heart

The purpose of my instruction is that all believers would be filled with love that comes from a pure heart, a clear conscience, and genuine faith (1 Tim. 1:5).

Most of us are a strange mixture of good and bad. We find a man who is a brilliant physician, but he wastes his money on gambling. We find the lady who is an outstanding actress, but what the public doesn't know is that she's an alcoholic. Often it is those who are most powerful that reveal the most painful weaknesses.

An instant of pure love is more precious to God and the soul, and more profitable to the church, than all other good works together, though it may seem as if nothing were done.
~ John of the Cross ~

Paul encourages Timothy to teach people the right and good type of love "that comes from a pure heart." The interpretation of "pure" translated here can be "clean" as opposed to "dirty." It grew to refer to things that were originally a mixture of good and bad, but have been purified. When the wheat is separated from the chaff, it is pure. An army that is quiet and disciplined is pure in the sense that it has become a first-class fighting unit. This is the kind of heart Paul wants the Ephesians to have – a heart that has been purified from all filth and impure desires.

We also need a pure heart. Your heart will be purified when the love of Christ urges you to give to others, and to seek what is best for them instead of focusing on your own enrichment, popularity and reputation. Love and a pure heart go hand in hand. You will only be able to know true love if you have a pure heart – and the more of God's love that is in your heart, the purer your love will be.

God of love, cleanse and purify my heart so that my love is pure.
Amen.

The Spirit in Our Hearts

It is God who enables us, along with you, to stand firm for Christ. He has commissioned us, and He has identified us as His own by placing the Holy Spirit in our hearts as the first installment of everything He has promised us (2 Cor. 1:21-22).

The Christians of our time celebrate the outpouring of the Holy Spirit on Pentecost Sunday. It was also one of the main annual Jewish celebrations. Many Christians, however, only have a vague idea of who the Holy Spirit is and how He works.

The Holy Spirit was given by God. He was a gift of God, just like Jesus was when He was born in Bethlehem. Like Jesus lived among them as someone in whom God lives, the Holy Spirit came as a gift from God to live in His disciples. Jesus was the God they could see and talk to. The Holy Spirit was the God they couldn't see, but who spoke inside them because He lived in their hearts. By living in them, the Holy Spirit brought Christ into being in their lives.

Jesus has gone to prepare a place for us, and the Holy Spirit has been sent to prepare us for that place.
~ Anonymous ~

This is still the Holy Spirit's work. He lives in you and He is the power of God working inside you so that you are conformed to Jesus more and more. A Spirit-filled believer is a Christ-filled believer. Thus the essential feature of the Holy Spirit's work is the extent to which you demonstrate the love of Christ, the joy of Christ, the peace of Christ and the goodness of Christ. The very best way to celebrate that gift of God on Pentecost is to allow the Holy Spirit to fill you anew with Christ. Do it today!

Come, O Holy Spirit, come today with renewal and live in me anew. Amen.

A Clear Conscience

The purpose of my instruction is that all believers would be filled with love that comes from a pure heart, a clear conscience, and genuine faith (1 Tim. 1:5).

Someone once said, "Your conscience is the voice inside that warns you someone is watching you." Is it the thought of someone else watching you, or the possibility that God is? Conscience has also been called "God's soft whispering in your inner being." Sometimes a guilty conscience frightens you and paralyzes you so that you can't act. It can also encourage you to be honest about something you are hiding. A French saying goes: There is no pillow as soft as a clear conscience.

Conscience tells us in our innermost being of the presence of God and of the moral difference between good and evil.
~ Billy Graham ~

Underlying the thought of a conscience is the knowledge inside you of what you have done. A clear conscience means you are comfortable with what you know about yourself. A guilty conscience means that you know God is not comfortable with what you know about yourself. The only way to really have a clear conscience is to confess every known sin before God so that He can forgive you and purify your thinking. Paul knew that a guilty conscience would arrest the flow of God's love in people that would otherwise have served Him devotedly. He knew that to have a clear conscience you have to live a pure life. He didn't want his co-workers to be hampered by sin from the past clouding their lives.

If there is anything on your conscience that undermines your work for Christ, don't postpone dealing with it straightaway. Let the healing power of Christ touch you anew and revive you. Allow Him to make you whole and clean like only He can do.

Lord Jesus, I plead for a clear and pure conscience. Amen.

Whom Do You Obey?

Slaves, obey your earthly masters in everything you do. Try to please them all the time, not just when they are watching you. Serve them willingly because of your reverent fear of the Lord (Col. 3:22).

Golfers often say, "Every shot makes someone happy." If you play a good shot, it makes you happy, and if you play a poor shot, it makes your opponent happy.

Paul puts a Christian focus on the daily work of Christians. It is much more than just a way of earning a living. It is more than the expression of your gifts and skills. It is even more than your contribution to the community. The Christian's daily work is an offering to God. Do their work in a way that pleases God.

Work is love made visible.
~ Kahlil Gibran ~

God is interested in your daily task and how well you do it. You may do the work to please your employer (in the hope of getting a promotion). You might do it to gain the respect and admiration of your colleagues. You might do it to please yourself because professionally, you are truly proud of your work.

But if you do it to glorify God and please Him, it raises your task to another level. It gives your daily work a spiritual dimension. This means that you live from your faith, not only in what you say, but also how you live. Your faith and deeds become one. Whom do you obey? Whom do you make happy? Whom do you please – your employer, yourself, your family; or all of them and God?

Lord, my God, grant that I please You above all, every hour of every day. Amen.

March

His light on my path helps me persevere through trying times.

So be truly glad. There is wonderful joy ahead, even though you have to endure many trials for a little while. These trials will show that your faith is genuine. It is being tested as fire tests and purifies gold.
~ 1 Pet. 1:6-7 ~

The hotter the fire, the purer the gold.
~ Charles Stanley ~

Holy God and loving Father,
You alone know how sincere
our desire is to believe like You expect us to.
So often we fail and disappoint You.
Teach us through the Holy Spirit the lesson of
perseverance up until the very end.
Grant that we will never doubt
Your unfailing love and grace,
or stop believing in Your empowering love.
Help us to persevere in spite of setbacks and disappointments.
Thank You that You know
and understand all our weaknesses,
and that You are always there for us,
and support us in our greatest need.
Grant that we will hold on to Your Word and Your grace.
Carry us through the cold winter season
into the spring of unshakable faith and trust.
Do this for us in Your undeserved goodness and
in the name of Jesus, our Master.

Amen.

Patient Endurance

Supplement your faith with self-control, and self-control with patient endurance, and patient endurance with godliness (2 Pet.1:6).

A young man felt called by God to join the ministry. He took the qualifying examination and failed hopelessly. He could have thought that he had misunderstood God. But he didn't. He retook the examination again the following year and passed one part, but failed the other by a single mark. He tried a third time, passed and became a powerful and effective minister of the Word. Through the years, thousands of people thanked God for this man's endurance; his failures helped them realize how perfectly human their shepherd was.

Patient endurance is one of the basic qualities of the Christian believer. In its very nature and being, it is focused on something in the distant future – the final return of Christ when He will reign as King. This means that Christians have to endure hard times and even suffering. It is making a comeback after every setback and starting over after each failure; it is keeping your eyes on the horizon.

> All things are possible to him who believes, yet more to him who hopes, more still to him who loves, and most of all to him who practices and perseveres in these three virtues.
> ~ Brother Lawrence ~

If you have stumbled in your faith somewhere along the way, for whatever reason, don't lose heart. Don't expect an easy and prosperous journey. It is said of Jesus, "Because of the joy awaiting Him, He endured the cross, disregarding its shame. Now He is seated in the place of honor beside God's throne" (Heb. 12:2). Expect hardship and disappointment, but hold on to Jesus – until the very end.

God of grace, grant me the patience to endure and persevere to the very end. Amen.

Grow in Your Knowledge of God

Supplement your faith with a generous provision of moral excellence, and moral excellence with knowledge (2 Pet. 1:5).

Many good Christians pay little attention to knowing God better, which stunts their spiritual growth. Although they get away with it up to a point, they complain that they sometimes don't know how and what to pray; they don't have enough time; they don't know what to say to God; their thoughts wander in all directions. Many simply lose heart and give up.

The truly great Christian disciples have one thing in common – they make time for God in their lives. They persevere in this through thick and thin, because it invigorates and refreshes them. They know God has always loved them and continues to love them in Christ. They know that, no matter how intense the pressure, they are in urgent need of regular contact with God. They also know that it is during the time they spend with God in solitude that they get new perspectives on life, new strength to really live life, and understand themselves better. When they face problems, they involve God in the matter and find that they are able to press ahead. They enter into the presence of God and experience the assurance that He accepts them, and come to know that they can accept themselves.

Prayer does not change God, but it changes him who prays.
~ Søren Kierkegaard ~

Many wrestle through crises, sickness, disaster, doubt and problems with newfound strength and power. They know where their secret lies: in the renewal that takes place as a result of their intimate walk with God. Try it and experience the amazement.

Holy Father, grant me time in Your presence, getting to know You more. Amen.

God Cares

Give all your worries and cares to God, for He cares about you (1 Pet. 5:7).

Many people are incurable worriers. They simply must have something to worry about otherwise they would be utterly miserable! They worry about their health, their finances, their family and their friends. They worry about the future, about "what is going on in the world," they complain about the weather, crime and violence, and they are frustrated because "things are going from bad to worse."

Peter had many real worries. He could lose his life any day due to the persecution of Christian believers. And so could the people he was addressing. The faith that he stood for could be wiped out. It could be undermined by false teachings, or by troublemakers, or by internal strife. It almost happened – and yet Peter knew that God was *there,* above all these things. He knew that God cared about him and about all the people who were threatened by these things.

> Worry does not empty tomorrow of its sorrow; it empties today of its strength.
> ~ Anonymous ~

God also cares about you, whether you are worried or not. He watches over you and He will see you through. Therefore, hand your cares over to Him: the real and the imaginary, the big and small. Don't hold anything back. Allow Him to take them all and then find peace in Him. He has the whole world in His hands. When Jesus was dying, He prayed, "Father, I entrust My spirit into Your hands!" (Luke 23:46). Why don't you also pray this now, in the thick of your worries? Peace is within your grasp.

Lord Jesus, take all my anxieties and worries and let me find rest in Your care. Amen.

Seize Every Opportunity

Live wisely among those who are not believers, and make the most of every opportunity (Col. 4:5).

Some people who run businesses have a sixth sense when it comes to opportunities in the business world. One businessman built up a large business by selling shoes for a manufacturer. One day he heard that the factory had hired transport to distribute their goods. He hired a truck and asked the manufacturer to let him deliver the shoes to the shops. It was not long before he ran his own transport business.

Paul encouraged the Christians of Colosse to be on the lookout for opportunities to recommend the gospel and to testify for Christ. He was in fact saying, "Develop a sixth sense and make use of every opportunity to speak and act for Christ." He was devoted to his task as a preacher and missionary.

In the middle of difficulty lies opportunity
~ Albert Einstein ~

The local Christian community had to go on proclaiming the gospel, putting the truth into practice and testifying about Christ. It was not only Paul's preaching that would untie the knot in Colosse. It was how the Christians lived, spoke and died that would confirm or deny the gospel. They would have to make the most of every opportunity to testify, do good deeds, show love and act responsibly.

We must do the same so that the gospel is reflected in our everyday lives. One way is to look out for the poor and weak, and take care of them. Another is to speak about Jesus. We must make the most of every opportunity to promote the gospel.

God of grace, enable me to have an open heart for every opportunity to serve You. Amen.

Doing God's Will

Epaphras, a member of your own fellowship and a servant of Christ Jesus, sends you his greetings. He always prays earnestly for you, asking God to make you strong and perfect, fully confident that you are following the whole will of God (Col. 4:12).

Many Christians find it difficult to know God's will for them. Young Christians experience this problem as having to determine what career choice would be best for them, or the choice of a marriage partner. Older believers battle to know God's will for their lives and the demands of serving Him. The difficult part is guarding against confusion.

Paul told the believers in Colosse that their friend and leader, Epaphras, was praying in earnest that God would help them realize His will for their lives. All his prayers were focused on building their spiritual well-being. Not one prayer was for healing or money, and neither for a kind of "God-please-help-me" request. Epaphras knew how difficult it was to know God's will and he pleaded with God to help them through this.

The will of God will never take you where the grace of God cannot keep you.
~ Anonymous ~

It would be a good idea for us to do the same. The more confused we become about God's will for our lives, the more we need His guidance to find it. Ask Him to reveal it to you.

Often you will find that the more difficult the choice is, the more likely it is that this is God's will for you. He seldom calls you to walk a path of moonlight and roses. Ask other, wiser Christians to work through the confusion with you. Test the different options and see if you are comfortable with the thought that God is really leading you in a specific direction. Pray, and pray in earnest, that God will reveal His will to you clearly.

Lord, my God, today I pray for all who seek Your will for their lives. Amen.

An Absent God

"Someday the groom will be taken away from them, and then they will fast" (Mark 2:20).

Time and time again when disaster strikes or murders are committed, we hear the question, "Where was God when this happened?" Perhaps you have experienced this kind of situation yourself and said, "If only God was there it wouldn't have happened."

When Jesus died, was raised, and ascended to heaven, the disciples were left on their own. This was not because God had let them down. By physically withdrawing from them, Jesus was saying to them, "Now you can't find refuge in My presence any longer. You're on your own. Go ahead with the instructions I gave you. From now on I'm with you in a different form. Now it depends on you." This is what Jesus meant when He said He would be taken away from them.

God is not far away from us. Rather He awaits us every instant in our action, in the work of the moment. There is a sense in which He is at the tip of my pen, my spake, my brush, my needle.
~ Pierre Teilhard de Chardin ~

There are periods of deep spiritual darkness: The stark tragedy of a specific situation; the overwhelming awareness of evil in a person's own life, or in the world in general; or simply just feeling spiritually forsaken. We are driven to despair, and fear that God will not ever again reveal Himself to us. This is how Jesus felt on the cross when He called out, "My God, My God, why have You forsaken Me?"

It is on occasions such as these that genuine faith draws from deep waters and says, "It is now as dark as midnight, but God will see to the break of day."

Ever-present God, visit those who endure the darkness until the day breaks again. Amen.

New Wine

"No one puts new wine into old wineskins. For the wine would burst the wineskins, and the wine and the skins would both be lost. New wine calls for new wineskins" (Mark 2:22).

When something we use often begins wearing away, we start looking for a new one. When a car is old, one part after the other starts giving in. The trouble of getting the car repaired every few weeks becomes too much for the owner. The expense rises and the inconvenience increases. Before long, he buys himself a new car. The seats are more comfortable, there are no scratches on the body, the brakes work well, the car runs like a dream – even the smell of the new car is breathtaking. The driver feels like a new person.

Jesus Christ was completely new. In many respects the old religion had lapsed into a sad state of obeying countless petty rules and regulations. There was no joy, no peace, no personal strength. And because it was difficult obeying so many laws, many people were saddled with a heavy burden of guilt there was no getting away from.

That is why we never give up. Though our bodies are dying, our spirits are being renewed every day.
~ 2 Corinthians 4:16 ~

Jesus wasn't there to simply patch up the old way of doing things. He proclaimed a new religion, a new concept of God and a new way of life. He breathed renewal.

In those days, there weren't any glass bottles; wine was stored in leather wineskins. As the wine fermented, the skins stretched and couldn't be used more than once. New wine would cause the skins to tear. The real question is: Have you tasted the new wine of Christ's empowering love yet?

Heavenly Father, renew everything in me through Jesus.

Amen.

You Can't Please Everyone

"To what can I compare this generation? It is like children playing a game in the public square. They complain to their friends, 'We played wedding songs, and you didn't dance, so we played funeral songs, and you didn't mourn'" (Matt. 11:16).

If you try to please everyone, you will eventually realize that you please no one. There comes a time when you cannot be a people pleaser all the time, on account of the fact that your principles differ from those of others.

Petty and immature people see differences as disagreement and this always causes resistance. If you don't agree with them and support their viewpoints you cannot really be their friend. If you are true to your principles, there will always be differences.

We find comfort among those who agree with us – growth among those who don't.
~ Frank A. Clark ~

A sensible person understands two very important things: The principles you made your own through Bible study, meditation and prayer, and the right of other people to feel strongly about their personal point of view. You have no right to force your views onto others, and trying to do so only creates a spirit of hostility where there should be love and understanding.

The fact that you don't agree with everybody shouldn't affect your relationship with others. As a Christian disciple, with Christ's love in your heart and mind, you must find it possible to love, even if there are differences of opinion and faith. It is impossible to agree with everybody, but don't let this keep you from loving those around you.

Lord and Master, Your wisdom helps me to respect and love people I don't agree with. Amen.

No Christian Spectators

Saul was one of the witnesses, and he agreed completely with the killing of Stephen (Acts 8:1).

There are people who believe they can play a passive role in life's issues and still remain true to the principles of Christ's teachings. They try to keep the faith, no matter how weak it may be. They think the fact that they don't want to become involved in something safeguards them from the responsibility of identifying themselves with Jesus' statement, "Whoever is not for Me, is against Me."

We read in Acts that Stephen was stoned to death because of his faith in Jesus Christ. Saul was a spectator – looking after the clothes of Stephen's murderers. Specifically through this act of not getting involved, Saul sided with the group that was stoning Stephen.

When you have to make a choice and don't make it, that in itself is a choice.
~ William James ~

As a Christian you will often find yourself in situations where you are called on to identify with, or distance yourself from, a given set of circumstances. No one who is a sincere and true disciple of the Living Christ can be a spectator and keep himself from making a stand for Christ.

When that which is right is at stake, you must stand up and be counted for Christ, otherwise you are denying Him. Give yourself to God under all circumstances and the power of His Holy Spirit will enable you and give you the courage to live up to your Christian convictions.

Savior and Lord, grant that I will never lack the courage to make a stand for that which is right and for the glory of Your name.

Amen.

Before It's Too Late

Starting a quarrel is like opening a floodgate, so stop before a dispute breaks out (Prov. 17:14).

Some of the greatest rifts in human relationships are caused by only a few sharp and badly chosen words. It is shocking that people will even resort to violence after the wrong interpretation of a seemingly innocent remark. Families and friends can be driven apart for years about something fairly insignificant.

An argument can only take place between two or more people. If you find yourself in such a situation, you can prevent it from getting out of hand by defusing the situation. Avoid the argument by refusing to get involved if it seems that tempers are starting to flare, or when the issue shows signs of reaching crisis proportions.

The difficulty in life is the choice.
~ George Moore ~

When things have cooled off and everyone calmed down, you will find that no harm was done because you said nothing to fan the flames.

If you follow Jesus' example, you will know how to make level-headedness triumph over anger and pride, and you will be able to withdraw from the argument, your dignity intact. Then you and all those involved will be thankful that peace has been restored because the heat of the moment has passed.

Holy Jesus, grant that I am never too hotheaded to stop before it's too late. Amen.

Religious Language

May the words of my mouth and the meditation of my heart be pleasing to You, O LORD, my rock and my redeemer (Ps. 19:14).

Exclamations of religious ecstasy are totally pointless unless they are the embodiment of insight. When David, who wrote this psalm, praised God, he did it for a specific reason and not by force of habit.

He praised God for His goodness, for saving him from his enemies, for His protection and guidance. When you say, "Praise the Lord!" it must be followed by the question, "What for?" Shouting "Praise the Lord!" or "Hallelujah!" in frenzied excitement is not good enough. These exclamations demand insight into why exactly they are used.

Religious clichés impede our spiritual growth if they are used without a second thought. They create a fixed pattern in our mind and dull our spiritual sensitivity so that we are not receptive to greater truths than we already know. The testimony of many Christians is so stereotyped and repetitive that it is ineffective because it lacks conviction. The Master warns against the use of empty phrases in our prayer life.

Praising God is one of the highest and purest acts in religion. In prayer we act like people; in praise we act like angels.
~ Thomas Watson ~

Make every effort to express your faith in modern terminology. Reveal your love for your Master in simple words that are easy to understand. It will not only refresh your faith, but also make the Living Christ real to the people around you.

Loving Master, grant me the wisdom to make my faith relevant by using modern and meaningful language. Amen.

Don't Act in Haste

Don't say, "I will get even for this wrong." Wait for the LORD to handle the matter (Prov. 20:22).

In any difference of opinion or hostility between people, there is always the tendency to get even. Hurt feelings, wounded pride, or a sense of injustice always bring out the worst in people. Then we tend to take matters in our own hands – and this has the ability to worsen an already unfortunate situation.

If feelings of disapproval and dislike are not stopped, they smolder until, as in the case of a fire, they grow and spread to such an extent that the situation becomes hard to control. These feelings can cause untold misery by affecting not only emotions, but also our entire viewpoint of the lives of other people – especially those close to us.

When you forgive, you in no way change the past – but you sure do change the future.
~ Bernard Meltzer ~

If you feel you have been treated or judged unfairly, remember that it is expected of you as a Christian to forgive. To succeed in overcoming the natural human reaction to seek revenge, hand yourself and everyone involved over to God, and allow Him to deal with the matter in His own time and way. Follow Jesus' example and ask for His grace to help you rise above your human tendencies and to reveal God's forgiving love. Then you will experience a feeling of peace that will heal your pain and feelings of being wronged.

Heavenly Father, even if I feel the pain caused by others, help me to forgive like You forgive me. Amen.

The Unstoppable Word

Each time Jehudi finished reading three or four columns, the king took a knife and cut off that section of the scroll. He then threw it into the fire, section by section, until the whole scroll was burned up (Jer. 36:23).

In the past, people have tried to prevent the message of God's truth from reaching those it was meant for. For close on seven decades of communist rule in Russia, the Bible was banned and Christians persecuted. Finally, communism was rejected. During the past decade, 20% of the population converted from atheism to the Christian faith and Bibles are freely available again.

In ancient Israel, Jeremiah persuaded his friend Baruch to bring the message of God to the king and his people. It told about God's judgment over both the king and the people, and at last it was read to the king. He had it cut up and burnt. Jeremiah immediately wrote everything down again and it has been preserved for all time in the book of Jeremiah. Long after the king tried to destroy the Word of God, we are able to read and hear the exact words the king tried to destroy.

The gospel is not speculation but fact. It is the truth, because it is the record of a Person who is the Truth.
~ Alexander MacLaren ~

Tyrants may ban or burn the Bible, but they cannot stop the message from spreading. The truth (about God) will become known. Your task as a Christian is not only to read and hear the gospel, but to encourage its spread, both in the world outside and in your immediate surroundings. If you live in a country where the Bible has been banned, keep it safe, cherish it, use it and make it known to others as far as you possibly can.

God of the Word, make the work of those who spread Your Word prosper. Amen.

God Is in Control

Then the king commanded his son Jerahmeel, Seraiah son of Azriel, and Shelemiah son of Abdeel, to arrest Baruch and Jeremiah. But the LORD had hidden them (Jer. 36:26).

We sometimes hear how God rescues people from a specific situation like a war, earthquake or other natural disaster. People survive an accident and know that if the hand of God had not protected them, they would certainly have died.

When Baruch took Jeremiah's message to the royal court, insiders warned him of the danger that awaited him and Jeremiah. They decided to hide until the danger had passed. They saw God's hand in everything and they surely thanked Him for their survival.

It is good for Christians to hear this story. God can intervene in situations where people are in danger because of their faith, and because they stand by what they know to be the truth.

If you should be arrested for being a Christian, would there be enough evidence to convict you?
~ Anonymous ~

In some countries, tyrants are still in positions where they have sole power. Millions of people suffer tremendous injustice. Some brave Christians have courageously started speaking out against this unrighteousness and the persecution of Christians.

God doesn't guarantee their safety for taking this courageous stance. But He is there in the whirlpool of conflict, and in many cases He intervenes on their behalf. God is never conquered by dictators. In the end, He is in control, whatever the outcome of the conflict might be.

Almighty God, protect those who are in danger because they remain true to You. Amen.

More Precious than Gold

The laws of the LORD are true; each one is fair. They are more desirable than gold, even the finest gold. They are sweeter than honey, even honey dripping from the comb (Ps. 19:9-10).

We tend to think of gold as an exceptional source of wealth. In fact, it is very unpredictable as far as price goes. For many years its selling price was $35 an ounce. Then, in 1980 it shot up to more than $800 an ounce. In 2004, it was valued at about $260. In 2006, an expert predicted that it would exceed the $1000 mark! Material values are unpredictable, unreliable and deceptive. Yet, in spite of this, people spend their lives worrying and stressing about these material values.

Our Scripture for the day was written 3,000 years ago. King David had deep insight into the course of world events, and also the value of things as compared to the truths and precepts of the Lord. He was a very prosperous man. He knew that in guiding humankind on how to live, God gave us something more precious than the finest gold. David obeyed God's precepts himself and did his utmost to use them as indicators for his faith and actions.

A man's heart is right when he wills what God wills.
~ Thomas Aquinas ~

Don't be like so many modern people who run down and despise the Lord's teachings. Jesus didn't do it. He said He had come to fulfill the law. He rated the law even higher by adding love to it. What we urgently need is to make the laws of God number one in our value system again, and to cherish them. We will be so much richer if we do this.

Help me, Father God, to place Your teachings at the top of my priority list. Amen.

Be Careful and Discerning

You are following a different way that pretends to be the Good News but is not the Good News at all. You are being fooled by those who twist and change the truth concerning Christ (Gal. 1:6-7).

Centuries ago, Jesus warned His followers to be careful: "Beware of false prophets who come disguised as harmless sheep, but are really vicious wolves" (Matt. 7:15). This warning is as relevant today as it was all those years ago, because we still have those with us who manipulate the Scriptures or present us with a weak version of the gospel.

They may succeed in presenting it in a very attractive and innocent way, but they are doing great harm by undermining the gospel and the church of Christ.

There is nothing that Satan more desires than that we should believe that he doesn't exist.
~ Bishop Wordsworth ~

There is no easy way to salvation, and anyone who shows no respect for Jesus' teachings must be regarded with suspicion. When Jesus called you to take up your cross and follow Him, He made it quite clear that He is the only Way. As you undoubtedly know, this means unreserved surrender to Christ and His commands.

Anything else, no matter how acceptable it may seem, is not from God. To help you identify these false prophets, Jesus said, "Not everyone who calls out to Me, 'Lord! Lord!' will enter the Kingdom of Heaven. Only those who actually do the will of My Father in heaven will enter" (Matt. 7:21).

Lord Jesus, keep my feet on the right way – Your way. Amen.

No Sunday Christians!

All who fear the LORD will hate evil. Therefore, I hate pride and arrogance, corruption and perverse speech (Prov. 8:13).

When you surrender yourself to Christ and you are dedicated, it is a permanent and unconditional act. The Lord gave a clear indication of this when He said, "Anyone who isn't with Me opposes Me, and anyone who isn't working with Me is actually working against Me" (Matt. 12:30).

The implication cannot be missed: Christians must identify with Christ in every aspect of their lives. By demonstrating it in the way they live, they attract others to Jesus because they are an example of His love.

It is a sad fact that very little of the godliness many people reveal during Sunday worship is seen in the way they do business. They are involved in shady business transactions; they show their dishonesty, through their social agendas and lack of compassion, understanding and love. These things have no place in the Christian faith, and are a total denial of Jesus Christ.

Do not let Sunday be taken from you ... If your soul has no Sunday, it becomes an orphan.
~ Albert Schweitzer ~

Your love for God must always be evident in your love for one another, and you should behave like you do in the house of the Lord on Sundays. Remember, as a Christian, you constantly live with, and are in the presence of, the Master. Turn away from everything unchristian and honor God the Father every hour of every day.

Give me the grace, God, to live to Your glory and honor every day. Amen.

The Mark of Distinction

"Your love for one another will prove to the world that you are My disciples" (John 13:35).

Each Christian church has its own distinctive teachings. In most cases, it is claimed that the teachings are inspired by the Holy Scriptures, yet in spite of this, these teachings can drive God's children apart and bring division.

This conflicting dogma has already caused much confusion and done great harm to the faith. People who have given up Christianity point to the division in the church and say, "See there, that's how Christians love each other!" Many earnest seekers don't know what they should believe anymore.

Our only business is to love and delight ourselves in God.
~ Brother Lawrence ~

The Master made it clear that His disciples would be known by their attitude toward one another. This kind of love is not selective, and chooses not to be displayed only in religious fellowships and gatherings. If someone loves Christ, they must also love other people who love Him. Failing to do this is denying the Master's instructions.

The obstacles that cause division between God's people are often very hard to overcome. Dogma, religious organizations, pride and control all contribute to estrange churches from each other. It is essential that the spirit of love increase so that we can overcome obstacles created by human thinking. We must also love those who have conflicting theological opinions. This is only possible if our love for the Master is the most important experience in our lives.

Grant, Holy Spirit, that I express my religious convictions with love and understanding. Amen.

How Can I Serve God?

Your love has given me much joy and comfort, my brother, for your kindness has often refreshed the hearts of God's people (Philem. 7).

Many people want to serve God, but don't know how. The result is inevitable – they experience a vacuum in their spiritual life and become frustrated because they feel that their lives lack fulfillment. They search in vain for ways to witness for the Lord and serve Him, but every avenue seems to be a dead-end. In their disappointment, they withdraw more and more, until, in many cases, they reject a faith that seems meaningless to them.

Every one of the Lord's disciples has a capacity for loving and there can be no better way of serving the Lord than to share the love of Christ with others. Love can encourage, save and give the helpless and the desperate hope. It can break down dividing walls, build relationships, bridge all gaps and heal all wounds. As Paul puts it, "Love is the greatest of all!"

Our Lord does not care so much for the importance of our works as for the love with which they are done.
~ Teresa of Avila ~

If you are looking for a way to serve the Lord, why not start by loving others in His name? A telephone call, a note, paying someone in need a visit, or contacting someone involved in the Lord's work can bring great joy and encouragement. Even more important, it will bring fulfillment to your own life while you serve the Lord in this way.

Use me, heavenly Father, to share Your love with others on the road of life. Amen.

The Power of Prayer

Are any of you suffering hardships? You should pray (James 5:13).

Very few people in our world today don't have problems of some kind or another. The media reports on wars, tribal conflict, disease, famine, drought, floods and many other disasters. There are those who suffer in their personal lives because of sickness or sorrow and some have financial problems. Others suffer a forced change in lifestyle that is a cause of concern to them when they think of the future. The fact that people are worried and upset is a fact of life – but what is the solution?

> You cannot alter the will of God, but the man of prayer can discover God's will.
> ~ Sundar Singh ~

To the person who is staggering under the pressure of worry and stress, the following might seem like a hypocritical statement, but what Paul says is the undeniable truth: "And we know that God causes everything to work together for the good of those who love God and are called according to His purpose for them" (Rom. 8:28). Irrespective of your current problem remember that the Lord has an eternal view of life. He will use your current circumstances "to work together" for your own good, on the condition that you trust Him to lead you. Golgotha is a classic example of this.

No matter how much you are suffering, never stop praying for the power of faith that will enable you to give yourself and your problem to God, and to trust Him to lead you out of the darkness into His wonderful light.

Hearer of prayer, I call out to You in my anxiety and need and know that You will hear and answer my prayer. Amen.

Christianity's Challenge

You must have the same attitude that Christ Jesus had (Phil. 2:5).

The different churches interpret Jesus Christ's challenge according to their own explanation of His message. For this reason, it is difficult to understand what Jesus' challenge to His followers really is.

One thing, however, is very clear. Those who call themselves Christians, and walk the road in fellowship with Him, must grow in grace and knowledge of their Lord, Jesus Christ, so that they can become more and more like Him. Any Christian who is satisfied with less than this has an incomplete gospel.

To walk in fellowship with the Living Christ and to grow in His grace and knowledge demands spiritual and mental discipline. You don't need to be a brilliant student, but the brain that you do have must be dedicated to Christ to the very best of your ability. Through dedication, your thinking must be set free from fear, hate, bitterness, greed, pride and any other destructive power.

> Growth is the only evidence of life.
> ~ John Henry Newman ~

If you feel incapable of meeting these high standards, call to mind all the wonderful promises in the Bible. The Scriptures insist that Christians must have Jesus Christ's attitude, and through this discover the Master's approach to life, share in His wisdom and experience His guidance.

If this challenge and truth sound too theoretical to you, always remember that the Master and His indwelling Spirit promises this to all who are willing to accept it.

Holy Lord Jesus, grant that I will reveal Your attitude in my life, in this way glorifying You. Amen.

The Reward of Christian Service

I am setting before you today a blessing and a curse – the blessing if you obey the commands of the LORD your God (Deut. 11:26-27 NIV).

No one with any spiritual insight serves God to be rewarded. To be capable of worshiping and praising God is enough reward in itself; it is dreadful and immature to think that you may be doing this for God so that He will do something for you in return. No person is in a position to negotiate with God.

God, in His eternal and boundless wisdom, owes nobody anything. It is impossible to serve Him without receiving a blessing, but it is important to serve Him for His own sake and not just for the blessings He pours out over you. Trying to serve God without an awareness of His indwelling Spirit only leads to frustration, disappointment and unhappiness.

We don't follow Him in order to be loved; we are loved so we follow Him.
~ Neil Anderson ~

When you forget about the self in your service to God, you will find that the Master comes close to you and you become aware of His indwelling Spirit that strengthens you.

You cannot possibly do God's work in His Spirit without becoming aware of His living presence. One of the deserving influences of serving Christ is that you are drawn closer and closer to Him and this inspires you to serve Him better.

Lord, my God, may the way I serve You not be spoiled by hidden motives or selfish desires. Amen.

Lies and Gossip

"God blesses you when people mock you and persecute you and lie about you and say all sorts of evil things against you because you are My followers" (Matt. 5:11).

Life can sometimes be hard if you are a sensitive soul. It is possible that you convince yourself that people are saying untrue and unkind things about you and this makes your life miserable. And then there are the people who find perverse pleasure in telling you what others say about you.

If what is said about you is true, you must do something constructive to neutralize the cause of the criticism. If not, you must rise above the negative comments and be spiritually strong enough to decide that you will not allow people to hurt or influence you with their mockery and snide remarks.

The only way to rise above the unfair lies and be free of the hurt it causes, is to live for God's approval and no one else's. It is impossible to stop people talking about you, but make sure their lies are totally false.

> The trouble with most of us is that we would rather be ruined by praise than saved by criticism.
> ~ Norman V. Peale ~

When you are battered by gossip, don't respond in the same way – don't stoop to their level. Bring the person to know God's love by means of prayer or other action. Always remember that God knows all about your pain, and if you involve the power of prayer and love in the matter, you are following the most constructive path.

Lord Jesus, help me through Your wisdom to handle lies in a constructive way. Amen.

Fasting

Why don't Your disciples fast like John's disciples and the Pharisees do? (Mark 2:18).

You have undoubtedly tried many things to move closer to God – prayer, worship, reading the Bible and joining a cell group. You might have devoted yourself to the church or to serving the community. Do you ever fast as an act of surrender and dedication? Some Christians do, and give the money they save in this way to the poor who don't have much to eat.

People in Jesus' time fasted as a token of remorse and confession. The original law of the Old Testament demanded that people should fast once a year. Later on, it was increased to four times. In Jesus' time, the Pharisees fasted twice a week. In the times of the apostles, Christians sometimes fasted for a specific occasion, especially when they prayed in earnest for a new missionary outreach (see Acts 13:2; 14:23).

Fasting is a divine corrective to the pride of the human heart. It is a discipline of body with a tendency to humble the soul.
~ Arthur Wallis ~

Jesus fasted when He was tempted in the wilderness and it is likely that He fasted four times a year as the old Jewish custom stipulated. He didn't give His disciples any specific instructions about fasting and neither did Paul.

If you are convinced that God wants you to go without food, do it. You might wish to do it from time to time as a sign of remorse and confession, or to be enabled to concentrate more on prayer and meditation. You may also fast as an act of love for Jesus, or as a way of showing your sincere concern for the millions of hungry people all over the world. Don't feel pressurized, but fast as a sign of your commitment to Him.

Jesus, You broke the bread at the Sea of Galilee. Break the bread for those who have nothing to eat. Amen.

Celebration

"Do wedding guests fast while celebrating with the groom? Of course not. They can't fast while the groom is with them" (Mark 2:19).

For some people, faith is a matter of unflinchingly abstaining from all the joys of life. Discipline is a fundamental part of Christianity, but they exaggerate this principle beyond all bounds. They not only deny themselves joy, but also deprive others of it.

Jesus often referred to the kingdom of God as a feast. We read that He often attended festivities of some kind. In this Scripture, He portrays Himself as the groom at a wedding and His followers as the groom's guests. Their weddings were not the half-day celebrations we know today, but often lasted a whole week. A wedding was a festive and a joyful occasion. With this, Christ was pronouncing a loud and clear "no" to everyone who wanted to turn religion into a long-faced, joyless endurance test. He was saying, "To live with Me is to celebrate life!" He wasn't propagating a carefree, irresponsible and artificial approach to life. He was positive, confident and joyful.

> The opposite of joy is not sorrow. It is unbelief.
> ~ Leslie Weatherhead ~

At best, life is not easy. As far as this is concerned, you and I are no different from anyone else. Celebrating life with Jesus is experiencing life with all its joys and sorrows, successes and failures with a cheerful heart and attitude; with a positive mindset and a trusting faith. It is to hope against hope, no matter how difficult the situation, and to seek the lovely, the good and the holy. How does this celebration fit into the framework of your approach to life? Change it today.

Father God, turn all our sorrow into pure joy in You. Amen.

Trust and Hope

The strongest among you will disappear like straw; their evil deeds will be the spark that sets it on fire. No one will be able to put out the fire (Isa. 1:31).

History is packed with remnants that were left behind when mighty people who seemed invincible were eventually defeated. When those who were driven by evil tendencies reached their end, it was an example of good triumphing over evil. This always created the possibility of a new beginning.

The leaders who ruled over Israel were no exception. They allowed and encouraged idolatry. They did not care for the poor and the weak. They were involved in corrupt and selfish practices and made a mockery of justice. They disobeyed God.

Those who keep speaking about the sun while walking under a cloudy sky are messengers of hope, and the true saints of our day.
~ Henri J. Nouwen ~

But, as always, God would have the last word. Isaiah prophesied that these people would be destroyed by their own evil deeds and that this would pave the way for a new order that would bring about peace and hope for the nation. He looked beyond the present and trusted God to restore peace.

No matter how powerful dictators might be, in the end they always get what they deserve. God will clear the way for peace, hope and of justice. If you look at the world around you today, there are situations that seem hopeless – but they aren't. Because God is God, He will pronounce judgment over the mighty and evil leaders and create the possibility of a better life. Never despair. Keep on trusting and hoping.

Almighty God, destroy the mighty that multiply evil, and establish Your government of truth and righteousness. Amen.

Follow Christ's Example

Don't lord it over the people assigned to your care, but lead them by your own good example (1 Pet. 5:3).

Authority and leadership require specific qualities. Simply being dynamic and decisive is not enough. And it is not enough to have knowledge or to be innovative, either. High on the list of priorities for leadership are the qualities of compassion for fellow humans and understanding, combined with sincere humility.

During His short earthly ministry, Jesus drew great crowds to Him, but in spite of His authority and power, He led by example. His teachings were not words only, but also actions. He was caring, and His loving compassion and understanding for all could be clearly seen. The Romans used their power to rule over the people, and the priests and scribes used their positions of authority to gain the admiration of the people. Jesus, however, used the simplest and most effective way, namely that of love, to draw people to Him.

Leadership is found in becoming the servant of all.
~ Richard Foster ~

If you are in a position of authority, remember that your power will be measured by the example you set, and not by the extent of your authority. To achieve this, look up to Jesus and the example He set. If you demonstrate the practices and character typical of Jesus in your dealings with people, your leadership role will prove to be successful.

Father God, enable me to show compassion and love for my fellow humans in all my dealings with others. Amen.

Jesus' Influence

Anyone who belongs to Christ has become a new person. The old life is gone; a new life has begun! (2 Cor. 5:17).

Religion is like a magnet to those who enjoy an argument. They take an obscure text from the Bible and spend precious time attaching a meaning to it that was never intended. It is possible to make religion so philosophical that it loses its sense and meaning for ordinary folk.

A meaningful faith must show practical results. It is of little use telling people to love God without showing them how that love should be revealed. Emphasizing the therapeutic value of forgiveness is not nearly enough. It is essential to reach beyond theory and to put love and forgiveness into practice.

> Setting an example is not the main means of influencing others, it is the only means.
> ~ Albert Einstein ~

You might be a zealous follower of Jesus, but if your spirit is rigid and confined, your faith will not count for much. It is when you live in the presence of God, and reflect on His gracious and loving personality, that you reveal to the world the kind of faith that is a blessing to all you come into contact with. They will know instinctively that you know Jesus and that He blesses them through you.

There can be no effective argument against a living and positive faith. When narrow-minded believers become honest; when lives are transformed by the redeeming love of Jesus Christ; when homes that used to be hell become heaven, then there can be no argument against the influence of the Living Christ in the lives of people.

Lord Jesus, grant that the quality of my daily walk will be the greatest argument for my faith. Amen.

Look Ahead

"Look! I am creating new heavens and a new earth, and no one will even think about the old ones anymore" (Isa. 65:17).

As time goes by, it is to your own advantage to consider how your faith helps you to walk the road in the world we live. You may have your own personal reasons why you feel either pessimistic or optimistic about the future. It will probably depend on the plans you cherish for the future, or the disappointments you experienced in the past. Try to focus on your personal situation and acknowledge the God who is the God of the Bible, as well as the Father of our Lord Jesus Christ.

We look ahead with hope in our hearts because, in addition to Him being the God of unlimited sources and initiatives, God is also the God of renewal and re-creation. His creative work goes on forever. Even if we are caught up in the past, God isn't. He is the God of the future because He comes to us from the future as the eternal Creator. As wonderful as His work was in the past, He is constantly seeking to create a new heaven and a new earth.

When considering the creation, the how and the when does not matter so much as the why and the wherefore.
~ R. de Campoamor ~

The book of Revelation ends with a dream God has for the future. His creative work is never finished. He is still making new things. He is able to create new things and new people from the destruction and decay of the past. Look around you and see if you can find God's wonders in your life and in creation, and bow down before the Creator God of worship.

Creator God, let me look ahead to Your future creations with hope in my heart. Amen.

The Human Word

So the Word became human and made His home among us (John 1:14).

In the days before e-mail, cell phones and computers, there was a trend to have what was called pen pals in different parts of the world. If you had something to tell your pen pal on the other side of the world, you wrote to them and they wrote back. Sometimes pen pals exchanged gifts. Gradually you got to know each other better and better. But to really know that person, you had meet him yourself, speak to him and spend time with him face to face.

This is what God did in Jesus Christ. He came to us Himself. Before this, He sent messages through the prophets. He spoke directly to people.

People could see Him, speak to Him, listen to Him and touch Him. This made all the difference. And knowing that He loved them urged people to love Him, too.

Jesus Christ is God in the form of man; as completely God as if He were not a man; as completely man as if He were not God.
~ A. J. F. Behrends ~

For a few short years the Everlasting, the Creator came to earth as a human being of flesh and blood. God's message took on a human shape. He grew, struggled, learnt, ate, worked, slept, suffered and died for us. But it was more than "with us and for us." It was for *you!* If Christ was God's Word to you personally, what is your word to Him?

Eternal God, thank You that You became human for a period of time so that I may shout Yes! to You. Amen.

A Light in the Darkness

The light shines in the darkness, and the darkness can never extinguish it (John 1:5).

The movie *Amazing Grace* is about the life of William Wilberforce and the campaign he launched to abolish slavery in the early nineteenth century. It is a story of compassion, pity, conviction, courage and perseverance. It can be said that Wilberforce truly "saw the light" because he saw how cruel and wicked the slave trade was, though everybody accepted it as fine.

Because his campaign challenged the rich, he was met with tough opposition from those who wanted to keep the slave trade going. But Wilberforce, convinced that he was called by God to free the world of this gruesome evil, pressed on until, after many years of toil, he achieved his goal. He was surrounded by darkness, but it never quenched the light of God that shone in his heart and life.

Darkness cannot drive out darkness; only the light can do that. Hate cannot drive out hate; only love can do that.
~ Martin Luther King, Jr ~

There will always be darkness in this world. In a certain sense it is a form of the chaos that ruled before creation that is trying to re-establish itself. The birth of Christ, a sign of the victory of light over darkness, is an indication from God that He will not allow darkness to triumph. This is why Christ's birth is a celebration of hope, joy, love and God's light. Each of us can contribute toward keeping that Light burning.

Jesus, Light of this dark world, shine in our darkness and light everything up. Amen.

April

His light on my path shows me
the power of the cross.

He took the humble position
of a slave and was born as
a human being. When He
appeared in human form, He
humbled Himself in obedience
to God and died a criminal's
death on a cross.
~ Phil. 2:7-8 ~

I, the Eternal Wisdom, was
mocked as a fool in a white
garment before Herod,
My fair body was rent
and torn without mercy
by the rude stripes of whips,
My lovely countenance was
drenched in spittle and blood,
and in this condition I was
condemned, and miserably
and shamefully led forth
with My cross to death. They
shouted after Me, so that:
Crucify, crucify the miscreant!
resounded to the skies.
~ Henry Suso ~

Eternal God and Father of our Lord Jesus Christ,
Love made You send Your Son
to this sinful world to be our Example and Savior.
He had to pay a humanly impossible price.
He had to become the Man of Sorrows
to make the joy of heaven possible for us.
He came to earth in poverty so that we
could enjoy the wealth of Your forgiveness.
He cast off His godly majesty so that
we could become children of the King.
He gave His love unconditionally so
that we could spread this love to others.
His life set a perfect example for us to follow.
He died a shameful death on the cross,
for our salvation, forgiveness and eternal life.
He was triumphantly raised from the dead,
so that we may be part of His triumphal procession.
Lord Jesus, Man of Sorrows,
make us willing to accept the challenges
of being Your children
and to live and die as Your faithful witnesses.
Thank You that those who are part
of Your cross also share in Your crown!
Thank You that those who suffer with You
will also live with You.
In the name that is above all names,
Jesus our Savior.

Amen.

Focus on Christ

When they looked up, Moses and Elijah were gone, and they saw only Jesus (Matt. 17:8).

A truly devout life is filled with rich experiences. You may belong to a vibrant church and the community you share with other Christians is a great inspiration to you. Your service to God might develop your personality far beyond your greatest expectations and you might feel that Christ is working through you. As you reflect on the time before you accepted Christ as your Redeemer and Savior, you are amazed and overjoyed at the difference He made in your life. The old life has made room for the new, and in your life, the right priorities now top the list.

Christ is a jewel worth more than a thousand worlds, as all know who have Him. Get Him and get all; miss Him and miss all.
~ Thomas Brooks ~

While you rejoice and stand in awe of all the wonderful things God has done for you, don't allow your joy and enthusiasm to sidetrack you from your love and devotion to Jesus Christ. When talking about everything Jesus has done for them, many believers turn the spotlight on themselves instead of on Jesus Christ. Without them noticing it, this egotistical attitude becomes part of their lives and it is detrimental to their spiritual experiences as disciples of Christ.

When Peter, James and John received their revelation and heard the Holy Voice speak, they got up from the ground where they had fallen face down in terror, and "saw only Jesus." This is the decisive moment of the Christian experience. No matter how wonderful your own spiritual experiences might be, they can only be credible if Jesus is the focal point.

Lord Jesus, I keep You at the center of my life, because when I have You, I have everything. Amen.

The Resurrection and the Life

Jesus told her, "I am the resurrection and the life. Anyone who believes in Me will live, even after dying" (John 11:25).

We human beings are a strange mix. It is in our nature to be selfish and yet we reach complete maturity when we love. We are lazy by nature, but realize our greatest achievements when we work hard. We are capable of the most atrocious wickedness, but also of unbelievable goodness. We are a continuous battlefield for growth and decay, and life and death are always close bedfellows, whether we are aware of it or not.

Jesus came to give life a new dimension – life in all its fullness. Yet death pursued Him for the greater part of His life. When He invited His disciples to follow Him, He told them it was not going to be a path of roses – more like taking up a cross. And many who followed Him died an early earthly death precisely for this reason – that they were His followers.

Our old history ends with the cross; our new history begins with the resurrection.
~ Watchman Nee ~

He *was* life to them and in Him they found a quality of life that death could not destroy. They hoped for the resurrection that He taught them would come at the end of time, but found that it came for them in the middle, and before they died. The "Jesus method" of life was not limited to any single phase, time or status. If you believed in Jesus and followed Him, His life and resurrection power was already alive and working in you – and continued after your death.

To Christians, resurrection is a promise for the future. But that future has already begun, because faith in Christ brings Him to life in your inner being. Therefore, rejoice – your resurrection has already begun!

Resurrected Master, live Your life in me. Amen.

Love Has No Price Tag

Mary took a twelve-ounce jar of expensive perfume made from essence of nard, and she anointed Jesus' feet with it, wiping His feet with her hair (John 12:3).

People who love beautiful and precious things will spare no expense or effort to get hold of a specific object or item they badly want. For one person it could be a painting, for another a veteran car and for another a postage stamp. Sometimes someone will give the one they love an expensive gift that they can barely afford.

Jesus was loved by His followers in spite of the fact that His family members hardly understood Him, and that His group of disciples were confused and uncertain themselves. On top of this there was the opposition of spiritual leaders who were supposed to believe in Him. The family in Bethany counted among those who loved Him most. Each of them loved Jesus in their own specific way. Martha met all His earthly needs; Lazarus witnessed about the great miracle that happened to him, and Mary with her unsparing love, worshiped Him. She expressed her love by the extravagance of her expensive gift to Him. She didn't do it to receive some favor from Him. She did it with a pure and sincere love.

God regards with how much love a person performs a work, rather than how much he does.
~ Thomas à Kempis ~

We can never pay Jesus for His great love for us. We can, however, express our love for Him in actions that tell Him, "I love You." Some people do it by working hard, serving in His church, others by soulful worship, uplifting music, or some special work of art. If you feel the need to show your love for Christ, do it now, do it big and don't count the cost.

Lord Jesus, grant me the grace to love You sincerely and to make sacrifices for You. Amen.

Evil Lurks All Over

Judas Iscariot, the disciple who would soon betray Him, said, "That perfume was worth a year's wages. It should have been sold and the money given to the poor" (John 12:4-5).

It is sad but true that most of us are a mixture of good and evil and that there are more troublemakers than honorable people. Even the best among us are at risk of suddenly and rapidly going bad.

In John's story about the events in Bethany, he set the scene with strongly contrasting role players. Lazarus was there, filled with love and praise for the Man who called him back to life. Martha was there, busily going about her humble duties. Mary was there, offering a fragrant token of her love. And Judas Iscariot was also there, his greed for money so strong that he scorned her offering of love.

> If you have been tempted into evil, fly from it. It is not falling into the water, but lying in it that drowns.
> ~ Anonymous ~

If Mary's beautiful gift of love was passed on to us through the ages, it is equally true that Judas is also alive and well among us. There are those who are willing to use the structures of the established church to play their own power games, promote their own publicity and twist the gospel to suit their own political agendas.

Christian believers must not be too shocked when, at some stage, leaders they trusted are involved with evil. It lurks around every corner and is forever on the prowl where people interact. Spreading the gospel of Jesus Christ places tremendous temptations on the path of Christ's most devoted servants. Pray for those who have fallen by the wayside; but also pray for those who didn't, so that they aren't snared as well.

Lord Jesus, protect Your servants in all temptations and trials.

Amen.

Hidden Agendas

Not that he cared for the poor – he was a thief, and since he was in charge of the disciples' money, he often stole some for himself (John 12:6).

One of the greatest truths about the devil is that he always appears in the form of "an angel of the light." So whenever people claim that they never think about themselves, but always act entirely in someone else's interests, watch out! Few people are genuinely unselfish.

Judas pretended to be a particularly caring person. At the time, John, who tells us the story, probably trusted Judas. But when he wrote down the story, he had seen right through Judas. Judas had shown his true colors by then, and was trying to enrich himself at the expense of the poor – and of Jesus. Judas loved money and would take someone else's gift to fill his own purse. The poor would see nothing of the money.

He that will play with Satan's bait, will quickly be taken with Satan's hook.
~ Thomas Brooks ~

There are robbers all around you who pretend to be knights in shining armor. Politicians proclaim their deep concern about "the poorest of the poor" while they are in fact seeking publicity for themselves. Churches and church leaders might make an appeal for donations to help the poor and they sometimes do praiseworthy work, but not always. Some are more concerned about their own welfare. There are businesses that do the same. Make sure that when you give, you can trust those who work with your contributions, and insist that they account for their stewardship.

Holy Lord Jesus, keep me from ever wearing the money-grubbing mask. Amen.

Let Love Flourish

Jesus replied, "Leave her alone. She did this in preparation for My burial" (John 12:7).

When you love someone deeply, you sometimes give them a gift that you actually cannot afford. A man might give his wife expensive jewelry even if they are in debt. He feels that this is a way of showing his deep love for her, more than a practical, useful gift would do.

This is one way of looking at the expensive gift of aromatic oil that Mary gave Jesus. And Jesus treasured that love because He realized it was given to Him in an act of deep, sincere devotion and worship. He knew that He was only a few days from His death. The cross was steadily coming closer and Mary had bought this expensive oil to anoint His body with. Did she sense what was coming, or did Jesus tell her? If she knew, she was probably thinking that it was better to do it then than wait until His death.

Love is the only service that power cannot command and money cannot buy.
~ Anonymous ~

There are many practical ways of honoring God and showing Him your love besides showering Him with beautiful things. But in the end, it is the giver of the gift's love that will decide what the gift will be. So many churches are decorated and adorned by people as an expression of their love for God and their gratitude to Him. Resist the temptation to criticize them and to speculate what they should rather have done with the money. Admire the love and dedication that motivated them to do it. Rejoice in the beauty and glory of these "gifts" because they are a token of love for the Lord.

Thank You, Father God, for all the beautiful gifts that bring You joy and glory. Amen.

The Gospel Speaks for Itself

When all the people heard of Jesus' arrival, they flocked to see Him and also to see Lazarus, the man Jesus had raised from the dead (John 12:9).

It is easy to be led astray by some aspects of Christianity. Some church groups are little less than social clubs. Some Christians are so involved in social and political activities that they forget the simplicity and truth of the gospel in the process. Some evangelists become so obsessed with money, that they forget the work of righteousness and truth implied in the gospel.

The truth is that the gospel speaks for itself when it comes to God's actions (and this is what the entire gospel is about), because that is where people see Him at work. And it has a mightier effect than many sermons. God acted through Christ's miracle of raising Lazarus from the dead. The truth and power of the gospel lie in the fact that God does act, and that is the central fact of Christianity. It was clear to the crowds that flocked to Bethany that God was busy with something very special.

There are two things to do about the gospel – believe it and behave it.
~ Susanna Wesley ~

Where Jesus is honored and glorified, God does special things. He changes people. He heals them. He transforms communities.

Search for the place where Jesus is at work. Focus on God and His deeds, those of both 2,000 years ago as well as today. Stay true to the things that are at the core: "He [Christ] is the beginning, supreme over all who rise from the dead. So He is first in everything" (Col. 1:18).

Heavenly Father, let me always keep in mind the mighty deeds You did through Jesus Christ. Amen.

Greet the King

The next day, the news that Jesus was on the way to Jerusalem swept through the city. A large crowd of Passover visitors took palm branches and went down the road to meet Him (John 12:12-13).

When royalty is visiting a place, detailed plans are made for the royal visit. Everything is cleaned and tidied up, things that need to be repaired are attended to, and nowadays security is regarded as the number one priority.

When the Israelites celebrated Passover, huge crowds gathered – some from faraway countries – and it became a gala event. They commemorated the Israelites' escape from Egypt centuries before. But rumors that the Man who raised Lazarus from the dead was also present spread like wildfire, and they also came to greet Him. They waved palm branches to indicate the royal status of the honored guest. Caught up in the emotion of the moment, they paid homage to Jesus with a greeting fit for a king. Little did they know that within a few days' time, He would be crowned with a crown of thorns. And no one could think that in centuries to come, millions would crown Him in many more coronations.

Many are willing that Christ should be something, but few will consent that Christ should be everything.
~ Alexander M. Stuart ~

Some people prefer to think of Jesus mainly as their Friend, their Savior or their Good Shepherd. Whatever your preferred image of Jesus might be, remember that He is also the King of kings, a person with royal status. The book of Revelation declares: "The whole world has now become the Kingdom of our Lord and of His Christ, and He will reign forever and ever" (Rev. 11:15).

Savior and Redeemer, I praise You as the King of my life. Amen.

The World Belongs to the Lord!

Then the Pharisees said to each other, "There's nothing we can do. Look, everyone has gone after Him!" (John 12:19).

Insight into human nature and the irony of history are the essential ingredients of a good story. We see it in movies, novels and plays. The Pharisees feared that if the great number of people who were ready to crown Jesus as King, succeeded in doing so, the priests would lose their authority and power, because the Romans would react with strict laws. They simply couldn't understand that this was the last thing on Jesus' mind. But the crowds that welcomed Him were just as wrong.

He had not come to be their type of king either. John said, "He came to His own people, and even they rejected Him" (John 1:11). Even though the multitudes honored Him on Palm Sunday, they had still not put their trust in Him as Lord and Savior. And the Pharisees believed that the whole world (that He had come to save) was starting to follow Him.

Anything that one imagines of God apart from Christ is only useless thinking and vain idolatry.
~ Martin Luther ~

The world belongs to Him – there is no doubt about that! It is His because He died on the cross to bring about salvation. It is so because He refused to become the political figure created by the wishful thinking of the crowds. It is so because He reigns in glory at the right hand of the Father. The Word of truth is spreading slowly but surely all over the whole world. The seed that He sowed in the hearts and lives of people grows across the entire world.

Pray faithfully that His cause will prosper and that more people will acknowledge Him and crown Him as their King.

We acknowledge You, Lord Jesus, as King in the hearts of people all over the world. Amen.

Working Things Out

His disciples didn't understand at the time that this was a fulfillment of prophecy. But after Jesus entered into His glory, they remembered what had happened and realized that these things had been written about Him (John 12:16).

It often happens that after we have listened to an expert discussing a series of events that took place that we say, "So this is what it was all about. I always wondered." We don't always understand everything when it happens, but later on we do.

Jesus' disciples didn't understand much of what He did or said. They found it difficult to grasp who He really was. He died, rose from the dead, ascended to heaven and sent them the Holy Spirit.

> Faith is deliberate confidence in the character of God whose ways you may not understand at the time.
> ~ Oswald Chambers ~

One way in which the Holy Spirit works is to explain the truth about Jesus Christ to us. He was still helping Jesus' disciples to work everything out long after Jesus had already left them.

Don't worry if you don't understand everything about God and Jesus at the moment. Accept that the Holy Spirit will explain it all to you one day, and then you will understand the truth. You build up your knowledge of Christ step by step, just like the first disciples. Just keep on reading your Bible regularly – focus on the New Testament. Learn everything you can and trust in the Holy Spirit to lead you to greater depths of understanding and insight. You must accept that God will keep some truths from you until you see Him face to face one day. On earth you must walk in faith and not by sight.

I praise and thank You, Father God, that You will interpret everything for me and explain everything in Your own time.

Amen.

The International Faith

Some Greeks had come to Jerusalem for the Passover celebration (John 12:20).

We associate certain traits with certain nationalities. Exquisite cuisine belongs to the French; engineering to the Germans; watches to the Swiss and business to the Israelis.

We also associate religion with the Israelis. The Jewish faith traveled far and people of various nationalities found firm ground on which to build their faith in the Ten Commandments. For a long time the Greeks were the leading nation in the ancient world. The Greek army conquered and occupied large parts of the world, their philosophy was among the very best and their architecture breathtaking. Some Greeks took up the faith of Israel and came to celebrate the Passover in Jerusalem. Little did they think that they would experience the birth of a new faith – a faith that would spread across all of Greece. God would not be limited to Israel. All over the world people would meet Him, not by means of the Law and the Commandments of Israel, but through the Prophet of Nazareth, Jesus the Christ.

> The gospel of Jesus Christ can make bad men good and good men better, can alter human nature, can change human lives.
> ~ David O. McKay ~

Christianity burst its banks, like a river in flood. When the Holy Spirit and the persecution from Rome drove the apostles far and wide, the news of Jesus Christ spread rapidly. The same would happen in Asia Minor, in Syria, North Africa and even in Italy. Tradition has it that Thomas took the gospel to India. Wherever you might go and whatever you do, be sure to pass on the message of Jesus' love.

Holy Father, through the Holy Spirit, make me a faithful witness of the gospel. Amen.

Read John 12:20-36

Followers of Jesus

"Anyone who wants to be My disciple must follow Me" (John 12:26).

When we were young, our parents warned us about keeping bad company. It seemed that "bad company" was found all over and was ready and waiting to pounce on unwary and innocent young people. The company you keep will affect you and eventually cast you in a certain mold.

On the night before the crucifixion, Jesus made it very clear to His disciples: To be Jesus' follower was not a walk in the park. Following Him was not a career leading to riches, fame and power. It meant going where He went; serving as He served. It meant being ready to die at any moment. Some of those listening to Him did die for Him. For most of His disciples, it meant lifelong service to others; to help them and to care for them – to glorify Christ. Following Jesus means obediently accepting any path He shows you. For many it meant an untimely death. For others, a long and tiring period of hard work. For many it might mean performing your daily tasks with humility, selfless loyalty and love.

The strength and happiness of a man consists in finding out the way in which God is going, and going that way too.
~ Henry Ward Beecher ~

For every Christian disciple, being a "follower of Jesus" means battling side by side with Him through toil and hardship; suffering and sacrifice; drudgery and effort. At times it will be exciting, but more often than not it will be a matter of patiently tolerating repetitiveness, but it will be done in love and with Jesus Christ. Discipleship has its own rewards and the greatest of these is simply being a Christ follower.

My greatest joy in life, Lord Jesus, is being Your humble disciple.
Amen.

Through Thick and Thin

"My servants must be where I am" (John 12:26).

People who have battled through tough times together develop a special bond of friendship, like soldiers who fight side by side in a war, or miners who survive a mining disaster.

During His three-year ministry Jesus and His disciples experienced many things: they witnessed miracles; stood firm through opposition and scorn; wrestled to get to know the truth of God; survived a storm on the Sea of Galilee, and started a movement that would have a tremendous influence on humankind. His suffering and consequent resurrection bound them to Him more than anything else. When the Holy Spirit came, they understood these things better.

> There is no other method of living piously and justly, than that of depending upon God.
> ~ John Calvin ~

To this day, people live and die for Him. A female physician once told Bryan Green, the Anglican evangelist, of a painful experience she had. She accidentally cut and poisoned her finger during surgery, which led to intense pain and suffering. On more than one occasion it seemed that her life was in danger, but eventually she recovered. She said, "I would trade this experience of pain and suffering for nothing else, because during it the presence of Christ was more real to me than ever before."

Whatever your trial or suffering, find Christ in it and journey with Him. Beyond the problem, anxiety and exhaustion, you will find that Christ surrendered Himself for you and that He will never let you down. Whether you sense His presence or not doesn't matter – He is holding you tight! Don't ever forget this.

Lord Jesus, let me always walk with You and trust You under all circumstances. Amen.

Love of Life and Love for God

"Those who love their life in this world will lose it. Those who care nothing for their life in this world will keep it for eternity (John 12:25).

Sometimes it is said of a deceased person, "He/she lived life to the full." This simply means that they had lots of energy and did many things. We also say, "He/she loved life," which means that they had many sources of joy and pleasure.

Jesus said that the road to true life, eternal life, is to let go of everything and hand it over to God. By that He meant that if you give yourself over in a selfish way to your personal health, riches and enjoyment, you will actually lose the life you seek. You end up absorbed in yourself, while your love for others steadily diminishes, distancing you from God. But if you give your life to God, you will get to know a new dimension, both here and in eternity.

No one ever lost out by excessive devotion to Christ.
~ H. A. Ironside ~

William Barclay tells the story of the life of Cosmo Lang. He had a strong personality with an overpowering ambition for worldly success. A friend, who was a devout Christian, convinced him to give his life to Christ and he became an Anglican minister. While he was studying, he went to the prayer chapel of the college one day to pray. While he was there, he heard an unmistakable voice saying, "You are needed." He finally rejected all his earthly ambitions in obedience to God. He later became the Archbishop of Canterbury.

God also needs you, whether you hear a voice or not. He wants you to give up all your selfish desires in obedience to Him and live for Him.

My spirit, my soul, and my body I dedicate to You, O Lord. I offer myself as sacrifice to You forever. Amen.

Being Afraid of Being Afraid

"Now My soul is deeply troubled. Should I pray, 'Father, save Me from this hour'?" (John 12:27).

Most of us are overcome with fear at some time or another. Some people's fear gets completely out of hand in certain situations. There is a long list of phobias, the technical name for ordinary fear, like agoraphobia (a fear of crowds) and claustrophobia (a fear of confined spaces).

Jesus was aware that He was facing death and He had to deal with the natural human fear of death. He didn't try to put on a brave face and pretend that He was not afraid. He was a real human being and no other occasion demonstrates His human dignity more than this one. Part of Him feared the cross, but He faced that fear, wrestled with the dilemma of going through with it or not, and then surrendered Himself obediently and courageously to His Father's will.

Fear knocked at the door. Faith answered and no one was there.
~ Anonymous ~

Don't be afraid of fear. The fact that Jesus knew what it was to be afraid shows that it is not a disgrace to feel afraid sometimes. Face up to your fear bravely and see it for what it really is. Then quietly and humbly ask God for extra courage. Ask Him to go through this fear with you, to hold you and let His strength work through you.

Think about how Jesus walked to the cross, quietly and bravely. Surrender yourself unconditionally to God, put yourself in His almighty care and trust Him completely. He will carry you through this.

Lord Jesus, help me to face up to fear and overcome it in Your name. Amen.

Glorify God!

"Father, bring glory to Your name" (John 12:28).

The human race is forever chasing after glory, and most people have a fervent wish to be famous. Sportsmen do their utmost to win championships because it will mean both money and glory for them. Those in the entertainment business strive for the limelight – they want their share of glory. It is the same with politicians who want to see their names in the newspaper and their faces on TV. The same thing happens in religious circles.

Those who crowded around Jesus after He had raised Lazarus from the dead were glorifying Jesus. But Jesus wanted God to be glorified. He knew that something much bigger than the raising of Lazarus was just around the corner – His crucifixion and resurrection. This was God's tremendous act of salvation and it had to draw people to Him. It had to point to the great Almighty God as the Great Savior of the world. It was also Christ's final act of obedience.

> The radiance of the divine beauty is wholly inexpressible: words cannot describe it, nor the ear grasp it.
> ~ Philimon ~

You are at your very greatest when you glorify God. Glorify Him for His goodness, His grace, His majesty and His love. Honor Him for His constant presence and His help. Love Him for His gentleness and grace, and thank Him for His abundant provision. There is absolutely nothing better that you can do than glorify God!

Holy Father God, help me to glorify You at all times. Amen.

Listen, God Is Speaking

Then a voice spoke from heaven, saying, "I have already brought glory to My name, and I will do so again" (John 12:28).

Sometimes people claim that God spoke to them. Jean d'Arc heard so many "voices" that people thought she was mentally disturbed. There are people who claim that God told them to do something. Many of these allegations are untrue – they are simply claiming God's authority to justify their own selfish aims.

God speaks throughout the entire Bible. When Jesus prayed to His Father and asked for glory to be brought to His name, "a voice spoke from heaven." Some of the people present heard it as the sound of thunder, and often in the Old Testament thunder was regarded as God's voice. Whatever sound they might have heard, God spoke to both Jesus and the crowd. God was saying to Jesus that He had already brought glory to His name by raising Lazarus and that He would do it again with the death and resurrection of the Son.

Words that do not give the light of Christ only make the darkness worse.
~ Mother Teresa ~

Does God ever speak to you? Do you listen for His voice during your daily prayers and when you read the Bible? Do you listen when you worship in church on a Sunday, or in your cell group, or in your conversations with friends? Sometimes God speaks by making you conscious of a certain matter that you need to know about. At other times, He speaks to challenge you; sometimes to comfort you, and always to encourage and assure you of His love.

Father God, urge me to listen and obey when You speak. Amen.

Everybody!

"When I am lifted up from the earth, I will draw everyone to Myself" (John 12:32).

Some activities are practiced in certain cultures only. Snake charmers are peculiar to India; eating fish and chips wrapped in a newspaper is unmistakably British. Jesus was universal. He was the Savior of *all* people. In biblical times, some Jews and also many "heathens" turned to Him. Soon the Greeks started believing in Him and also the Romans. Augustine was one of the early church fathers, and He was from Africa. Columba, another devout church father, was from Ireland. He took the message of Jesus to the island of Iona on the coast of Scotland and used it as a base from which to introduce Jesus to the northern part of Britain. Today, millions of people believe in Jesus and He is worshiped from Fiji to Finland, Chile to China, and Namibia to New Zealand.

The gospel is not speculation but fact. It is truth, because it is the record of a person who is the Truth.
~ Alexander MacLaren ~

Christ is universal because He personifies God's love to all people and because He died for all of humankind. His cross is much more than an adornment. It is a proclamation, a symbol of life through death. It is God's word to a world of violence and evil. It looks ahead with hope for the future and declares that God loves, that God forgives and that God saves.

If you have always believed in Jesus, devote yourself to Him anew. If you have never believed in Him, give yourself to the Man of Golgotha and to God. Let Christ's dying blood flow into your heart until it overflows with compassion toward all people. And let that love, His love, be your reason for living.

Lord Jesus, give me the faith to reach out to all people with Your salvation message. Amen.

Do You Believe?

Jesus shouted to the crowds, "If you trust Me, you are trusting not only Me, but also God who sent Me" (John 12:44).

Some people accept that there is a "supreme being," but they say they cannot believe anything more than that. This means that they think there is "something" bigger, better and higher.

Jesus is not in this category. He is not a "something." He is a "He!" He is real, a person of flesh and blood. People saw Him in the flesh, the same as all other human beings. They met Him, touched Him, spoke to Him, responded to Him and had a relationship with Him. They even knew His family. They knew Him as the son of the carpenter on the street corner. And even if they did accept that God would one day send a Messiah, He would be a royal figure, not an ordinary carpenter.

God is best known in Christ; the sun is not seen but by the light of the sun.
~ William Bridge ~

Those who experienced Jesus' sincerity and love found it difficult to associate "this man down here" with "that God above." And those who responded to Him were not the normal "religious types." Even Jesus found it difficult to convince them that He was the one sent by God. "You don't believe only in a carpenter," He said, "you are accepting the God of eternity."

Believe in Jesus Christ and find your God and your life in Him. He is the greatest proof of the only true, personal God that has ever existed.

We thank You, Lord our God, that You are the God and Father of our Lord Jesus Christ and therefore also our God. Amen.

Before the Passover Celebration

Before the Passover celebration, Jesus knew that His hour had come to leave this world and return to His Father (John 13:1).

We like celebrating great events and honoring special people with formal ceremonies. We like ceremonies where wreaths are placed at the foot of statues to honor those who died in wars. A mother's eyes are filled with tears of longing when she looks at a photograph of the son who never returned from the war. A widow will wipe a tear from her eye when looking at the photo of the man she hoped to grow old with. These things can happen any time.

Jerusalem was packed with pilgrims who had come to celebrate Passover and to commemorate the liberation of the Israelites from Egypt some twelve or thirteen hundred years earlier. But behind the scenes, something much more sensational was happening. In a secluded room, Jesus was unobtrusively preparing for death.

God often visits us, but most of the time we are not at home.
~ Joseph Roux ~

He was preparing the disciples for the trauma awaiting them. He gathered them together in the upper room and certain sacred things took place. He spoke to them, shared a meal with them, washed their feet and prayed. Today, no one knows anything about the Passover that was celebrated that day – only about the crucifixion, death and resurrection of Jesus Christ.

It is good to celebrate the important Christian feasts, but it is even better to allow God to break through to you and speak to you in a moment of silence or during an ordinary, everyday event. He is not bound to the great festivities only – He can come to you any day and at any moment. He could be trying to get through to you today.

Holy Father, come to me now in the awe of this moment. Amen.

Where Are You Headed?

Jesus knew that the Father had given Him authority over everything and that He had come from God and would return to God (John 13:3).

An elderly lady was in hospital, seriously ill. The family members had been called and were gathered around her bed. The curtains were drawn and she lay motionless for hours. Then the physician quietly entered the room and nodded to the family. He took her pulse, laid his hand on her head and listened. Finally he looked at the family, shook his head and said, "I'm afraid she is going downhill." The old lady suddenly opened her eyes and replied, "This lady is going nowhere, and when she does go somewhere, it will be up!"

Jesus always knew that He came from the Father, but now He was intensely aware that He would soon return to the glory He had to leave to come to earth. He could look beyond the pain, deceit, cruelty, mockery and unrighteousness and take pleasure in the joyous homecoming He knew awaited Him in His Father's house.

Heaven will be the perfection we have always longed for. All the things that made earth unlovely and tragic will be absent in heaven.
~ Billy Graham ~

A person ought to know where they are headed. Look beyond the suffering, loneliness and loss of everything you treasured. Look up to God. Look at Jesus. Think of heaven that is your final destination. Think of the reunion with the loved ones you were separated from so long; of the love that will triumph and the earthly trials and tribulations that will be something of the past. Think of the Father's glory and the presence of Jesus in all His glory and greatness. Do you know where you are headed?

Lord Jesus, help me through the Spirit to look beyond the present and see the glory of heaven. Amen.

Look at Your King

Pilate said to the people, "Look, here is your king!" (John 19:14).

We often say sarcastically, "There is none as blind as those who will not see." This refers to what we call "selective perception." We don't see everything in sight. We see the things we are interested in, that excite us or that frighten us.

As today's Christians we must stop our normal activities and look at Jesus. Let us choose to see Him and remind ourselves of His crucifixion. Look with eyes of faith at the historical occasion in Jerusalem two thousand years ago. Take note of what Pilate said to the crowds, "Here is your king!" The priests chose not to see Jesus. Suddenly the Caesar of Rome – whose rule they hated – was the king they wanted to see.

Through the ages, people chose to see the crucified Jesus as their King – or they chose another they preferred above Jesus to dominate their lives and rule their hearts. Two thousand years later He is still on the throne. Caesar is history.

Jesus does not give recipes to show the way to God as other teachers of religion do. He Himself is the Way.
~ Karl Barth ~

Choose the King you want to look up to and serve Him to the best of your ability. Choose the One who rules from the cross and who has a crown of thorns on His head. His kingdom is coming!

Lord Jesus Christ, I bow before Your throne and acknowledge You as my only King! Amen.

Broken Hearts

When all the crowd that came to see the crucifixion saw all that had happened, they went home in deep sorrow (Luke 23:48).

Death is a bewildering moment. When an elderly person dies, it is difficult to accept straightaway that someone who was here yesterday is gone today. When a young person dies of an incurable disease, it seems like such a waste; you can't help thinking of what that person could have achieved.

The crowds who saw Jesus die on the cross went home with broken hearts. They were hoping for wonderful things He was still going to do. Some hoped He would set Israel free from Roman oppression. Now that dream had died with Jesus. Others believed that He was the promised Messiah. Then there were those who loved Him for His uncomplicated love of people, and through that love they got to know God and love Him.

Earth has no sorrow that heaven cannot heal.
~ Thomas Moore ~

The disciples were probably more shocked than anybody else. There was enough reason for everybody to feel deep sorrow. Even God was sad – it was His Son they killed.

When you are sad, always remember that Jesus will comfort you. He walked the road to Golgotha; He knew suffering, anxiety and loneliness, and He reaches out to you in your affliction. You do not walk alone, Jesus walks with you. And when you come back home in tears, dealing with all the stress and heartache, He will stay with you until you can face the world again.

Loving Savior, comfort everybody with a broken heart. Amen.

Rebel or Savior?

You brought this man to me, accusing Him of leading a revolt. I have examined Him thoroughly on this point in your presence and find Him innocent (Luke 23:14).

People still "examine" Jesus and always come to the wrong conclusion. Some say that He was just an ordinary teacher and that His followers made such a fuss about Him because they thought He was going to start a protest movement. Others thought He was a well-disguised rebel looking for the opportunity to start an uprising. Others thought His miracles were simply fables and exaggerations. The theories about Jesus are endless.

There are some sciences that may be learned by the head, but the science of Christ crucified can only be learned by the heart.
~ Charles H. Spurgeon ~

Jesus' miracles made them believe that He had greater power than any human being. Evidence proved that He made the blind see, cast out demons, raised the dead, calmed the stormy sea and touched lepers to heal them. When He taught people about God, He spoke in uncomplicated terms so that even the most simple could understand.

Think fresh about Jesus today and come to your own conclusion. You can write Him off as a rebel, an instigator, a prophet or just a pleasant person who lived long ago. Or you can recognize Him as the One who saved you, died for you, was raised from the dead for you, and who gives you hope for the future. Follow Him in the spirit to Golgotha, hear Him pray for those nailed to the cross and prepare yourself to meet Him after His resurrection. Glorify Him as your Savior and Redeemer.

Lord Jesus, once again we walk the way of suffering with You, hereby intensifying our love for You. Amen.

Make the Right Choices

Then a mighty roar rose from the crowd, and with one voice they shouted, "Kill Him, and release Barabbas to us!" (Barabbas was in prison for taking part in an insurrection in Jerusalem against the government, and for murder.) (Luke 23:18-19).

Crowds can behave in a notoriously fickle way. They may fully support a sports star today and turn their backs on him tomorrow. On Palm Sunday, the crowds in Jerusalem praised Jesus as their new King and a few days later demanded that He be crucified. They were willing for Barabbas to be set free and wanted Jesus crucified. Barabbas was in prison because he had committed murder and led an uprising. Conversely Jesus avoided political involvement and brought the people healing, hope and abundant life.

As in those times, strange choices are made in the world of our day. Sometimes we choose war instead of peace, weapons rather than bread, money rather than righteousness, and despair instead of hope.

> Destiny is no matter of chance, it is a matter of choice, it is not a thing to be waited for, it is a thing to be achieved.
> ~ William J. Bryan ~

You and I also need to make choices and the options are not always that obvious. It seems easy to choose between Jesus and Barabbas, but deciding between a truth and a lie can be difficult, especially if the right choice is the unpopular one. Bribery can approach us in different guises and sometimes employment depends on how willing one is to agree to dishonest practices. We are constantly choosing between Jesus and Barabbas. Not only during Easter does it become a matter of conscience. We must always be wide awake, and often it is only the guidance of the Holy Spirit that will help us make the right choice.

Holy Spirit of God, help me every day to make the right choices.

Amen.

Let Him Save Himself

The crowd watched and the leaders scoffed. "He saved others," they said, "let Him save Himself if He is really God's Messiah, the Chosen One" (Luke 23:35).

From the cradle to the grave, we have to struggle to survive in an environment which is often competitive and aggressive. This means we have to acquire the knack to cope, play according to the rules, and in general take care of ourselves. These are forms of self-preservation.

Jesus lived for others and not for Himself. He taught others, healed and befriended them, led them and always put them first. Even on the cross He prayed for His enemies, forgave the criminal next to Him and asked John to look after His mother. His whole mission on earth was to save others.

God gives the cross, and the cross gives us God.
~ Madame Guyon ~

The leaders of the time misunderstood the purpose and aim of His life. To meet God's requirements, Jesus had to save others by not saving Himself.

Easter is a fresh reminder that the purpose of Jesus' suffering and death was to save us, and to replace our self-satisfaction with concern for others. Ask yourself how you can change so that you will care more for others, give selflessly, and be driven by love. Remind yourself that the focal point of the Easter story is Jesus' loving self-sacrifice, for you and the entire human race. It is at the foot of the cross where you become a new creation.

Crucified Master, fill me with Your sacrificial love. Amen.

The Mystery of the Cross

So You're the Messiah, are You? Prove it by saving Yourself – and us, too, while You're at it! (Luke 23:39).

People like watching magic tricks and sleight of hand. Circus performers take your breath away with their stunts. Magicians and conjurers leave people dumbfounded by their tricks.

Crowds in Palestine undoubtedly flocked to Jesus, not as much to hear what He had to say about God, but to be present when He performed a miracle. Many could probably not tell the difference between His mighty acts and the entertainment provided by magicians. One of the criminals on the cross expected Jesus to perform another miracle by saving Himself and them too. *What on earth,* the criminal might have thought, *is the use of performing miracles if you can't use this skill to save yourself in a critical situation like this?*

> The cross alone is our theology.
> ~ Martin Luther ~

Because of the way he reasoned, he didn't realize that a miracle was indeed taking place. Right next to him, the holy God of love was performing the great miracle of the salvation of humankind. Magic tricks amuse for a short while, but they have no permanent worth. The miracle of salvation and redemption is for all time. It changes lives, saves souls, changes evil people into good ones and brings faith to doubting hearts. The wonder of the love of Christ, manifested by His death, means eternal life for those who first despaired but then believed and hoped.

Easter acknowledges the cross of Jesus Christ as the miracle of God's grace, which it is indeed. Change the criminal's words and say, "You are the Christ of God, save me now and forever!"

Crucified Savior, save us by Your miracle of love. Amen.

The Final Dedication

Then Jesus shouted, "Father, I entrust My spirit into Your hands!" (Luke 23:46).

On Good Friday we commemorate Jesus Christ's crucifixion with gratitude. We do this with a mixture of amazement, sorrow, thankfulness and mystery. In spite of all the explanations, there is always something about the crucifixion that challenges human comprehension. It is the moment when we kneel down and wonder how a man who died centuries ago can put us right with God.

In His dying moments Jesus called out, "Father, I entrust My spirit into Your hands!" Death was not the moment of sacrifice – it was its completion. Jesus dedicated Himself to the Father all His life. As a child, He told His worried parents that He had to be busy with the things of His Father. At His baptism in the Jordan, Jesus dedicated Himself, not to His choice of work, but to God's. During His temptation in the wilderness, He subjected Himself to His Father's will, and in Gethsemane He once again surrendered Himself to God. All along the road He walked, He said yes to God. He made His mission of the salvation of humankind His first priority.

Give your all to Christ, who gave His all for You.
~ Anonymous ~

Good Friday is an appropriate time to ask yourself how strong your devotion to God really is. To what extent you have surrendered yourself to Him? Even though you did give your life to Him at some stage, it is possible that you have let Him down and fled, like His disciples did? Have years of painful experiences worn away your faith? Today, look at Jesus on the cross and say for the first time, or once again, but with sincerity, "Father, I entrust my spirit into Your hands!"

Father God, let Your will be done today and every day of my life.
Amen.

An Independent Opinion

When the Roman officer overseeing the execution saw what had happened, he worshiped God and said, "Surely this man was innocent" (Luke 23:47).

Soldiers are usually hardened people. Warfare makes those involved tougher than they would otherwise be. Being a soldier is not for the faint-hearted.

The officer in charge of Jesus Christ's crucifixion was of a senior rank, a centurion. He had been part of military life for many years and had probably served in various places. To be put in control of a hundred soldiers meant that he was no fool. To be in control, often in difficult circumstances, you had to be sharp-witted. You had to earn the respect of those under you.

> God can never receive too much praise.
> ~ Anonymous ~

This officer probably knew something about the farce that Jesus' hearing turned out to be. It is very likely that he saw right through the hypocrisy of the priests and of Pilate and was on guard while his soldiers mocked Jesus. He was in no way unfamiliar with death, and blood was nothing new to him. It was highly probable that he had heard about all the miracles.

While watching Jesus' last moments, Pilate quietly spoke words that revealed insight and conviction. He could see that Jesus was not an ordinary criminal and he was undoubtedly disappointed that Roman justice had sunk so low to allow this good man to die. His considered opinion was "surely this man was innocent" (v. 47). And, like thousands through the ages, he praised God. Join him today in doing the same!

Lord, our God, we live to praise You. Amen.

Who Rolled the Stone Away?

They found that the stone had been rolled away from the entrance (Luke 24:2).

When someone is healed from a serious illness, we might say, "The age of miracles has not yet passed." During Easter we celebrate one of God's greatest miracles of all time – the resurrection of Jesus from the dead!

The question at that moment was, "Who rolled the stone aside?" How did Jesus' dead body come to life again and how did He leave the rock tomb when a heavy stone was covering the entrance? At the time, the guards that were specifically appointed to prevent the body from being stolen fabricated the story that the disciples stole the body. By means of a mighty act of His power, the Eternal God rolled away the stone, brought His Son back to life and by doing this, and introduced a new era in history.

> Without the resurrection there will not be a Christianity – Christianity stands or falls with the resurrection, and this single factor makes Christianity remarkably one of a kind.
>
> ~ Steve Kumar ~

That same God still rolls away stones. He rolls away the stone of our unbelief that declares, "This is impossible! Dead people don't return to life!" He rolls away the stone of our desperation that claims, "In the end, He is also subject to nature and death." He rolls away the stone of our fear and says, "I entered death and tasted the glory of resurrection from death. And so will you!" There is only one explanation of what happened that first Easter morning in the garden – God! Don't seek or ask for any other answer: "Death is swallowed up in victory. O death, where is your victory? O death, where is your sting?" (1 Cor. 15:54-55).

Living Lord Jesus, because You live, Your children will also live.

Amen.

May

His light on my path shows me the power of the Holy Spirit.

Just as you can hear the wind but can't tell where it comes from or where it is going, so you can't explain how people are born of the Spirit.
~ John 3:8 ~

Walk so close to God that nothing can come between you.
~ Anonymous ~

Holy God, we worship You as the Giver of new life.
Blow through our lives, O Spirit.
Cleanse us of all contamination and impure thoughts;
of lack of love, selfishness and intolerance.
Give new life to our entire being.
Blow through the hearts of all who are distressed.
You are the Comforter that the Savior promised to the sad.
Raise them up who snap under the burden of their sorrows
and give them new courage for life.
Blow through Your church, O Spirit,
and bring a God-willed revival.
Transform communities that work out of love for You
and make Sundays of everyday life.
Blow, O Spirit, through our country, its leaders and all its people.
Work in a powerful way for reconciliation, tolerance and peace.
Let the Father's name be glorified, Christ's attitude live in us,
and let Your fruit, O Spirit, become visible in our lives.
Be, O Spirit of God, to all of us,
the breath of a truly Christian life.
In the name of our Risen Savior, Jesus the Living Christ.

Amen.

Shallow Spiritual Water

When He had finished speaking, He said to Simon, "Now go out where it is deeper, and let down your nets to catch some fish" (Luke 5:4).

Jesus gave the above instruction to His despondent disciples. They had been fishing all night, without success. Despite physical fatigue, disappointment and the fact that they knew Jesus was not a fisherman, they obeyed Him.

Christ gave us His Spirit in our hearts to make us holy. He calls on His followers to venture bravely into deeper spiritual waters, and not flounder in shallow muddy water. Too many of His children waste their spiritual strength on the surface, without ever reaching for the abundant depths.

Like the early church of Laodicea, we are neither hot nor cold. Because we are lukewarm, we cannot reach, or make use of, the full depths of the life that Christ has in mind for us through His Spirit.

If this is happening in your spiritual life at the moment, make a decisive and honest effort to do something about it. Be as serious in your approach to your spiritual growth as the situation deserves. Ask the Spirit to let you take to heart the challenge in John 15:4-5: "Remain in Me ... you cannot be fruitful unless you remain in Me." Don't settle for second best. If His Spirit leads you to the full depths of your relationship with your Savior, you will be rich and strong, surging forward to where Christ wants to take you and use you.

There is no better evangelist in the world than the Holy Spirit.
~ Dwight L. Moody ~

Holy Spirit of God, lead me to the depths so that I may fearlessly follow Christ. Amen.

Spiritual Maturity

And now, just as you accepted Christ Jesus as your Lord, you must continue to follow Him. Let your roots grow down into Him and you will overflow with thankfulness (Col. 2:6-7).

One of the dark clouds hovering over the Church of Christ is the large number of immature disciples – people who claim to love Jesus, but because their love lacks substance, their witnessing is ineffective. They need to be fed milk because they are still babies in the faith, though they should already have been on solid food long ago.

These people gave their lives to Jesus with great sincerity, but there was no spiritual development. The Word tells us to evaluate our spiritual progress in all honesty. The point of departure for spiritual growth is primarily a personal meeting with God through His Son, Jesus Christ. God leads us to the Word incarnate through His Word. We dare not stop short at this meeting, but allow the Holy Spirit to lead us to deeper knowledge of the Living Christ.

Spiritual growth consists most in the growth of the root, which is out of sight.
~ Matthew Henry ~

In doing so, we gradually reach spiritual willingness to discipline and feed our thoughts from the sources God has made available to us: His Word, prayer, meditation, worship and spiritual conversations. This leads to increasing obedience to His will as the Spirit reveals it in our hearts. Without us being aware of it, the image of Christ is revealed more and more in our lives as we grow toward spiritual maturity. Our faith blooms to the enrichment and adornment of that part of earth we occupy in His name.

Thank You, Holy Spirit of God, that You help me grow to spiritual maturity. Amen.

A Faith Lamp

Go to a shop and buy some for yourselves (Matt. 25:9).

There are many things in life other people can do for you. An architect can design a house for you; a building contractor can build it for you; the service station can service or repair your car; a medical doctor can treat your illness. One thing, however, you must do for yourself – believe in Jesus Christ as your personal Savior. There is no way that your faith lamp will burn with someone else's oil.

For some people, all their lives they are part of the wedding procession of the Lamb, but their hearts are never completely involved. Then, panic-stricken in their crisis hour, in terror of dying, they call for help. Then they cling to mother or father; to husband or wife; to church or preacher: "Give us some oil – it's getting dark around us." It is of no consequence if these people *want* to help them. What matters here is what they *cannot* do. Salvation cannot be divided. A parent can't believe for their child, a friend cannot be converted on behalf of a friend. Each of us must perform our own act of faith. You get this oil only if you go and buy it for yourself.

Salvation is God's way of making us real people.
~ St. Augustine ~

Thus we are cast back on to God – the only One we can receive faith oil from. He charges us nothing – the price has already been paid (see Isa. 55:1). We cannot borrow this oil, steal or beg for it. We must have our own personal certainty of faith.

We may have beautiful lamps – all the outward forms of religion – but if we don't have faith oil, our lamps will go out and we remain unsaved. Only God can keep us from that disaster if we come to Him in time.

Holy God, and in Jesus Christ, my Father, thank You that I may say through the Holy Spirit, "I know that my Savior lives."

Amen.

A Spirit of Love

We know how dearly God loves us, because He has given us the Holy Spirit to fill our hearts with His love (Rom. 5:5).

The certainty that God loves you can bring about a mighty turnaround in your spiritual life. It inspires your thinking, broadens your view, gives you new confidence, creates enthusiasm and makes your daily existence meaningful. All of this is the work of the Holy Spirit who continuously reminds you of the strong bond between you and the Source of true love.

The stronger this love between you and God is anchored to the foundation of faith and reality, the more strength and inspiration you draw from it. This is confirmed by the ripple effect of your love for your fellow humans. To say that you love Christ and yet refuse to lighten the load of an underprivileged person is a blatant denial of that love. If you truly love God, it brings you to a clear and sometimes painful awareness of the needs of others, and creates in you the urgency to do something about it.

All God can give us is His love; and this love becomes tangible – a burning of the soul – it sets us on fire to the point of forgetting ourselves.
~ Brother Roger ~

If you claim to have the love of God in your heart, it will find expression in your words and deeds. In this the Holy Spirit is your sympathetic Teacher. This love enables you to desire the best for those you meet. It includes heart and mind, as well as the will and emotions. It is the conscious effort to seek nothing else than the very best for others with the help of the Holy Spirit. The Source of this love is God Himself, as revealed in Jesus Christ and cultivated in our hearts by the Holy Spirit.

Spirit of Love, illuminate my heart and my thoughts, so that Your love will become visible in my life. Amen.

Blessed Assurance

For all who are led by the Spirit of God are children of God (Rom. 8:14).

The Holy Spirit always leads us to the core truths of the gospel: Fatherhood and childhood; salvation; certainty of faith; and heirship. These are great and glorious salvation truths. Praise the Lord!

It is unacceptable to claim that the human being is "nothing." Admittedly, Scripture does often remind us of the insignificance and brevity of the human life. But the re-creative theme of the New Testament is that God loved people so much that He sent His Son to the world to reconcile us to Him and to renew us so that we may become what God intended us to be.

We are so unspeakably valuable to God that He invites us to call Him Father. The Spirit leads us to rejoice in humble gratitude about the truth that Christ delivered us from our sin and made us children of God. As we stand in awe of this wonderful truth, we are also told to forget our sinful past and to concentrate on being a child of the King.

It's a good thing God chose me before I was born, because He surely would not have afterwards.
~ Charles H. Spurgeon ~

An unfailing certainty of God's Fatherhood does not presume smugness, complacency or pride. It is the practical and concrete result of an ongoing relationship with the Living Christ. No longer a slave, but a child and an heir: An indescribable miracle of God's love and grace.

I praise and thank You, O Father God, that I am baptized in the name of the Father, Son and Holy Spirit; that I am Your child and that Your Spirit assures me of this. Amen.

Forward on Our Knees

Devote yourselves to prayer with an alert mind and a thankful heart (Col. 4:2).

Must a person present their needs and wishes to God and then leave it to Him to answer in His own good time without constantly reminding Him? Or must you keep on asking? This has been a debatable point among the praying followers of Jesus throughout the ages.

The fact of the matter is that both arguments may be correct. Sincere prayer is not regulated by a rigid set of rules. God's Holy Spirit is at work in the hearts and lives of His children. "True prayer is a state of mind that creates a channel between the Almighty God and the insignificant human being. Just human sin can block this channel" (George Allan). It is amazing how the Holy Spirit adapts to the life, background and personality of the person and guides him into the godly presence by way of one of many roads.

Prayer is not conquering God's reluctance, but taking hold of God's willingness.
~ Phillips Brooks ~

The way of prayer, under the guidance of the Holy Spirit, doesn't always follow the most well-known route, but often takes the path that God chooses according to your personal needs. The result is always surprising and encouraging. Whatever prayer route you take, it is essential to travel it with faith and be aware of His holy and loving presence.

In the training school of the Holy Spirit, you will quickly learn to handle prayer positively. Prayer is not a panic button you press in times of crisis. In time, you will recognize answered prayers and thankfully praise the way in which God brings His works to fulfillment in your life.

Help me, O Hearer of prayers, to watch and pray through the guidance of the Holy Spirit. Amen.

The Test

"Your love for one another will prove to the world that you are My disciples" (John 13:35).

The test of true Christian discipleship is love. There is so much heartlessness, envy and character assassination in our world that sometimes we feel overwhelmed by these destructive powers. Unless we constantly pray and watch, we will be flooded by these attitudes. Christ expects a lot from His followers, and it is our obedience to His demands that distinguishes us from those who don't acknowledge Christ's rule in their lives.

To remedy a lack of love, we must experience the guidance of the Holy Spirit as a reality in our lives. We must develop a love for Christ that will become a driving force in our lives. Then we will tend to our own wounds instead of wounding others and serve humbly instead of trying to rule over others. This is the only formula a Christian can follow to live and work in this world that is so sadly lacking in love. The essential difference between believers and unbelievers is the love believers have for each other. It is a quality that should be clearly visible in our lives.

The God of love and the love of God constrain you to love one another that it may at last be said of Christians as it was at first, "Behold how they love one another."
~ Ralph Venning ~

Christ is the source of all true love. If we find it difficult to love, we must open up our lives to His Spirit and allow Him to love others through us. Then the world will know without a doubt to whom we belong and we will pass the test of discipleship. In following our Master's example, love will even enable us to win over those who hate us. Jesus demonstrated this to us on the cross when He prayed for those who nailed Him to it.

God of love, help me to be generous with my love, whether it is deserved or not. Amen.

Is Happiness a Vain Hope?

If you look carefully into the perfect law that sets you free, and if you do what it says and don't forget what you heard, then God will bless you for doing it (James 1:25).

Happiness is the one thing all people persistently strive for and yet it seems to elude most people most of the time. Happiness is like a butterfly: as long as you chase it, it will stay out of your reach, but when you are sitting down peacefully, it will settle on your shoulder. Happiness does not depend on external conditions, but on your deepest inner attitude toward God and life. With God at the center of your life, it is possible to experience rich and ongoing happiness, even in the most trying times.

There is no duty we so much underrate as the duty of being happy. By being happy we sow anonymous benefits upon the world.
~ Robert Louis Stevenson ~

It is not asking what you can get out of life, but what you can put back into it. The highest form of giving is giving something of yourself – to God and your fellow humans. Then you experience the highest form of happiness.

Many people look for happiness in material things. People who put their trust in material things don't own their possessions, their possessions own them. "And what do you benefit if you gain the whole world but lose your own soul?" (Matt. 16:26).

The road to happiness is not found in a change of circumstances, but in changing our way of thinking. J. M. Barrie said if we bring sunshine to the lives of others, we will not be able to avoid its reflection in our own. Honest and unselfish service to God and your fellow humans is happiness in a concrete form is something God desires for all of us.

Lord of joy and happiness, grant that I may find true happiness through the Holy Spirit. Amen.

The Thunder of Silence

"In repentance and rest is your salvation, in quietness and trust is your strength" (Isa. 30:15 NIV).

We get to know God by being quiet in His presence. The hustle and bustle of modern life hardly contributes toward acquiring a calm heart. Our quality of life is greatly determined by appointments, agendas and many other matters that make it extremely difficult to become quiet with God.

This daily rush has probably also invaded our spiritual lives to a great extent. We are too busy to worship; too busy for fellowship; too busy to read the Word in silence; too busy to spend time in prayer. This stampede has made the program of our spiritual growth totally meaningless. The faster we run, the more overwhelmed and impoverished we become; the more powerless our spiritual lives and the shallower our relationship with our Lord, the Source of our strength.

O God, make us children of quietness and heirs of peace.
~ Clement of Rome ~

Remember in such circumstances that there is a place of silence and solitude – with God. There we can be alone, but never lonely: God is always there! The wonderful part is that He is waiting for us, ready to fill us with new strength when the burden of life becomes too heavy for us; to renew us and refresh us so that we will be able to meet the raging demands of life and triumph over them in His glorious name.

Jesus is our perfect example. He regularly made time to be alone with His Father in silence. This was the secret to His ability to complete His work in a level-headed and calm manner.

God of the great silence, teach me to follow You to green pastures and quiet waters despite my rushed life. Amen.

The Folly of an Unforgiving Heart

"If you forgive those who sin against you, your heavenly Father will forgive you. But if you refuse to forgive others, your Father will not forgive your sins" (Matt. 6:14-15).

There are some people who stubbornly and willfully refuse to forgive if they have been wronged. Yet, forgiveness is one of the essential qualities of a true Christian. When Peter asked Jesus how many times a person should forgive, Jesus answered, "Seventy times seven!" (Matt. 18:22). He wanted to point out to Peter how extensive this virtue is. Forgiveness should be a perfectly normal attitude for the Christian disciple.

> Forgiveness is not
> an occasional act;
> it is an attitude.
> ~ Martin Luther King, Jr ~

The tragedy of people who are unforgiving is that they cause themselves more harm than anyone else. Withholding forgiveness from someone is breaking down the bridge you have to cross yourself. You rob yourself of God's forgiveness. If you are serious about demonstrating Jesus Christ's attitude, you dare not have any unforgiving thoughts in your heart.

You can't love Christ, and nurse bitterness toward someone at the same time. Then strife and frustration are etched on your being instead of the pureness of Jesus.

Refusing to let go of an unforgiving spirit proves that your pride and hurt feelings are more important than a happy and healthy relationship with the Lord. Then it is impossible to confess, "I believe in the forgiveness of sin." Forgiveness is the death knell of vengeance and bitterness.

Merciful God, through the Holy Spirit, give me faith that is big enough to overcome an unforgiving attitude. Amen.

Firm Gentleness

"God blesses those who are humble, for they will inherit the whole earth" (Matt. 5:5).

Gentleness means kindness and friendliness in your interaction with others. It is the exact opposite of self-assertion where you and your own interests come first. Self-assertion is in fact a denial of God and His omnipotence to intervene or take action. Gentleness is acknowledging your total dependence on God and living accordingly. It creates a deep and genuine selflessness.

Gentle people are contented, in contrast to those who are greedy. The latter are the "grabbers" in life and they desperately cling to everything they can get hold of. Gentle people are the "givers" who want to make others happy. God smiles through their eyes.

Nothing is so strong as gentleness, nothing so gentle as real strength.
~ Francis de Sales ~

Jesus is the epitome of gentleness: "See, your king comes to you, gentle and riding on a donkey" (Matt. 21:5 NIV). His gentleness was not soft or weak, but decisive and powerful. He taught us to forgive those who wrong us and to return evil with good.

The world doesn't belong to the brutal, but to the gentle – and so does God's new world. Behind every gentle person stands an Almighty God who takes care of them. Only the Holy Spirit can lead you to this Christian virtue (see Gal. 5:22-23). And this virtue leads you into God's kingdom.

Teach me, O Spirit of God, to live to the glory of God with gentleness in this world. Amen.

Yearning for God

As the deer longs for streams of water, so I long for You, O God (Ps. 42:1).

Unconditional surrender to God's will brings incredible happiness and blessing. Christ Himself said, "God blesses those who realize their need for Him, for the Kingdom of Heaven is theirs" (Matt. 5:3). This indescribable blessing begins when we realize our total inability, and place our full trust in God, obeying His will to such an extent that, we become citizens of His kingdom.

The world says, "Grab everything you can, and hold on to what you have." The Christian says, "He must become more and I must become less."

There is not a heart but has its moments of longing, yearning for something better.
~ Henry Ward Beecher ~

Most people find it difficult to be dependent. Our independence and self-reliance mean so much to us. But this independence is an illusion – the big lie that Satan plants in our hearts. The rich fool's sin was not that he was rich, but that He left God out of the equation.

Can you be happy if you hand over control of your life? Yes, if you hand it over to Jesus Christ. Then you will know a quiet happiness that no one can take from you. Real happiness in life can only be found when you have become completely dependent on God.

The essence of sin is selfishness and self-interest. The essence of salvation is surrender and dedication. Then your thirst is quenched and your hunger satisfied, because the Good Shepherd has brought you to green pastures and quiet waters where there is peace.

Lord Jesus, thank You that You fulfilled my yearning for God and that the Holy Spirit led me to surrender. Amen.

Mercy

"God blesses those who are merciful, for they will be shown mercy" (Matt. 5:7).

In Christ's parable of the Good Samaritan, we have three people with contrasting views of life. The robbers say, "Everything that is yours, is mine – I take it." The priest argues, "Everything that is mine is mine – I keep it." The Samaritan's outlook on life is, "Everything that is mine, is yours – I share it."

Mercy or compassion comes from God and is a fruit of the Holy Spirit. He takes a sinful, self-centered person and gives him a new heart – a heart like God's that truly cares, feels and loves. God would like to see that we are merciful, like Him. According to Antonie Ruler, mercy is generosity, compassion and a forgiving nature. It means that God's children feel for others because they love a God who does the same.

The Lord is full of tenderness and mercy.
~ James 5:11 ~

This beatitude (see Matt. 5:7), one of eight statements made by Christ about people who are blessed, teaches us that in the kingdom of God it is all about people. Christ laid down His life because He cared for people and He also expects it from His followers. He even expects that we should love our enemies, because, "If you love only those who love you, what reward is there for that? Even corrupt tax collectors do that much" (Matt. 5:46). It is a demand unique to Christianity that we must love our enemies.

Mercy or compassion is to look through other people's eyes, think with their minds, and feel with their feelings. It is identifying with them and having compassion for them.

Loving Father, give me a heart that beats warmly for the needs of others, so that I will always treat them with understanding, compassion and love. Amen.

The Bloodstained Road

"God blesses those who are persecuted for doing right, for the Kingdom of Heaven is theirs" (Matt. 5:10).

The gospel of Jesus Christ is pure and honest. It speaks of persecution, insult and of carrying the cross and suffering. Christ never misleads His followers. He didn't come to make life comfortable for us, but to save us and give us eternal life.

For a moment, think about the people Christ is talking to here. They belonged to the then familiar world, and the gospel crashed like a wave over the entire world at a time when Christians were severely persecuted. In their own homes they experienced being cut off from their families if they became Christians. Physically they would suffer torture, torment and death in the cruelest ways.

Either He will shield you from suffering or He will give you unfailing strength to bear it. Be at peace, then, and put aside all anxious thoughts.
~ Francis de Sales ~

This is how Jesus calls on His followers to take up their cross and follow Him. Will we be willing to stay faithful to Him until death? Will we be able to walk the bloodstained road of the martyrs if it is expected of us? If we are willing, we will be a tremendous encouragement to fellow believers.

Nobody ever suffers in vain for Christ. He is always with us, supporting us as He promises in Hebrews 13:5. Inspired and supported by the Holy Spirit, we can endure any suffering for Christ's sake; He gives us gladness on earth and rewards in heaven.

Help me, Spirit of God, to shoulder my cross and carry it behind the great Carrier of the Cross without grumbling. Amen.

Courtesy

"Do to others whatever you would like them to do to you" (Matt. 7:12).

Courtesy is free, and it yields surprising dividends in the form of improved human relationships. It creates happiness, peace and understanding when it is sincere. It is a Christian virtue that we must diligently strive for.

Unfortunately, people are often courteous or respectful only in certain circumstances. They will, for example, be considerate and kind when they try to please a loved one. Because this behavior doesn't come naturally to them, however, they soon get tired of it and can't keep it up. Consequently, they soon lapse back into their old ways.

> Without respect, love cannot go far or rise high: it is an angel with but one wing.
> ~ Alexandre Dumas ~

To be truly effective, courteousness must come from your deepest being. It mustn't be a conscious act, but an intrinsic part of your conduct; a natural expression of your true self. If it comes naturally to you, you enrich your own life as well as those you come into contact with. "Courtesy is one of the attributes of God, who sendeth His rain on the just and on the unjust; for courtesy is the sister of charity" (St. Francis of Assisi).

Cultivating a spirit of courteousness is inseparably linked to the Holy Spirit. If you are at peace with yourself, you will be able to live in peace with those around you. You find peace with yourself only when you are at peace with God.

Holy Spirit of God, cultivate in me a spirit of courteousness toward all people because they have been created in the image of God. Amen.

Overcoming Fear

The angel reassured them. "Don't be afraid!" he said. "I bring you good news that will bring great joy to all people" (Luke 2:10).

Fear is a destructive feeling and can have far-reaching effects on a person's emotions. It is not limited to the physical aspects of life, but can cause much more harm to your mind and spirit. Many lives have been wrecked because fearful people couldn't cope with the situations they were caught up in.

Here's vital and valuable advice for you when you're fearful: "You need not be afraid of sudden disaster ... for the LORD is your security" (Prov. 3:25-26). Christ is beside you to hold you in every situation in life because He loves you. When the icy fingers of fear grab at you, hold on to this thought and open up your heart to the whisperings of the Holy Spirit. Use His means of grace available to you: the Bible, prayer, fellowship with other believers, praise and worship of God. Slowly your fear will diminish and finally the love of Christ will drive it out.

The remarkable thing about fearing God is that when you fear God, you fear nothing else, whereas if you do no fear God, you fear everything else.
~ Oswald Chambers ~

This world has become a maze of fear. Fear already began with the Fall: "I heard You walking in the garden, so I hid. I was afraid because I was naked" (Gen. 3:10). We fear for this world; we fear the unknown; we fear for our children, for our bank account, for our health; we fear loneliness, old age and that great final fear – death.

There is only one place to go with all our fears: to Christ. He defeated the cause of our fear: sin, Satan and death. The Holy Spirit teaches us not to fear; we have reason to rejoice.

Spirit of Grace, You know the fear that hides in my heart. Bring the light of Christ's love to drive away all my fear. Amen.

Fearless Witnesses

Then Peter stepped forward with the eleven other apostles and shouted to the crowd (Acts 2:14).

Archimedes claimed that with an unmovable rock and a lever, he could move the earth. Peter found that "Rock" in the Eternal Rock, Jesus Christ! He also found the lever – the power of the Holy Spirit ... and he turned the world around! After Pentecost, the world would never be the same again because Peter had surrendered completely to the Holy Spirit.

Nuclear power has always existed, though it was only in our time that people started tapping this source. In the same way, since the beginning of time, God has always been Father, Son and Holy Spirit, but it was only with Christ's ascension that His children learnt the true power of the Holy Spirit: "You will receive power when the Holy Spirit comes upon you. And you will be My witnesses, telling people about Me everywhere" (Acts 1:8).

The world is not waiting for a new definition of the gospel, but for a new demonstration of the power of the gospel.
~ Leonard Ravenhill ~

A witness has experienced something personally and can give a first-hand account of the particular event. His testimony is based on personal observation. Spirit-filled people are always on fire for the Master. They love with a glowing love; they believe with fiery hearts; they serve with burning zeal. The fire in a child of God is the Holy Spirit enabling us to become powerful instruments in God's hand.

The power of Peter's testimony lay in the fact that he knew Jesus personally and accepted Him as Savior. By the power of the Holy Spirit, he was made into a fearless witness for Christ.

Lord Jesus, inspire me through the Holy Spirit to be a burning witness of Your salvation and love. Amen.

Peacemakers

Do all that you can to live in peace with everyone (Rom. 12:18).

The breathtaking pace of our lives today leads to raw nerves and flaring tempers. People who are normally peace-loving crack under the pressure. Ill feelings and misunderstandings are the inevitable result, and people become estranged from one another. This is by no means the life a child of God is meant to live.

Peace is not the absence of war, it is a virtue, a state of mind, a disposition for benevolence, confidence, justice.
~ Baruch Spinoza ~

To create good relationships means you contribute anything to the benefit of others. This is not a form of escapism from problems, but rather a purposeful effort to overcome them. It is a road to peace, even through strife, because it is God's work you are doing. Make the world a better place by rooting out weeds of bitterness and planting flowers of peace.

There are, however, people who are storm centers for trouble and warped relationships. They are always the cause of discord at home, in the church and in the community. Fortunately, there are also the people who build bridges, heal bitterness and make the world a better place. They are the children of God who have learnt self-discipline and humility through His Holy Spirit and who reflect the attitude of their Master.

As a peacemaker, you create a positive living space in which everybody around you can live, work and relax in peace. It is not an unreachable ideal or an empty dream. In Christ it is a feasible reality because He is the Prince of Peace.

Holy Spirit of God, help me to really make a contribution toward peace in this broken world. Amen.

Self-Confidence

I can do everything through Christ, who gives me strength (Phil. 4:13).

Losing your self-confidence is a problem all of us struggle with at some stage or another. It can happen gradually and unnoticed, or it can take place all at once with a traumatic experience. It can reach such alarming proportions that it finally drives you to despair. Then it is good to call to mind God's words in Genesis 1:27: "So God created human beings in His own image. In the image of God He created them."

Always hold on to your worthiness: you are a unique creation and you have been created in His image.

Go quietly and spend time with your heavenly Father in prayer, and remember that you can always go to Him and bare your soul to Him. After all, He is your Father! He knows you through and through. He gave you particular gifts and He sees great possibilities in you. Remember that God has great expectations for you and that His love will enable you to meet them.

It is not your business to succeed, but to do right: when you have done so, the rest lies with God.
~ C. S. Lewis ~

No matter how humble your task might be, if you do it to the glory of God, it will bear the stamp of worthiness. Through His Spirit, you will become one of the people who move forward in Christ's strength.

Thank You, Creator God, that I am a creation of Your hands and that You have a plan for my life. Inspire me through the Holy Spirit. Amen.

Gratitude

Give thanks for everything to God the Father in the name of our Lord Jesus Christ (Eph. 5:20).

Thankfulness is a Christian virtue that lends a special quality to our lives. We must never forget what God did for us in Christ. Our behavior and actions are rooted in the sentiment of thankfulness. "A thankful heart is not the greatest virtue, but the parent of all other virtues" (Marcus Cicero). It is not only the memory of the heart, but also praise to God for His unfathomable goodness.

The secret of being thankful is to live thankfully. This was Albert Schweitzer's philosophy in life: "In gratitude for your own good fortune you must render in return some sacrifice of your life for other life." In gratitude to God for life, you must live positively, productively and victoriously. In gratitude for your opportunities, you must use them as challenges to succeed in His service. In gratitude for your happiness, you must strive to make others happy. In gratitude for the beauty you see in His creation, you must make a contribution toward conserving and protecting His creation.

The hardest arithmetic to master is that which enables us to count our blessings.
~ Eric Hoffer ~

Our primary and greatest thankfulness is toward God who set us free through Christ from eternal death and sin. Add to your prayers of thankfulness, a life of thankfulness. If you follow the Holy Spirit's guidance in this, you will get to know true happiness – because a thankful person is a happy person.

Holy Spirit of God, make my whole life a song of thankfulness for Your love and grace. Amen.

Forget the Past

No, dear brothers and sisters, I have not achieved it, but I focus on this one thing: Forgetting the past and looking forward to what lies ahead (Phil. 3:13).

A person's memory is a wonderful gift from God. The Bible calls on us to remember the day of the Lord, to never forget His mercy and to think of the Creator in our youth. If we want peace of mind, however, we must learn to forget certain things.

We must forget the sins we have already confessed. The devil is only too keen to remind us of these. But God has forgiven us in Jesus Christ and He looks at us as if we have never sinned. Sin from the past needn't eat away at our hearts like a cancer. Learn from your mistakes and be more careful and sensible in future.

We must forget the petty arguments and misunderstandings of the past. We are all human and we mustn't nurse the faults of others in our hearts like a festering sore. We must also forget the good deeds we have done. We don't do good deeds to impress others, but because we are thankful to God for the underserved salvation He brought about through Jesus. Good deeds must be done only to glorify Him.

It is always the case that when the Christian looks back, he is looking at the forgiveness of sins.
~ Karl Barth ~

Refuse to remain in the dark valley when we should have reached the hills of a new dawn. Prayerfully and obediently we must allow the comfort of God to lead us into the light. He does this through His Comforter, the Holy Spirit.

Holy Spirit, Comforter of the sorrowful, help me to remember to forget the things that are bad for my spiritual growth. Amen.

Mountaintop and Valley

No, despite all these things, overwhelming victory is ours through Christ, who loved us (Rom. 8:37).

Sometimes you will find yourself on a mountaintop of spiritual ecstasy where the presence of Christ is an absolute reality. He Himself took the disciples down into the valley where they became deeply aware of their powerlessness and incapability – and this immediately after they shared a mountaintop experience with Him (see Luke 9:28-34). We will experience both the mountaintop and valley, but we know that the Lord will be with us every step of the way.

It is curious that physical courage should be so common in the world and moral courage so rare.
~ Mark Twain ~

It is encouraging for us to know that Paul knew what it was to be in the depths of spiritual despair. Yet he rose again to great heights of spiritual strength and experience. We must listen attentively when he emphasizes the highs and lows in his life, because the Holy Spirit wants to bring something to our attention through Paul's experiences.

You will have your share of mountaintop and valley experiences, but you will have to decide for yourself where you choose to stay on.

Too few of Christ's followers see themselves as victorious children of God. As a child of God, you must believe in your worthiness as a person. You must live like a worthy individual and develop a balanced self-image. It will give new quality to your existence and you will live on victorious soil to His honor and greater glory; a worthy image – bearer of God's love and power.

Almighty Father, I make my life available to You so that Your Spirit can develop it to its full potential. Amen.

Christian Joy

Always be full of joy in the Lord. I say it again – rejoice! (Phil. 4:4).

It is necessary to remind one another regularly that Christianity is a great joy. So many people have this false notion that a Christian must be dressed in black and go through life with a long face. At one stage, Oliver Wendell Holmes wanted to become a church minister but decided against it as many ministers he knew "looked so much like undertakers."

How many people are put off Christianity by our lack of joy? A little more Christian cheer would undoubtedly make this world a better place. Christianity is supposed to bring joy back into life and add flavor to our daily existence, like salt seasons food. The Christian has good reason to be joyful!

Rejoicing is clearly a spiritual command. To ignore it is disobedience.
~ Charles Swindoll ~

There is, of course, a right and wrong kind of joy. The world's joy is superficial, like that of the Prodigal Son in the country of sin and promiscuity. Let us not forget the joy of the homecoming feast in his father's house where the boy belonged.

God Himself is the source of the Christian's ongoing joy. It is through His Son that we become children of God. Christ says in John 16:22, "I will see you again; then you will rejoice, and no one can rob you of that joy."

Robert Louis Stevenson said, "When a happy man comes into a room, it is as if another candle has been lighted." Christ said, "You are the light of the world" (Matt. 5:14).

Source of all joy, thank You that I may have a share in bringing the message of joy to the world. Amen.

Dealing with Depression

Weeping may last through the night, but joy comes with the morning (Ps. 30:5).

Some Christians always seem cheerful and happy, while others struggle through spiritual darkness. Some people live life joyfully and seem to be unfamiliar with depression. There are those who have the ability to flourish in spite of setbacks, while others are discouraged and paralyzed when they pass through the valley of affliction. The God-fearing Job confesses, "So I looked for good, but evil came instead. I waited for the light, but darkness fell" (Job 30:26).

Some of God's most sensitive children also went through similar experiences. Many threatened to give up hope and, like Elijah, went and sat under a tree, wishing to die. Even our Master was sometimes distressed, for example in the dark shadows of the Garden of Gethsemane. Spiritual dejection is not necessarily synonymous with spiritual failure. It becomes a problem when you stop trying to move out of the darkness into the light.

When you come to the bottom, you find God.
~ Neville Talbot ~

Put your relationship with God right. Cut out everything in your life that causes division between you and God. Don't rate your own needs and desires higher than your duty to obey His will. "Commit everything you do to the LORD. Trust Him, and He will help you" (Ps. 37:5).

If depression is separating you from God, bring it to Him and experience His comfort and support in the dark times.

O Holy Spirit, O Holy God, in times of darkness bring me to a clearer understanding of Your unfathomable love for me. Amen.

Remain Faithful

"Remain faithful even when facing death, I will give you the crown of life" (Rev. 2:10).

Faithfulness is a word with an impressive emotional content. Our lives are crisscrossed with it, especially in our relationships. Here one thinks of the patriot's faithfulness to his country of birth; the soldier; the guard; the police officer who stays faithful until death; faithfulness in marriage, where people stay together through thick and thin for many years and face the world outside together.

The highest form of faithfulness is our faithfulness to God. This faithfulness is a fruit of the Holy Spirit (see Gal. 5:22-23). It is also faithfulness to Christian principles, even if it means going though fire. The principles in your life are the things that bind you to God: your faith, His Word, prayer, your sacramental vows, your marriage vows. It also means being faithful to your Christian calling in God's world. It is to place first things first and the ability to discern those things that really matter. It is being faithful in your task of witnessing, giving your tithe in His service, and holding on to God during suffering.

It is better to be faithful than famous.
~ Theodore Roosevelt ~

Those who remain faithful to God are richly blessed. He knows how tough temptation is – He will keep us going and make sure that we are not tempted beyond our abilities. No one will pluck us from His hand. If we are faithful, Christ will profess us before the Father like we profess Him before people. He will also give us "life" as a crown. This is true and abundant life: on earth and also in the hereafter where we will share in His glory forever.

Holy Spirit of God, enable me to remain faithful to God until death. Amen.

Human and Godly Sympathy

Blessed are those who help the poor (Prov. 14:21).

True sympathy doesn't lie as much in words as in quiet togetherness. It lies in being there for others so that when they reach breaking point, the bottled-up feelings can be shamelessly set free in a torrent of liberating words or tears. Knowing that there is a friend who suffers with you, and is willing to be quiet and listen, is often better than a thousand comforting words.

In our expression of sympathy, we are mainly expected to be available; to serve as a sounding board so that those who are suffering can work through their feelings and distress knowing that there is a friend who understands and who is prepared to listen.

No matter how precious and needed human sympathy may be, it is inevitably limited. But there is Someone who understands perfectly and whose sympathy is complete: "This High Priest of ours understands our weaknesses, for He faced all of the same testings we do" (Heb. 4:15).

> God does not comfort us
> to make us comfortable,
> but to make us comforters.
> ~ J. H. Jowett ~

Because Christ became human Himself, He understands the pain we go through and He also understands our needs. God is able to help: "All praise to God, the Father of our Lord Jesus Christ. God is our merciful Father and the source of all comfort. He comforts us in all our troubles so that we can comfort others. When they are troubled, we will be able to give them the same comfort God has given us" (2 Cor. 1:3-4).

God of comfort, grant me the grace not to buckle under my sorrow, but to live from the certainty of Your love. Amen.

The Great Comfort

He comforts us in all our troubles so that we can comfort others. When they are troubled, we will be able to give them the same comfort God has given us (2 Cor. 1:4).

Suffering and trials weave a special kind of beauty into the believer's life. After all, God did promise that all things, also pain and sorrow, will work together for the good of His children. We sometimes discover the most precious treasures in the darkest valleys of life.

Paul had first-hand knowledge of the Father's compassion during his trials and challenges. He learnt that God is "the source of all comfort" and comforts us in any circumstance (see 2 Cor. 1:3). For this reason, Thomas Moore could rejoice: "Earth hath no sorrow that heaven cannot heal."

When you are in the dark, listen, and God will give you a very precious message for someone else when you get into the light.
~ Oswald Chambers ~

This comfort flows directly from our fellowship with God. It often happens that our own sorrow is relieved while we comfort others. Our hearts become sensitive to others because of the trials and sorrow we have wrestled with ourselves. Our highest calling is to glorify Him by spreading His love and comforting others in His name.

The memory of our own sorrow creates a tender atmosphere that hovers over a house like the silence that descends after prayer. That is why there is a blessing in every burden and affliction in our lives. We must simply receive the grace through the Holy Spirit to see it and share it with others. In so doing, our own sorrow is toned down and we are able to reach out to others with a comforting hand and heart.

Holy Comforter, let Your healing love enfold my heart so that I will be tender in my contact with others' grief. Amen.

Peace of Mind and Heart

"I am leaving you with a gift – peace of mind and heart. And the peace I give is a gift the world cannot give. So don't be troubled or afraid" (John 14:27).

In our merciless search for progress, both adults and children are placed under tremendous pressure. The demands become higher, and more and more is expected of the individual. Thus the stress becomes worse, and people all over seek relief from the unbearable burden.

Naturally, there are manmade tranquilizers that are used in vast quantities. We should be thankful that these remedies bring relief to some people. To many, however, it is a trapdoor to addiction. Unfortunately, all manmade products have negative side effects.

> A great many people are trying to make peace, but it has already been done. God has not left it for us to do; all we have to do is enter into it.
> ~ Dwight L. Moody ~

In the end, there is but one way to be sure of the rest for body and soul that we yearn for: "I wait quietly before God, for my victory comes from Him" (Ps. 62:1). To know God and become quiet in His holy presence is the formula for true peace. In this the Holy Spirit is our Leader and Teacher. We must discover this power of God again so that we can be strengthened in silence from on high.

This is why our Lord achieved success in the bitter tests of life, and emerged triumphant! He invites the weary and burdened and waits for them to accept His invitation. With Him we find the peace of God that transcends all understanding.

Lord Jesus, my Savior, I praise and thank You for the peace that I have inherited from You through the quiet working of the Holy Spirit. Amen.

The Ministry of Intercession

They will pray day and night, continually. Take no rest, all you who pray to the LORD (Isa. 62:6).

A prayer program that goes no further than our own needs, is a diminished form of God's intention with prayer. It is by the incredible grace of God that we are intercessors in His kingdom.

By means of intercession, we become co-workers of the Great Intercessor, Jesus Christ. Our prayers become part of His perfect prayer. We pray in the name of Jesus Christ for His church on earth; for our fellow humans in need; for God's called servants in their work; for heathens and for God's representatives; for the unhampered spreading of the Good News. The whole spectrum of God's involvement with humanity is covered by our prayers because the Holy Spirit teaches us to pray, even when we don't know how to.

We are never alone during intercession, but are closely united with millions of God's children all over the world. Accordingly, we may not devote only our leftover time and strength to this. From the start, we must fulfill the noble and lofty calling of intercession to the very best of our ability. The rich fruit this bears in our own lives and in the lives of others will naturally be part of it. We never pray for others without a part of the blessings flowing back into our own lives.

Where there is much prayer, there will be much of the Spirit; where there is much of the Spirit, there will be ever-increasing prayer.
~ Andrew Murray ~

O Hearer of prayer, thank You that I may be a co-worker of Jesus Christ. Make me faithful, sensitive and attentive to know Your will. Amen.

Hope = Christian Optimism

You will not grieve like people who have no hope (1 Thess. 4:13).

We use the word *hope* to describe various perceptions. We say, "I hope there is a rise in the price of gold," or "My husband is ill, but I hope he'll get well soon." Then it is purely a matter of the everyday expectations of life. But the word also has a much deeper meaning.

In the Tate gallery in London there is a striking painting by the artist Frederick Watts. The title is *Hope*. A woman is sitting on a globe. She is blindfolded and holds a lute in her hands. Except for one, all the strings of the lute are broken. Her finger touches that one string and her ear is bent toward the lute, listening. She is waiting to hear the sound from that one string. She has hope; she believes only the best in the worst circumstances.

Totally without hope one cannot live. To live without hope is to cease to live.
~ Fyodor Dostoevsky ~

As long as we hope, life can never get the better of us. We won't double over under the load of our problems and trials. We know that God can bring the best from the worst circumstances. Where there is Christian hope, the night is never so dark, loneliness never as painful, and fear never as terrifying. Christian hope is optimism grounded on God's omniscience and supreme wisdom. It is that hope for the future that fills a heart with joy, even when it wants to break.

Hope is the unwavering trust of the Christian in the eternal goodness of God. Where the world sees only a hopeless end, the Spirit-filled child of God sees an endless hope!

Unchanging God and Father, thank You for Your Word that fills me with hope. Strengthen me daily with Your hope. Amen.

With a Song in My Heart!

Be filled with the Holy Spirit, singing psalms and hymns and spiritual songs among yourselves, and making music to the Lord in your hearts (Eph. 5:18-19).

Throughout the entire Bible there is an appeal to God's believing children: "Praise the Lord!" Singing and thankfulness for salvation go hand in hand. A person that does not sing is like spring without blossoms. A thankful person is a singing person and a singing person is a happy person, irrespective of their circumstances in life.

God's creation abounds with song and music: the trees rustling in the wind, the rhythmic surging of the waves, the spattering of raindrops against the window, the swaying of grain in the fields.

For those who listen, nature sings in a thousand ways to the glory of God. Song is proof that God is present in our hearts. The world will know by our praises that God is the King of our lives.

There was jubilant song at Christ's birth. Jesus sang a song of praise with His disciples at the Last Supper. One day in heaven the singing of the saved will be heard. We must practice for this in the meantime!

Singing gives us courage in affliction. Like Paul and Silas, we must be able to sing in the night of our trials and tribulations. We are witnesses of the cross, but also of the glory of Christ's triumphal procession through the ages.

There is not one blade of grass, there is no color in this world that is not intended to make us rejoice.
~ John Calvin ~

Praiseworthy God and Father, make me a praise-singing disciple through the Holy Spirit and may my song to Your glory never grow silent. Amen.

June

His light on my path lets me triumph over fear.

"I am leaving you with a gift – peace of mind and heart. And the peace I give is a gift the world cannot give. So don't be troubled or afraid."
~ John 14:27 ~

Faith activates God – Fear activates the Enemy.
~ Joel Osteen ~

Almighty God who enables us to triumph over fear,
we worship You in Your holiness, majesty and peace.
Assure us once more that when You are with us,
we have no reason to fear anything.
Thank You that You transform our fear into peace. Your Word
reassures us that we will always find courage and hope with You
and that Your will for our lives is sure to be done.
We praise and thank You that Your Spirit always inspires us to hope.
While we lift up our hearts in songs of praise,
we feel the fear subside
and Your peace descending deep into our soul.
Praise the Lord! Thank You that in our quiet time with You,
when Your Spirit speaks to us and we listen to You,
we discover the Source that drives away all our fear,
and replaces it with the peace of God
that transcends all understanding.
We pray this in the name of the Prince of Peace:
Jesus who triumphs over fear and anxiety.

Amen.

Fear: Our Greatest Enemy

God has not given us a spirit of fear and timidity, but of power, love, and self-discipline (2 Tim. 1:7).

Fear is undoubtedly our greatest enemy. According to legend, a man was on his way to Constantinople one day when an elderly lady asked him to give her a lift. He agreed and they continued the journey. When he took a closer look at her he started getting worried and asked her, "Who are you?" The woman answered, "I am cholera." Deeply upset, the man asked her to leave the vehicle. But she persuaded him to take her with him by promising she would let no more than five people die.

As proof of the sincerity of her promise, she gave him a dagger and told him this was the only weapon she could be killed with. She added that she would meet him again in two days' time and if she had broken her promise, he could run her through. One hundred and twenty people died in Constantinople in those two days. The man who had given her a lift was furious. When he found the lady, he lifted the dagger to stab her. But she stopped him and said, "I kept my promise. Only five people died of cholera. The others all died of fear."

Fear is never a good counselor and victory over fear is the first spiritual duty of man.
~ Nicolas Berdyaev ~

This is an apt testimony of life. Where disease causes the death of thousands, fear causes the death of tens of thousands. From the cradle to the grave, fear casts its dark, ominous shadow over the lives of human beings. It paralyzes the human spirit, breaks down his resistance, disarms him in battle, makes him unfit for his task in life, and brings terror to his deathbed.

But there is deliverance from fear in God!

Thank You, Almighty Father, that You drive foolish fear from our hearts. Amen.

The Perverse Rule of Fear

I heard You walking in the garden, so I hid. I was afraid because I was naked (Gen. 3:10).

Biologists say that fear is not only a universal phenomenon, but it is also the first emotion that develops in humans and animals. All creation is ruled by fear. Each human being comes into this world tainted with fear even before being born. That fear multiplies in leaps and bounds as our knowledge and experience increase.

As a child, you may have caught a bird in a snare, and later when you held it in your hand, felt its terrified heartbeat. The bird had no knowledge of you or any human being and had no reason to fear you, except by instinct.

> The only thing we have to fear is fear itself.
> ~ Franklin D. Roosevelt ~

Fear is as old as humankind itself. It goes as far back as paradise. Adam and Eve rebelled against God because of their disobedience and ate the forbidden fruit. Immediately their hearts were filled with fear and when God came along in the evening for fellowship with them, as He always did, they hid from Him. When Adam's Creator called out to Him, "Where are you?" Adam was hiding from God in the dark shadows because he was afraid.

Through sin, fear acquires perverse dominion over our lives. The Lord's Word teaches us how to break this domination so that we can continue on our pathway with God, with courage and dignity.

Holy Father God, we are being corrupted by sin and forced into fearfulness. Grant that we will not become estranged from You by fear. Amen.

In His Safekeeping

He led His own people like a flock of sheep, guiding them safely through the wilderness. He kept them safe so they were not afraid (Ps. 78:52-53).

Anyone who owns valuable jewelry or diamonds is relieved once these valuables have been handed over for safekeeping to a trustworthy person whose job it is to keep valuables safe. Knowing that these articles are locked away in a safe, the owner is not afraid of suffering loss and he has the peace of mind that is so necessary if you want to live life to the full.

Peace of mind in your spiritual life is much more important than the issue of your worldly goods. On a spiritual level, a life of doubt, anxiety and fear without any peace of mind can become a real nightmare.

The wise man in a storm prays to God, not for safety from danger, but for deliverance from fear.
~ Ralph Waldo Emerson ~

If you want peace of mind and tranquility to become a reality in your life, it is of the essence that you cling to your faith in Jesus with all your might. Believe in His promise that He will always be with you and never let you down (see Heb. 13:5). Go to Him with every situation that makes you anxious and trust Him to protect you against all fear, anxiety and evil. Then you will experience the peace of God that surpasses all understanding.

Resist the onslaughts of evil that fill you with fear. Place yourself in God's safekeeping now and forever. Rest assured that He will keep you safe.

Protect me, Lord, in all circumstances and keep me safe so that I will overcome my fear. Amen.

Love Is Stronger than Fear

Such love has no fear, because perfect love expels all fear. If we are afraid, it is for fear of punishment, and this shows that we have not fully experienced His perfect love (1 John 4:18).

A well-known painting by Max Gabriel is, in essence, a portrayal of our text for today. There are copies of it in many art galleries. The original is kept in the Louvre in Paris. It is known as *The Last Token*. It depicts a scene from the days when Christians fell prey to bloody persecution because of their faith. One of these Christians, a beautiful young woman, is on the point of being savaged by wild animals. She is standing against the stone wall of the amphitheater. Above her, spectators are sitting row upon row, eager for the spectacle to begin. The iron gates through which the wild animals enter the arena have been thrown open. A starved and furious tiger is rushing toward the woman. She is dressed in white with a dark cloak covering her head and shoulders. A pure white rose lies at her feet, thrown from the arena by a loved one. Her upturned eyes see only the person who threw the rose.

Fear knocked at the door. Faith answered and no one was there.
~ Anonymous ~

The hatred of the people pronounced a death sentence on her and at any moment the bloodthirsty tiger will kill her. Yet a single rose changed the whole scene. There was no wild animal for her, no blood-soaked sand, no shrieking crowds – just a pure white rose and love that would make her triumph over cruelty and hatred. Love is indeed stronger than fear!

God of love, our hearts rejoice when we consider what Your love does; that You sent us Your Son to atone for our sins. Amen.

How Do You Defeat a Monster?

The Word gave life to everything that was created, and His life brought light to everyone (John 1:4).

If you are not completely certain that Jesus Christ has taken over your life, it is so simple to make sure. Join me in praying the following prayer and believe it with your whole heart and very being: "Lord Jesus, I am a wicked sinner. But I believe that You died on the cross for me. I now surrender myself to You unconditionally – body, soul and spirit. At this moment I accept You as my Redeemer and Savior. Hear my prayer for Your name and Your love's sake. Amen."

Believe with your whole heart that this is so. You are now a child of God, a new creation. So, from this moment on, start acting like a subject of the kingdom of God, a follower of the Living Christ and a saved child of God. This new birth is one of the mightiest weapons that we have against Satan, because now we have received "life" from Jesus and together with it, His nature. Fear is the character and nature of the Evil One. God does not give us a spirit of fear, but of courage and love and self-control (see 2 Tim. 1:7).

Jesus came treading the waves; and so He puts all the swelling tumults of life under His feet. Christian – why afraid?
~ St. Augustine ~

Paul writes to the Corinthians and says, "Everything belongs to you" (1 Cor. 3:21). Now you live your life together with Jesus Christ and you rule together with Him – also over fear (see Rom. 5:17 and Luke 10:20). Stand firm in this new relationship with Jesus Christ. Rejoice in your problems; they give you the opportunity to prove your strength. Rejoice in this and conquer the monster of fear in Jesus' powerful name.

Thank You, Redeemer and Savior, that I can defeat the monster of fear in Your name. Amen.

Babylon or Golgotha?

"Do not fear the king of Babylon anymore," says the Lord. "For I am with you and will save you and rescue you from his power" (Jer. 42:11).

Satan wants you to see all the negative things in your life so that you become upset and frightened. God, however, wants you to look up to Him and find peace in His completed salvation for you.

What is it that you fear? It might be fear itself, a family problem or financial circumstances. It could also be problems in your community or with the authorities. Fear will destroy your vision in life if you accommodate it.

In Colossians 2:15 we read the comforting words that Satan and his evil rulers and authorities have been disarmed and destroyed. You can stop identifying with fear. Feelings of fear might still remain in your life, but you aren't ruled by feelings anymore. Resist them through faith in the cross at Golgotha, and Satan will flee from you.

The essence of faith is being satisfied with all God is for us in Jesus.
~ John Piper ~

If you are controlled by fear to such an extent that it makes you feel helpless, ask a fellow believer who has gained the victory already and was set free by the blood that flowed at Golgotha, to encourage you. Fear can lead to illness, failure, despair, confusion, frustration and ultimately an early death. Don't keep on living in Babylon, but find true life at the foot of the cross!

Jesus, the Triumphant, thank You that I can gain victory over fear through You. Amen.

Positive Fear

Serve the Lord with reverent fear, and rejoice with trembling. Submit to God's royal Son, or He will become angry, and you will be destroyed (Ps. 2:11-12).

People experience fear as a negative concept, but sometimes it offers us moral medication. It works in a mystical and hidden way in all our physical and social circumstances. It stimulates initiative. People work hard because they fear poverty. Because we fear pain, we avoid things that hurt us or make us sick. It works the same way in the moral sphere. Because we fear that we will cause God sorrow, we live in line with His will. It draws our attention to spiritual dangers and motivates us to make the right decisions.

In its own way, fear is a pain. It has the nature of an incentive and rouses us from a lukewarm state. Fear is normally focused on the future, because it is a reaction to something we expect to happen. It is an early warning sign of dangers to come.

I fear God, yet I am not afraid of Him.
~ Thomas Browne ~

When we serve the Lord in fear and trembling, it is a positive form of reverence and respect for God's greatness and majesty.

This kind of fear is completely different to the fear that is a destructive and negative emotion and the result of transgression and sin. It keeps us inside God's directives so that we may lead a safer and blessed life.

The choice is yours. You either live in positive fear before God, or you live in fear and trembling in a place of sin and misery. Each form of fear has its own requirements and its own reward.

Loving Father God, I approach Your majesty in fear and trembling, but also with love. Amen.

The Origin of Fear

All have turned away; all have become useless. No one does good, not a single one (Rom. 3:12).

Our fleshly nature submits to the devil and consequently carries his sinful nature. But God gave us a different nature (see 2 Tim. 1:7).

Excessive obstinacy and lack of co-operation in the youth can arise from lifelong feelings of fear. Abuse and ill-treatment by parents result in negative reactions in a child's physical, emotional and intellectual composition which are often carried over into adulthood in the form of intense fear. Sometimes they rebel against any form of authority and discipline. It often takes professional treatment and the grace of God to free these children from their fear.

As we are liberated from our fears, our presence automatically liberates others.
~ Marianne Williamson ~

Different types of accidents can be the cause of neurotic fear. A car crash can cause its victims to be terrified of traveling by car. The experience of being in an elevator that gets stuck can cause fear of confined spaces in any form. Abnormal relationships between parents can become the breeding ground for fear in their children. A parent's alcohol abuse can contribute to a child's fear and instability.

Thus the causes of fear can multiply, but it can always be traced back to sin that takes its bitter toll every day. Only a genuine meeting with Jesus Christ can bring deliverance: "Oh, what a miserable person I am! Who will free me from this life that is dominated by sin and death? Thank God! The answer is in Jesus Christ our Lord" (Rom. 7:24-25).

Holy Lord Jesus, thank You that Your suffering and pain set me free from my fear. Amen.

Fear Is Transferable

When the 300 Israelites blew their rams' horns, the LORD caused the warriors in the camp to fight against each other with their swords. Those who were not killed fled (Judg. 7:22).

Parents that are constantly terror-stricken can easily pass this fear on to their children. Many of the problems caused by fear and anxiety among the youth can be traced directly back to the parents. The child is indoctrinated with the attitudes of the parents in the fragile sensitive years of their youth. When they reach adulthood, their hearts are the seedbed in which the devil grows fear.

A mother seeks help for her daughter. But the mother is filled with fear, frustration and hate herself. Consequently, the child experiences mental strain and emotionally she cannot develop past her teens, even if she is already twice the emotional age. Strife and arguments between the parents causes the daughter to develop a fear of adulthood.

Fear is a tyrant and a despot; more terrible than the rack, more potent than the snake.
~ Edgar Wallace ~

Fear among the management of a firm can be passed on to employees – so badly that the business can fold. Fear among the staff of a school can be carried over to the learners, with tragic results. Fear within a nation can be passed on in a way that sours the entire framework of the community.

This is why Gideon told all the terrified soldiers in his army to go back home. He gained a resounding victory with the brave band of 300 who remained. The Word of God often tells us not to fear. God knows that fear escalates and is passed on. It grows like a weed and if it is allowed to take root in your heart, it will spread to the lives of those around you.

Lord Jesus, with Your victory at Golgotha You made all fear disappear from our lives. Amen.

The Consequences of Fear

A glad heart makes a happy face; a broken heart crushes the spirit (Prov. 15:13).

Medical practitioners find that heart problems, stomach ulcers and many other ailments are caused by fear and anxiety. Cheerfulness is like medicine, but a panic-stricken and broken spirit subdues a person's cheerfulness. Proverbs 29:25 says, and rightly so, "Fearing people is a dangerous trap, but trusting the Lord means safety."

Fear of people, whether it is an employee or employer, a husband or wife or competition in the business world can be "a dangerous trap." Remember what Job said: "What I always feared has happened to me. What I dreaded has come true" (Job 3:25). If there is fear deep inside you, deal with it now, otherwise it can lead to your downfall later on.

Fear closes the ears of the mind.
~ Sallust ~

Some people hear about illnesses that run in their families and then just take it for granted that they suffer from the same disease. Soon fear has them in its iron grip and paralyzes them. If there is any part of your life that has been infiltrated by fear – no matter to what extent – deal with it immediately, otherwise it will grow out of all proportion and become a monster that brings about sickness, untimely death and all kinds of problems.

Rejoice in the Lord and believe with conviction that He will take all your fears away, and tell yourself this often throughout each day.

Lord Jesus, thank You that You set me free from the bondage of fear. Amen.

Fear Leads to Failure

Therefore, tell the people, "Whoever is timid or afraid may leave this mountain and go home" (Judg. 7:3).

Gideon was aware of the sly power and destructive danger of fear among his soldiers. He knew that he would be better off with a handful of fearless warriors than a whole army of cowards. Fear is like an electrical short. It robs you of all real power and brings about failure and destruction. Two thousand men left Gideon because they were afraid and in the end only 300 remained. With the fearless 300, Gideon was able to achieve a magnificent victory.

Fear is an attitude of failure sent from damnation to destroy us. Do not accommodate it in your thoughts or heart. Rejoice on the road to victory in the face of every problem. The Word repeatedly warns us against failure caused by fear. You can take a stand in faith and joy and gain the victory, or you can give way to fear and see your life disrupted and heading for failure. Be strong and move ahead triumphantly. Learn to stand firm in the Lord under all circumstances.

He has not learned a lesson of life, who does not every day surmount a fear.
~ Ralph Waldo Emerson ~

"Don't be afraid. Just stand still and watch the LORD rescue you" (Exod. 14:13). The flesh tries to pull you into fear and anxiety. Become still before God's omnipotence and He will bless you with victory upon victory. Fearlessness is being still and having faith. Fear, on the other hand, is a constant and useless struggle. Every time the Lord's children come up against a problem, He says to them, "Don't be afraid." So don't be afraid, and you will live life triumphantly and joyfully.

Thank You, Lord Jesus, that You also set me free from fruitless fear. Amen.

Overcome Fear with the Truth

"You will know the truth, and the truth will set you free" (John 8:32).

Many people have been freed from the demon of fear by the simple truth of our text today. God's Word is Spirit and the Spirit liberates: "The Spirit alone gives eternal life. Human effort accomplishes nothing. And the very words I have spoken to you are spirit and life" (John 6:63). "For the word of God is alive and powerful. It is sharper than the sharpest two-edged sword" (Heb. 4:12). There is nothing stronger than the Word. When the Word is the guiding force in your life, you will develop freedom from fear and you will be in full control in all circumstances.

> When I walk through the darkest valley, I will not be afraid, for You are close beside me.
> ~ Psalm 23:4 ~

The best way by far to deal with fear is to overcome it before it gets a grip on you. The best time to resist an onslaught is right at the beginning. It would be foolish to fight back after the enemy has already overpowered you. It's the same with the spiritual struggle – the time to act is at the beginning. To wait days, weeks or months is giving the enemy a hold over your life. Stand on the Word of God the minute a problem comes up. If you have faith, nothing is impossible (see Matt. 17:20). "For I can do everything through Christ, who gives me strength" (Phil. 4:13) and, "No, despite all these things, overwhelming victory is ours through Christ, who loved us" (Rom. 8:37).

Find a promise in the Word of God that is appropriate in your situation. Let it become part of your heart and thoughts, and praise God for it. In such a way, the Word builds a stronghold around you: "His faithful promises are your armor and protection" (Ps. 91:4).

Thank You for the truth of Your Word, O God, that enables me to overcome fear. Amen.

Defeat Fear with God's Word

It is God who arms me with strength and keeps my way secure. He makes my feet like the feet of a deer; He causes me to stand on the heights. He trains my hands for battle; my arms can bend a bow of bronze (2 Sam. 22:33-35 NIV).

When you confess the power of the Word of the Lord, the Word becomes a protective shield that wards off the poisoned arrows of evil. Your tongue becomes a tree of life. If, however, you yield to circumstances and start giving in to fear, you fall prey to the enemy. Then your tongue becomes a crack in the wall of your spiritual protection. Your shield is destroyed by negative behavior and you open the door to the enemy called fear, and he comes in and takes control of your life.

Develop a victorious attitude based on the Word of God. Defy your fear and every frustrating situation. Treat the Word of God as if you are being directly spoken to through it.

Do not lose heart, then, my brother, in pursuing your spiritual life.
~ Thomas à Kempis ~

At first it might not come through strongly, but persist until the truth drives the enemy away. Stand firm, rooted in victorious attitudes with the help of the Spirit of God. Say to yourself, "He makes my road ahead prosperous." Tell yourself this in faith and with conviction.

For many years you believed the devil and his scary stories. Now give God a fair chance to prove Himself in your life through His Word. He will make your "way safe." The Word will soon take root in your life and have a radical influence on your approach to fear and anxiety. Believe, and it will be so!

I praise You, Father God, that You make me triumph over fear through Your Word. Amen.

Surrender Your Fear to God

So if the Son sets you free, you are truly free (John 8:36).

Only Jesus Christ can set you free from fear. This is our point of departure to victory over incessant fear. There must be a true meeting with Jesus and a meaningful relationship between you and your Savior, based on your faith in His omnipotence and love.

Confess your feelings to the Lord, without embarrassment and without taking into account any of your current thinking patterns. Don't be ashamed of sharing your secret fears with Him. In Christ you can be victorious because He is always with you. You can live a meaningful life again because God keeps His hand over you. He works out His plan for your life: "He trains my hands for battle; He strengthens my arm to draw a bronze bow" (2 Sam. 22:35).

Spiritual victory comes only to those who are prepared for battle.
~ Anonymous ~

Make enough time to worship Jesus and confess your love for Him. Let your spirit reach out to Him through these truths and do this in a spirit of worship. Allow your spirit to take pleasure in the presence of Christ.

You were born to be a winner. You can overcome any obstacle the enemy uses to block your way. You are a soldier who can bend the toughest bow. There is a condition, however, and it is unavoidable – you must first be freed by the Son. Then you are truly free from fear.

Thank You, Father God, that You didn't create me to live in fear, but to triumph over fear through Your Son. Amen.

Defeat Fear with Trust

I praise God for what He has promised; Yes, I praise the LORD for what He has promised. I trust in God, so why should I be afraid? What can mere mortals do to me? (Ps. 56:10-11).

Unfailing trust in the Living God destroys fear. The Bible reminds us of this often: "Those who fear the LORD are secure; He will be a refuge for their children" (Prov. 14:26), "Do not throw away this confident trust in the Lord. Remember the great reward it brings you!" (Heb. 10:35) and, "Don't be afraid. Just stand still and watch the LORD rescue you today" (Exod. 14:13).

Learn to be still before the Lord in faith and trust and to look up to Him in times of anxiety and fear. Fear flourishes in anxiety and confusion. God, in His omniscience, has already worked out all the answers. Turn to Him confidently and see how He carries you through the sea of fear, unharmed.

Feed your faith and starve your doubts to death!
~ Andrew Murray ~

Refuse to press the panic button – remain calm in the knowledge that God is in control. Don't allow Satan to rule your life through fear. You are in a position to stand back and watch God rescue you.

Soon the enemy will disappear. This has got nothing to do with your spiritual abilities to defeat the enemy, your dynamic personality, or your good works, but it is solely because the omnipotence of Christ has been released in your life.

In safe and confident trust, Lord Jesus, I build up my hope on You to overcome fear. Amen.

Overcome Fear

Don't be afraid. Just stand still and watch the LORD rescue you today. The LORD Himself will fight for you (Exod. 14:13-14).

When you have put your trust in God, you must relax completely and get away from the battle zone. It is the Lord's battle now, not yours. If you insist on fighting the battle yourself, your fear will only grow and your problems become worse.

Leaving the battlefield is by no means an indication of a reckless faith. Surrendering to the Lord takes courage. Then walk the road with your Savior. You will find an indestructible fortress or shelter in showing respect for His Word. You dare not lose trust in God. Persevere on your pathway, following Jesus, and He will take care of you and protect you. After all, the final victory is in His almighty hands.

The seed that you sow in your character in this way will sprout. Give it a chance to grow to maturity in your life – then it will bear fruit. A problem can so easily take root in a person's life. Don't allow this to happen to you. Be patient and relax, and God will keep His promises time and time again.

The only saving faith is that which casts itself on God for life or death.
~ Martin Luther ~

Your trust is now based on Jesus Christ. He is in you and you are in Him. Now you have every right to say, "I can do everything through Christ who gives me strength" (Phil. 4:13). You are more than a winner and because of your faith in Christ, nothing is impossible for you (see Matt. 17:20).

Holy Spirit of God, make me steadfast in my struggle against fear. Amen.

Overcome Fear with Praise

Save us, O LORD our God! Gather us back from among the nations, so we can thank Your holy name and rejoice and praise You (Ps. 106:47).

When the people of Israel praised and worshiped God, the walls of Jericho crumbled and toppled down. In prison, Paul and Silas sang hymns of praise to the glory of God and He sent an earthquake to set them free. When the armies of Ammon and Moab advanced on Israel and God's people started singing and praising Him, God gave them the victory (see 2 Chron. 20:22).

Victory comes when you cultivate a spirit of victory in your deepest being; defeat when you have cultivated a spirit of defeat. You can choose to sing songs of praise like Paul and Silas, or to complain and grumble in self-pity. Good things happen to us if we praise God in worship – irrespective of how we feel at that particular moment.

God can never receive too much praise.
~ Anonymous ~

Recently I read about a missionary in Mexico who was in prison. He complained non-stop and said that God had forgotten him. Then God spoke to him through His Word: "I will never fail you. I will never abandon you" (Heb. 13:5). Since then, the Lord became so real to Him that he sensed the eternal presence of God. Together with that came the deliverance of his spirit. Two days later he was released from prison in an inexplicable way.

Your enemy "fear" can be conquered by seeking the Lord in His Word, and by letting worship and praise and songs of thankfulness that come from your very being, rise up to Him.

Let our chief goal, O God, be Your glory, and to enjoy You forever.
Amen.

Defeat Fear with a Positive Faith

We know that God causes everything to work together for the good of those who love God and are called according to His purpose for them (Rom. 8:28).

Progress in your spiritual life is often hindered by fear. This is Satan's work. There are many tests in your spiritual life before promotion comes. The only way to reach a higher standard in your walk with God is to keep on praising and worshiping Him, in spite of failure and defeat. Then you operate in the sphere of faith and that is an atmosphere in which Satan cannot exist. The devil works where things are negative – and fear is negative.

God is able to reverse every failure and every mistake you make, every attack of the Evil One, and turn it to His honor and glory. The devil wants to hurt you through fear, but God wants to use every negative attempt of evil to bless you.

A little faith will bring your soul to heaven, but a lot of faith will bring heaven to your soul.
~ Dwight L. Moody ~

Don't fail your test. Worship the Lord with sincere faith in your heart. Praise His holy name.

God is busy purifying and perfecting you. Be excited about it. Be thankful to God who trusts you with problems. Let your faith in Jesus Christ carry you through any situation and every fear will flee from your heart, replaced by thankful praise and worship: "Praise the LORD! Give thanks to the LORD, for He is good! His faithful love endures forever" (Ps. 106:1).

Lord, my God, I praise and thank You because You are my shield and protection against fear. Amen.

Overcome Fear with Joy

With joy you will drink deeply from the fountain of salvation! (Isa. 12:3).

Joy is a fruit of the Holy Spirit and part of God's nature. Fear is neutralized when you identify with the gladness of God: "Don't be dejected and sad, for the joy of the LORD is your strength!" (Neh. 8:10). By focusing on gladness, you take the feelings of fear inside you captive and rob them of all power. Bring your problems to the Living Christ – joy and victory will follow.

Our strength lies in our joy and gladness in the Lord. Gladness is a stronger characteristic than fear. Fear is from hell. That is why Paul cautions us: "Always be full of joy in the Lord. I say it again – rejoice!" (Phil. 4:4). If there is gladness in your heart, there is an uninterrupted flow of strength into your daily life. It is just a matter of the right attitude – the spirit of gladness in the Lord!

> The whole point of the letter to the Philippians is: I do rejoice – do you rejoice?
> ~ Bengel ~

If you want water from a well, you need a bucket and a rope. If you want the water of life, you need to use the bucket of salvation and the rope of faith. In this manner, you can draw water from the fountains of blessing. Live with the attitude of gladness every day.

Many people complain under difficult circumstances. This spirit and attitude must be destroyed. Constantly develop an attitude of gladness. It is not without reason that the wise Proverbs writer says that a cheerful person is a healthy person; a dejected person becomes exhausted. Gladness gives you freedom, while fear binds you with steel chains of your own making. Joy is like medicine. Choose joy.

Spirit of the Living God, thank You for the joy that You generate in my heart. Amen.

Overcome Fear with Thanksgiving

If you do not serve the LORD your God with joy and enthusiasm for the abundant benefits you have received, you will serve your enemies (Deut. 28:47-48).

Learn to be content with the things you have, and be thankful for them. The alternative is that you will always be hounded by fear. A restless spirit and a greedy heart are sinful. Be glad and rejoice in the situation you find yourself. Don't accept unpleasant conditions as permanent, but in the meantime learn to rejoice and be content. Then God will lead you to more blessings.

Be thankful for your home, your spouse, your children and friends, and rejoice in these as gifts from the Lord. There might be room for improvement in your circumstances, but rejoice in the blessings you enjoy at present. Be thankful for what God has given you and don't complain about the shortcomings in your life.

A thankful heart is not only the greatest virtue, but the parent of all other virtues.
~ Cicero ~

Our text for today reads, "If you do not serve the LORD your God with joy and enthusiasm for the abundant benefits you have received, you will serve your enemies." It is necessary to be thankful, because God regards ingratitude as a sin and it leads to fear and anxiety. Don't see only the negative things around you; see the goodness and grace of the Lord instead. That is how you are set free from fear.

Lord Jesus, even if I go through dark depths, I will not fear, because I am thankful that You are with me. Amen.

Overcome Fear with Faith

Strengthen those who have tired hands, and encourage those who have weak knees. Say to those with fearful hearts, "Be strong, and do not fear, for your God is coming" (Isa. 35:3-4).

Christ is in every true believer. He lives in your heart through faith (see Eph. 3:17). You have received fullness and abundance (see John 1:16; 10:10), and Lord, you have the power and authority to do His works (see John 14:6). You have evil underfoot (see Luke 10:19) and you are seated with God in the heavenly realms along with Christ (see Eph. 2:6). Therefore, you can confidently say to those who have lost heart, "Be strong! Don't be afraid!" It is positive and active power to act in Christ's name. Say, "I resist the spirit of fear, because I am strong in Jesus Christ."

This secret is revealed to us in John 8:32: "You will know the truth, and the truth will set you free." You are set free from fear when you stand firm in the Word of God, because the Word reveals the truth, and through the Word the Holy Spirit drives all fear from your heart and life. Refuse to listen to your feelings and emotions because they will only deceive you. Walk in the light of the Word of God. If you have faith, there is no fear and nothing is impossible (see Matt. 17:19-20).

Faith is the refusal to panic.
~ Martin Lloyd-Jones ~

Circumstances may convince you to be afraid, but Jesus asks you to look beyond circumstances and see only Him in His omnipotence. If you believe and act positively and in faith, it will bring you victory. Actively release your faith, and you will see the destruction of fear.

Almighty Master, help me through the Holy Spirit to take action against fear in faith. Amen.

A Winner's Mentality

In this way, God disarmed the spiritual rulers and authorities. He shamed them publicly by His victory over them on the cross (Col. 2:6-15).

Because of your faith in Christ, and the fact that you surrendered to Him, you are now a soldier in His army. The victory is guaranteed in advance, because He destroyed fear and disarmed the evil forces. Because you believe in the triumphant Christ, the Conqueror, Satan already lies prone at your feet, defeated. This is why you must refuse to allow fear in your life again. After all, you have the power of God behind you.

James calls on us to show a winner's mentality in everything we do: "So you see, faith by itself isn't enough. Unless it produces good deeds, it is dead and useless" (James 2:17). Faith must be active. Slumbering faith is not worth much. Faith enables us to move forward in God's perfect will. It is crucial to make time to pray and seek God's will. God did not separate the Red Sea before Moses lifted his staff in faith. This was a positive act of faith, born of a winner's mentality.

Faith is the bird that sings while it is yet dark.
~ Max Lucado ~

If we obediently pray and believe, God always makes His miracles happen. Things that look like insurmountable problems are removed by God's omnipotence, and we can move ahead fearlessly from one victory to the next. Our thoughts must always be dominated by our faith in God. Then we can join David in saying, "In Your strength I can crush an army; with my God I can scale any wall" (Ps. 18:29).

Thank You, Heavenly Father, that we may have a winner's mentality through our triumphant Christ. Amen.

A Positive Act of Faith

Don't you realize that you become the slave of whatever you choose to obey? (Rom. 6:16).

Your will is the overriding factor in your battle against fear. Either God or Satan can work in your life, depending on which one of them has taken possession of your will. When God created humankind, He gave us a will of our own. Morally, you are a free agent. If you choose to give way to fear, frustration and failure, these negative qualities will dominate your life. Choose to be set free from fear and be joyful through Jesus Christ, and the Lord will act for your sake – but you must first make this decision.

Day after day you make decisions that determine the course of your life. Many of the decisions are taken with hardly a thought to what you are doing. Perhaps you have accepted fear and defeat as a way of life without realizing the implications. You mistakenly think this is the fate you were allotted, and when you have problems, you prepare yourself for a long and tiring struggle.

Faith is extending an empty hand to God to receive His gift of grace.
~ A. W. Pink ~

Perhaps you have lived a life of the flesh for such a long time that you view God's miracles as an exception to the rule.

God brings you back to His Word: "I tell you the truth, if you had faith even as small as a mustard seed, you could say to this mountain, 'Move from here to there,' and it would move. Nothing would be impossible" (Matt. 17:20).

Holy God, hear my prayer and give me fearless faith in all circumstances. Amen.

Overcome Fear with Righteousness

You will be secure under a government that is just and fair. Your enemies will stay far away. You will live in peace, and terror will not come near (Isa. 54:14).

Sin is the seedbed of anxiety and fear. Sin always clears the way for fear and evil always results in fear. Ultimately, confusion and fear dominate your whole life. A righteous life will finally destroy all fear: "Your enemies will stay far away."

> We gain strength, and courage, and confidence by each experience in which we really stop to look fear in the face ... we must do that which we think we cannot.
> ~ Eleanor Roosevelt ~

Fear may force its way into someone's life through circumstances beyond their control. A child who was molested lives in permanent fear. His frustration and inability to deal with fear often lead to a nervous breakdown or even suicide. Fear is allowed to rule a child's life because of the sins of others. Counseling and professional guidance can help the child and rid him of the effects of his bad experience so that he can live a happy life again.

Establish a basis of righteousness again in a country and the forces of evil can be made to retreat. An illustration of this is Gideon's brave band of 300 who dramatically defeated the mighty army that advanced on Israel.

Approach God now. Repent and confess your sins. Even if you are the victim of unfortunate circumstances, the fact remains that you gave way to fear and confusion. Choose righteousness today and find your way to God: "Come close to God, and God will come close to you" (James 4:8). The victory is within your grasp.

Heavenly Father, I come to You with my fear. Please release me from it. Amen.

Overcome Fear by Prayer

I prayed to the LORD, and He answered me. He freed me from all my fears (Ps. 34:4).

Our hearts should always hunger and thirst for God. It is exciting to long for God. If you pray to Him, He will answer you and give deliverance. You need only pray a simple prayer: "My Father God, in the name of Jesus Christ I surrender myself to You. I seek You with all my heart. Let me not be put to shame." Then say to yourself: God has answered my prayer and will set me free from all my fear! This is God's tried and trusted method: He hears and saves when sinners ask Him to!

Perhaps you have never put God first in your life and have never given Him a fair chance. If you confess Christ as your Savior and Redeemer, hold on to that confession. Maintain a positive attitude toward God's forgiveness and grace in your life.

Is it not wonderful news to believe that salvation lies outside ourselves?
~ Martin Luther ~

If you have lost a precious treasure, you will look for it day and night until you find it. If you seek Him, you will find Him. Go to Him, stay with Him and soon the darkness will lift and the light of joy will shine brightly again: "He satisfies the thirsty and fills the hungry with good things" (Ps. 107:9).

Sometimes the Lord leaves you in the wilderness so that your longing for Him grows stronger. True faith that sets you free from fear is born in a yearning and hungry heart. Allow the Spirit of God to minister this saving truth to your hungry and thirsty heart.

As the deer longs for streams of water, so I long for You, O God. I will put my hope in You! You are my Savior and my God!

Amen.

Overcome Fear with Love

Such love has no fear, because perfect love expels all fear. If we are afraid, it is for fear of punishment, and this shows that we have not fully experienced His perfect love (1 John 4:18).

Perfect love is made possible by living in God's presence. Fear cannot survive in God's presence. If we love one another, God lives among us and assumes total authority. God's love thrives where there is an atmosphere of love.

Most of our problems are caused when we allow hate and fear to dominate us instead of love. Develop the ability to release love in every difficult situation, rather than fear, hate and self-pity. Motivated by compassion and love, Jesus healed the sick, for example, the leper in Mark 1:40-41. Love is the essence of God's character and nature. Hatred is in Satan's nature. We must learn to strive for love and to put it into practice.

If you judge people, you have no time to love them.
~ Mother Teresa ~

When we counsel people held captive by the chains of fear, it is of the utmost importance that we be permeated by Christ's love, that the person in need of help will feel it physically. Compassion and sympathy for our fellow human beings can become reality only if the love of God is in us.

Go aside and meet with the Living Christ in total love and devotion. Tell Him that you love Him, that you love your fellow human beings, your marriage partner, family and friends. And yes, that you also love your enemies. Fill yourself with His love while you worship Him. Cherish this love daily. The alternative is that evil will sneak into your life and bring fear back with it. Often repeat after Peter, "Lord, You know everything. You know that I love You" (John 21:17).

O Lord, reveal Your love also through my life and attitude.

Amen.

The Law of the Vine

"Remain in Me, and I will remain in you. For a branch cannot produce fruit if it is severed from the vine, and you cannot be fruitful unless you remain in Me" (John 15:4).

Paul's heartfelt prayer for the Ephesians is, "Christ will make His home in your hearts as you trust in Him. Your roots will grow down into God's love and keep you strong" (Eph. 3:17). To live in Christ is a daily task of faith. Every new victory is made possible by faith. If you ignore external circumstances and walk in faith, Jesus lives in you. You can move to a new level of love and into an atmosphere where it is impossible for fear to exist.

To stay in Jesus means a life of faith where the fruits of the Spirit flourish. You are the product of your words and deeds from day to day, and living in Jesus radically changes the pattern of your thoughts and conduct. When you are worn down, live in Him and stand firm, no matter how long your trials last. Stay where you chose to be, *in Jesus Christ!* In His name, lay to rest the fears that still threaten your life. Fear is an enemy that has already been destroyed by Jesus and it cannot survive in His presence.

> To the pure in heart nothing really bad can happen. Not death but sin should be our great fear.
> ~ A. W. Tozer ~

Jesus cautions you throughout His Word not to fear the enemy. Fear is an attitude that cannot be defeated by any human being. To live in Jesus Christ and to walk in love, peace and gladness, is your only defense against fear invading your life.

Lord Jesus, make me a fruitful branch that remains part of the vine, and let me walk fearlessly. Amen.

Identifying with Christ

So you should also consider yourselves to be dead to the power of sin and alive to God through Christ Jesus (Rom. 6:11).

When you are born again, you become one with Jesus Christ and identify with His death, burial and resurrection. You now have the life of God in you (see John 10:28). God Himself lives in you (see 2 Cor. 6:16). Your body is now a temple of the Holy Spirit (see 1 Cor. 6:19-20). You are filled with the fullness of God (see Eph. 3:19). Through the Word, you share in His divine nature (see 2 Pet. 1:4).

Therefore, stand firm in Jesus Christ. You live for God. You are dead to fear, failure and defeat. You live in victory, joy and in the power of His resurrection (see Phil. 3:10). Identify with this new life and nature. You are a new creation (see 2 Cor. 5:17). The old things have passed away. Fear belongs to the old life and is from Satan. Stop identifying with the person you used to be and identify with the new life of Christ in you.

Christ is a substitute for everything, but nothing is a substitute for Christ.
~ H. A. Ironside ~

Your new identity in Christ is fearlessness. Destroy the lie called fear. Take every thought captive under the Word of God. Fear is something of the past and has no place in your life. Regard yourself as healed from fear, which can only operate in you if you are unfaithful to the Christ-nature in you. When you are under pressure and at risk of falling back into your old ways, confess your identification with the living Christ and overcome your fear in His powerful name.

Lord Jesus, it is an overwhelming but joyful truth that I may identify with You. Amen.

The Lord Is My Helper

We can say with confidence, "The LORD is my helper, so I will have no fear. What can mere people do to me?" (Heb. 13:6).

Whatever your problems in life – illness, disaster or apparent failure – refuse to be afraid, for fear is your deadliest enemy. The Lord is mighty enough to give you victory if you refuse to be afraid: "Even when I walk through the darkest valley, I will not be afraid, for You are close beside me" (Ps. 23:4).

Whether the cause of your fear is poverty, business issues, family problems or shortcomings in your personality, you must train yourself in the skill of never giving in to fear. Fear from inside will destroy you more quickly than the enemy from outside. Fear makes you believe that you are a failure and falsely convinces you that there is no way out of the dark swamp of fear. The Lord says to Joshua through Moses, "Do not be afraid or discouraged, for the LORD will personally go ahead of you. He will be with you; He will neither fail you nor abandon you" (Deut. 31:8).

The oldest and strongest emotion of mankind is fear.
~ H. P. Lovecraft ~

Your greatest stumbling block is unbelief, because unbelief is fear. But God can carry you through every crisis: "Do not be afraid of the nations there, for the LORD your God will fight for you" (Deut. 3:22). If you believe this with all your heart, you needn't fear anything.

Fear can cut off your supply of faith and then God cannot act. Faith allows God to crush the enemy called fear. So you have a choice. Fear and be destroyed or believe and be a winner. Jesus Christ lives in you and He knows no fear. Why should you be afraid?

Holy Father, I will not fear, because You bring me peace of mind.
Amen.

God Is Your Protector

God is our refuge and strength, always ready to help in times of trouble. So we will not fear when earthquakes come and the mountains crumble into the sea. Let the oceans roar and foam. Let the mountains tremble as the waters surge! (Ps. 46:1-3).

In conclusion, confess with me: "God is my refuge and protection. He is my help. He rescues me from every problem. I find shelter in the Almighty and enjoy the protection of the Almighty. Therefore I will not fear. He will instruct His angels to protect me wherever I may go. Because I sincerely love Him, He will save me and hear me when I call on Him (see Ps. 91). If God is on my side, what should I fear?"

Constantly remind yourself of God's promise in Isaiah 41:10: "Don't be afraid, for I am with you. Don't be discouraged, for I am your God. I will strengthen you and help you. I will hold you up with My victorious right hand." Whatever your circumstances, God always tells His children not to fear. He knows that they can be victorious if they are not afraid.

Trust the past to God's mercy, the present to His love, and the future to His providence.
~ St. Augustine ~

Rejoice in the Lord. You are very special to Him. Jesus is your Savior – also from anxiety and fear. Just trust God at all times. Relax and be still at the feet of Christ. Your fear has become God's opportunity. Grab hold of it and fear no longer.

God of grace and love, thank You that the resurrection of Your Son overcame all fear. Amen.

July

His light on my path helps me deal with sorrow.

He was a man of many sorrows,
aquainted with deepest grief.
~ Isa. 53:3 ~

Earth hath no sorrow that
heaven cannot heal.
~ Thomas Moore ~

God of grace and comfort,
You know that if we nurse our grief
it becomes an unbearable burden in our lives;
You know that if we hold on to it for
too long it consumes our hearts.
Therefore, we plead that You will bless our
grief and help us part with it;
help us to let go of the luxury of a sad memory.
Help us, Lord, not to cling to our cross;
but to put something better in its place
and free us from grief.
We know, Father, that our sorrow cannot undo anything,
cannot bring back a single day.
We confess, God of love,
that prolonged grief can destroy our souls and let hope die.
Comfort our hearts and help us to conquer grief.
Let us try to comfort others so that
we may experience true happiness.
We know that we are able to do this
only if You walk with us.
We thank You for Your comfort in our sorrow.
In the name of Jesus,
who knew sorrow and grief and conquered it.

Amen.

God's Training School

He was despised and rejected – a man of sorrows, acquainted with deepest grief. We turned our backs on Him and looked the other way. He was despised, and we did not care (Isa. 53:3).

The fact that sorrow, suffering and pain are realities is the point of departure in God's training school of mercy, love and peace. Not even our Master was spared sorrow. A prophet foretold 700 years before His birth, "He was a man of sorrow, acquainted with deepest grief." He had to empty a bitter cup of suffering in Gethsemane and died a cruel death on a cross. This is why Jesus understands suffering better than anyone else. He grieved for Jerusalem (see Matt. 23:37) and wept at the grave of His friend Lazarus (see John 11:35). Because He understands our grief, He gave us comfort by sending His Holy Spirit.

When your heart is broken, you don't need theological explanations or complicated discussions; you need the healing presence of God. He knows and understands. Your loved ones try their best to comfort you. But deep inside you know (and so do they) that they cannot comfort you, because they don't know what you really need.

No affliction or temptation, no guilt nor power of sin, no wounded spirit or terrified conscience, should induce us to despair of help and comfort of God.
~ Thomas Scott ~

That is why people's well-meaning words cannot help or comfort you – even if they went through this dark valley themselves at some stage. You must work through it yourself and discover that God is always with you. The best any person can do for you is just to sit quietly with you in your sorrow and pray that God will give you strength that He will help you understand and give you peace of mind and heart.

Lord Jesus, it is good to know that because You experience grief Yourself, You understand. Amen.

Nobody Escapes Grief

What I always feared has happened to me. What I dreaded has come true (Job 3:25).

At some point in our lives we all grieve. This is an experience that we don't understand before we have been there ourselves. There are, however, certain truths that we should take note of beforehand, to help us when the dark moments come. It will help us to understand better, and also to comfort and encourage grieving friends. Jesus proved this when Martha and Mary lost their brother, Lazarus. He shared in their grief in a way that really helped and comforted them.

There are better things ahead than any we leave behind.
~ C. S. Lewis ~

When someone close to you dies, the broken emotional bond leaves you with a painful feeling of loneliness. This is brought about not only by death, but also when someone you love breaks off the relationship; when a marriage ends and a family is torn apart; enmity between friends; and many other things. Sorrow may also be caused by illness, your job, your financial situation, or conflict with others.

In order to cope with sorrow and grief you need to understand that pain is life-shattering and can tear your life into pieces. It is nothing less than an onslaught on your own life. The grieving process is your reaction to loss. Your thoughts, feelings and behavior are affected to such an extent that it could be seen as a serious illness.

The question then is whether your Christian faith is strong enough to carry you to say, "Even when I walk through the darkest valley, I will not be afraid, for You are close beside me" (Ps. 23:4).

Lord Jesus, You understand. Please comfort me in this dark period of my life. Help me not to lose my way in my grief. Amen.

Nobody Told Me

To all who mourn in Israel, He will give a crown of beauty for ashes, a joyous blessing instead of mourning, festive praise instead of despair (Isa. 61:3).

When the famous author C. S. Lewis wrote about his grief after his wife's death, he said, "Why didn't anybody tell me?" This is just one of the many questions that arise in people's minds in times of grief; questions that cry out for answers – in vain. It is simply because, no matter how praiseworthy their efforts, no human being can be of real comfort – only God can!

The best we can do for others who grieve is to tell them how deeply and sincerely we feel for them in their loss. At most we can guide them to God and remind the bereaved that they can trust Him. Through His Holy Spirit, and in His own time, He will give comfort like a spring shower in the barren desert.

How strange this fear of death is! We are never frightened at a sunset!
~ George MacDonald ~

The author G. W. Bristoff said, "When hearts are broken, people don't need explanations. They need the healing presence of God." The pain is too severe for others to understand. But the Omnipotent God understands. He loves you and cares for you and He can do far more than you could ever think or pray for. Real comfort cannot be found in people. Real comfort comes from God.

You want to cry out, "Is there anybody who understands my grief and emptiness?" Yes, we may answer, God knows. He knows everything!

God of comfort, let me never forget that You know everything about me. I turn to You for comfort in this dark hour. Amen.

See God in Your Grief

Our present troubles are small and won't last very long. Yet they produce for us a glory that vastly outweigh them and will last forever (2 Cor. 4:17).

The mother of a lost son, entangled in vulgar sin, said, "There are things worse than death." Only those who battle through similar situations will know what destructive sorrow can be unleashed by life. The troubles Paul mentions in 2 Corinthians can be caused by many things: disabled, children, the failure of a business venture, bankruptcy, a loved one who becomes addicted to drugs or alcohol, a painful divorce, a family member in prison. These and many other situations can cause death to seem like deliverance.

> The purest suffering produces the purest understanding.
> ~ John of the Cross ~

But sometimes it is through our grief and suffering that we are pulled back to our anchors and realize that we have drifted away from God's comforting love. "Before I was afflicted I went astray, but now I obey Your word" (Ps. 119:67 NIV). Apart from sin, sorrow is one of humankind's most serious problems. This is why we dare not allow grief to go to waste, but rather try to find what God wants to teach us through it. "Yet what we suffer now is nothing compared to the glory He will reveal to us later" (Rom. 8:18). According to the Word, suffering and sorrow do not hit us by mistake. Seen in the right perspective, this condition enriches our existence in a very special way.

The purpose of suffering is a mystery to humanity, but we know that everything works together for the good of those who love God (see Rom. 8:28).

Holy Spirit of God, stand by me in my moments of suffering and keep me from despair. Amen.

Suffering Is a Process

"You will not grieve like people who have no hope" (1 Thess. 4:13).

Sorrow and suffering caused by the death of a loved one is more than a crisis: it is a process. This process has more than ten stages to work through. The process varies according to the person and the situation. The acute phase may last for as long as three months. If there is no relief after this period, professional counseling is required.

Children experience sorrow more intensely. Young people are inclined to attacks of sorrow that older people don't experience in similar situations. When a relationship ends, you sometimes hear the heartless remark, "There are plenty of fish in the sea." Such a statement reveals blatant ignorance of the real sorrow young people experience.

Whether you are young or old, you must work through the grieving process. It is personal. No one can go through it on your behalf. Leroy Joesten says, and rightly so: "You feel the need for being comforted and supported, but you also need to be caringly challenged to deal with your own sorrow."

Suffering like Jesus comes before reigning with Jesus.
~ Anonymous ~

Do not despair – tackle the process bravely. When the time comes – and there is no fixed timetable – you will be given the strength to carry on with the wonderful gift of life without any feeling of betrayal tainting the memory of your beloved.

Fortunately, believers have the advantage that unbelievers don't. Paul told the Christians, "You will not grieve like people who have no hope" (1 Thess. 4:13).

Lord of comfort, I call to You in this crisis hour. Help me to accept this healing process as a challenge and discover Your love and mercy behind it. Amen.

Love Heals Sorrow

The LORD gave me what I had, and the LORD has taken it away. Praise the name of the LORD! (Job 1:21).

If we didn't love, we wouldn't have our hearts broken. It is the memory of all the situations and occasions that brought love into our lives that makes the grieving process what it is.

For years Job enjoyed the love of his children and he loved them abundantly. In spite of his confusion and grief in the dark hour when God took them from him, he knew that his love could not be destroyed even by death, because "love will last forever" (1 Cor. 13:8). It was in fact Job's love that enabled him to accept his loss and still praise God.

To turn away from God in our sorrow is to grieve without help. This leads to tension and despair that does not do love any justice. God cannot help or comfort a rebellious heart. God wants to help because He is love. And because His Son also died, He understands perfectly. C. S. Lewis said, "You can accept what God did without knowing how it works. In fact, you will most certainly not know how it works before you have accepted it."

The greatest happiness of life is the conviction that we are loved – loved for ourselves, or rather, loved in spite of ourselves.
~ Victor Hugo ~

God never puts His children in a furnace if He is not there with them. If I don't grow spiritually in my sorrow, my suffering is nothing but loss. Knowing that God is always there makes my sorrow bearable. When Jesus wept at Lazarus' grave, the bystanders said, "See how much He loved him." Let this be your comfort: Love makes you mourn, but your Comforter mourns with you because He is love.

Loving Father, You know how love tears my heart apart because I am separated from my loved one. Thank You that nothing can ever separate me from Your love. Amen.

Why?

Why didn't I die as I came from the womb? (Job 3:11).

After the death of a loved one there are many questions that cry out for answers: Why *my* loved one? Why did God allow it? Why didn't God heal them? Is there anything more I could have done? To know that you could have done nothing to prevent death is no comfort. You are confronted with the choice of trusting God unconditionally or turning away from Him in bitterness. How does a believer adapt to loss? There is no simple solution or easy answer, but there are four ways that slow down the grieving process:

Denial: Denying your feelings doesn't relieve the pain. On the contrary, pretending that you aren't hurting just makes things worse.

Playing it down: To put on a brave front and pretend to be strong is to bottle up your sorrow; eventually you will explode. No matter how strong you are, the pain won't disappear. It is just a subtle form of escapism.

> Grief is the agony of an instant; the indulgence of grief the blunder of a life.
> ~ Benjamin Disraeli ~

Idealization: To idealize the person you've lost does not work either. Admitting the truth, even only to yourself, about the good and the not-so-good in that person's life, is the only way to be set free, to regain your equilibrium and speed up your recovery.

Isolation: To withdraw, alone with your memories, slows down and hampers the grieving process. The way to healing is to walk with courage and perseverance – straight ahead!

Give yourself time to adapt. The one you have lost would want you to laugh, cry, serve and fully live life. The time has come again to live life to the full.

Holy God, I am laying all my questions at Your feet, knowing that You will take it from here. Amen.

Remember to Forget

"Forget all that – it is nothing compared to what I am going to do. For I am about to do something new. See, I have already begun! Do you not see it?" (Isa. 43:18-19).

When Jesus raised Lazarus from the dead, He said to the bystanders, "Free him so that he can go home." (Lazarus' hands and feet were still wrapped in burial cloths.) When a loved one dies, we must let them go and not begrudge them their new life with Christ. It is difficult, but possible.

God expects us to let go of the past and our deceased loved ones and leave them with Him. Only then can His perfect will for our lives unfold. We don't deny our loved ones by carrying on with life. Our loved ones will forever live on in our memories. It is only human to remember the good and forget the bad. Just like an artist has the right to position the subject of his painting in such a way that a blemish is camouflaged, we have the right to remember the good. We also tend to exaggerate our forgiveness of those who are taken from us, and are mercilessly unforgiving toward ourselves. We blame ourselves for so many things that we could have done, said or prayed.

Forgiveness is all-powerful. Forgiveness heals all ills.
~ Catherine Ponder ~

This attitude makes our feelings of guilt exceed all reasonable limits. Self-reproach is not fair to you or to God's forgiving love. Knowing that God forgave all your transgressions in Christ Jesus tones down your sorrow and gives you peace of mind. It is human to cover up weaknesses with the cloak of love and to draw a curtain of love across imperfections. Forgive yourself as you forgave your deceased loved one. God has already done it.

Living Lord Jesus, it is so difficult to part from a loved one and then to live with self-reproach. Thank You that Your Holy Spirit enables me to carry on with life. Amen.

Phase One: Shock

Martha said to Jesus, "Lord, if only You had been here, my brother would not have died" (John 11:21).

The words from today's Scripture passage are the words that a shocked Martha, Lazarus's sister, said to Jesus when He arrived. The death of a loved one always comes as a shock – whether it is sudden or after a long illness. Because it is unexpected, it is always a shock.

Although we expect the loss of a person after a terminal illness, we still go through the grieving process. Often this begins even before death occurs. When death comes, the loss is still a cruel reality. An inexplicable longing takes hold of us and there is suddenly a void with which we cannot make peace.

At this stage of the grieving process, friends and bystanders don't really know what to say or do. Just be there for them. The person involved wants to talk to someone about their loss, to tell them about their indescribable sadness. They also want to be assured that it is not wrong to be sad.

Death is as the foreshadowing of life. We die that we may die no more.
~ Herman Hooker ~

God knows your heart and He understands that the source of your sorrow is love. He will give you the strength through His Holy Spirit to wrestle through this stage and to triumph in His name.

Holy Spirit, keep me from holding God accountable for my sorrow. Bring me back to His heart and His love every time. Amen.

Phase Two: Numbness

O LORD, how long will You forget me? Forever? How long will You look the other way? How long must I struggle with anguish in my soul, with sorrow in my heart every day? (Ps. 13:1-2).

Numbness or the inability to feel, think or react in a normal way is an extremely difficult but essential part of the grieving process. Things around you look unreal and nothing really moves you. And you don't really mind. You walk around in a daze and you find it very difficult to think clearly and make decisions.

People in this phase usually don't have the strength to work through the "whys?," even if they repeatedly ask the question. This is not the time for advanced theological argument or discussion. It is better to simply agree that the loss is a heavy burden that causes deep sorrow and intense spiritual suffering.

It will greatly comfort you if you can see God's hand in both your losses and your crosses.
~ Charles H. Spurgeon ~

Yet, even during this stage, you can be sure of God's comfort and care – like Christ cared for Martha and Mary when Lazarus died. In this phase, you tend to isolate yourself. Denial and isolation act as buffers against the overwhelming realization of the reality of separation. Guard against isolation becoming a way of life, otherwise it will become increasingly difficult to return to reality. Feeling painfully alone doesn't mean you must despair. God's plan for your life is much bigger than your loss. Jesus wants to be your companion in your grief. Know that God understands your sorrow and that He wants to carry you through this period.

Loving Father, You are my only anchor and hope. Thank You for the comfort of Your Spirit. Amen.

Phase Three: Guilty Feelings

The LORD is compassionate and merciful, slow to get angry and filled with unfailing love (Ps. 103:8).

During stage three, there is confusion between fantasy and reality. People so often say in this situation, "It feels like my loved one has just gone out for a while and will be back soon." Especially children find it easy to hide in a fantasy world. It is a normal phase of the grieving process, especially if the loss was sudden. But it is also a difficult phase.

After the funeral of their child, parents often don't touch his or her room. A sermon on this subject can help them realize that death brings sorrow, and that they can accept it, in faith. Accepting that your loved one has died is not being disloyal. Once you understand that, the conflict between fantasy and reality can be dealt with.

During this phase, feelings of guilt might also surface. The person who is grieving might say, "Shouldn't we have gone to another doctor for a second opinion?" Or, "Did we really do everything possible to prevent this from happening?" If guilty feelings occur with reason, as a result of unresolved hurt or misunderstanding preceding the death, they must be addressed.

You never lose the love of God. Guilt is the warning that temporarily you are out of touch.
~ Jack Dominian ~

Through God's grace, we must get to the point where we know that we needn't feel guilty about the death of a loved one. Life and death are in God's hands – leave them there.

Merciful and compassionate God, thank You for the assurance that You have already forgiven me. Amen.

Phase Four: Releasing Emotion

When Jesus saw her weeping, and the Jews who had come along with her also weeping, He was deeply moved in spirit and troubled (John 11:33 NIV).

In the grieving process, it is necessary to open the floodgates for emotion. It doesn't mean that you haven't already expressed sorrow. During every stage there is emotion being expressed in varying degrees. When, however, you start accepting reality, it seems as if your emotions are given free rein. This is also normal: a person in mourning should not hold back their emotions. Remember that tears are a mechanism from God to help you with the grieving process.

Tears have a tongue, and grammar, and language, that our Father knoweth.
~ Samuel Rutherford ~

It is not realistic to say that we should be strong and not cry. Jesus shed tears. Emotions shouldn't be bottled up. Releasing emotion serves a purifying and healing purpose, especially when shared with others. Christ said, "God blesses those who mourn, for they will be comforted" (Matt. 5:4 NIV). Tears soften our grief and speed up the healing of our wounds. Thank God for the liberating and healing power of tears. They tone down our sorrow, bring acceptance of God's will and ultimately leads to recovery.

When John speaks of a new heaven and a new earth, he says, "He [God] will wipe every tear from their eyes. There will be no more death or mourning or crying or pain, for the old order of things has passed away" (Rev. 21:4 NIV).

Holy Master, thank You that I may follow Your example and shed tears. Thank You for the comfort of the Holy Spirit. Amen.

Phase Five: Painful Memories

I have no peace, no quietness. I have no rest; only trouble comes (Job 3:26).

It is difficult coping with the pain caused by the memories of a deceased loved one. This pain will last much longer than the short period between the death and funeral of the person. It might last months or even years. We go to church and the place next to us is empty. We meet a trusted friend of the deceased. We hear a song that the deceased loved. We go on holiday to a place with so many memories. This emotion must be acknowledged, otherwise it can have a negative effect.

During this time, you need someone with whom to share your grief; someone who has a sympathetic ear for your pain and longing. Praise and thank God if you have found such a friend. It is necessary and liberating to talk openly about your grief over a period of time. It has a healing effect to lay bare your feelings and work through them.

When doubts filled my mind, Your comfort gave me renewed hope and cheer.
~ Psalm 94:19 ~

Coming to terms with your grief is a gradual and taxing process. It requires time and involves pain, but this is the way to go. To deal with the pain and accept it, and adapt to the idea living without your loved one means you will also have to manage your memories. It is a tremendous help to share this phase with people you trust. Don't forget to share it especially with your heavenly Comforter.

Heavenly Comforter, thank You that You use my memories to lead me back to life again. Amen.

Back to Life

Why should I fast when he is dead? Can I bring him back again? I will go to him one day, but he cannot return to me (2 Sam. 12:23).

When you have gone through the grieving process with the help of the Holy Spirit, and feel that at last you have regained control of your life, you have reached the crucial period: back to life! You must reaffirm that you emerged from your grief stronger than you went into it. If you have accepted your loss, your pain is now bearable and the memories are no longer accompanied by hurt. Then you can start living a new life.

At this point you might discover a clear understanding of God's will and purpose for your life. You might be pleasantly surprised to find out how much God loves you and how much He cares about you. But you must still guard against hasty and impulsive actions. God wants you to make your decisions in prayer. If you hold on to your grief too tightly, you can miss out on a new, meaningful life.

The lust for comfort murders the passions of the soul.
~ Kahlil Gibran ~

Open yourself up to the rest of your family or a new opportunity when you have worked through your grieving process. Take on new responsibilities and live with purpose.

David mourned the death of his child for seven days before he spoke the words of today's Scripture. You and I must pray to be guided and helped by the heavenly Comforter to do the same.

Holy Spirit, Comforter of our hearts, enable me to return to life courageously and with purpose. Amen.

Problems with Grief

Submit to God, and you will have peace; then things will go well for you (Job 22:21).

The revolt and anger you may experience in the grieving process is a serious problem, especially for devoted children of God. Admit these feelings without hesitation and talk about them with a trusted friend. It will help you gain perspective. Your anger could be directed at another person. You may feel death occurred as a result of poor medical care, negligence, a reckless driver or something else. It could even be aimed at the deceased, if the person was responsible for their own death. Sometimes it builds up intense anger toward God because He allowed the person to die. It could also be anger directed at yourself because you feel you could have prevented it.

Anger toward the deceased, toward God and toward yourself is responsible for substantial and deep feelings of guilt. Deal with these feelings: Talk to God about them during your quiet time. Also talk to a trusted friend or a professional counselor. If you don't, it could lead to serious despondency and depression. Make sure you experience God's forgiveness, and then live accordingly.

A really intelligent man feels what other men only know.
~ Charles Montesquieu ~

Sometimes you start negotiating with God and yourself: If God answers my questions, if God comforts me, I will pray or go to church again. These are not reasonable conditions and they solve no problems. Surrender yourself unconditionally to God's love and obey the promptings of the Holy Spirit.

It is normal to be sad after the death of a loved one. This heartache does, however, need attention and must be dealt with accordingly.

Help me, O Master, in this perplexing time with emotions that are hard to handle. Amen.

What to Tell the Children?

"There is more than enough room in My Father's home. If this were not so, would I have told you that I am going to prepare a place for you? When everything is ready, I will come and get you, so that you will always be with Me where I am" (John 14:2-3).

One of the most difficult things concerning death is what to say to the children. How can they understand the death of a mother or father, or a family member they love? Maybe we have a problem explaining death to them because we have a problem with it ourselves, and find it difficult to accept. Only when we have overcome our own fear of death, can we explain it to children.

Kids today learn a lot about getting to the moon, but very little about getting to heaven.
~ David Jeremiah ~

Children will understand that Jesus prepared a home for them and that He is waiting for those who love Him. But to tell a little child that Jesus needs his or her mommy more than they do will only cause bitterness toward God. It is better to say, "Your mommy is with Jesus, and one day we will be with her and Jesus."

Just like most children are no longer unfamiliar with the mystery of birth, they should not be excluded from the mystery of death. Because children think of death as rejection, they should not be rejected further by being sent away. Even if our attempts to protect our children are motivated by the best intentions, they may suffer emotionally. Their most urgent need is the assurance that they will be taken care of by those closest to them. Tell children about a loved one's death at the right time and place. Then support them in their grief and sorrow.

Lord Jesus, Friend of children, take them in Your arms and bless them and help us support them in their grief and confusion.

Amen.

Acceptance

Death is swallowed up in victory (1 Cor. 15:54).

There are a few factors that condition the kind of grief we experience and the way we deal with it. One is the community's expectations and customs in a time of sorrow: a visit to the home of the bereaved; sending a note or a card expressing our sympathy; a handshake or a hug; a meaningful word of comfort. Experiencing the reality of death together, in our hope for the future, is the kind of support the Christian community owes those in mourning.

Another factor that conditions our grief is our attitude toward death. Realize that death is a reality to be reckoned with. It is part of the established earthly order of things.

What we can do is help to soften the cruel reality of death. We can talk about the dearly departed. The funeral nowadays does not expose the bereaved to so much raw grief as in the past when the coffin was brought into the church, followed by a long ceremony at the open grave.

One short sleep past,
we wake eternally, and
death shall be no more;
death, thou shalt die!
~ John Donne ~

We must believe Jesus' words that the spirit of the person does not die but goes to its eternal home. Knowing that our loved one is in God's care is of immense comfort. We mourn, but not like people who have no hope. We have the hope of a better life where the mortal body is clothed with the immortal: "Death is swallowed up in victory."

Almighty God of life and death, thank You that You go through the dark valley with us. Amen.

Adapting Takes Time

And the one sitting on the throne said, "Look, I am making everything new" (Rev. 21:5).

A contributory factor that influences the grieving process is the way in which the person died. If death was sudden and unexpected, it comes as an immense shock. If we were expecting it, we have already worked through part of the grieving process. This is a facet we must understand. A man may know for months that his wife suffers from a terminal illness. Every time he takes her to the doctor, the grieving process reaches a deeper level. By the time she dies he has already dealt with his grief in part.

In such cases the unenlightened might wonder why the man, after so short a time, doesn't seem to be so sad and mournful anymore. They might comment that it didn't take him very long to adapt to life without her. But during her illness he adapted gradually and started mourning sooner than the community realized. If he starts showing an interest in someone new, it must not be interpreted as unfaithfulness to his first wife. He has already gone through the process and emerged a new person, ready to take on life with all its demands again.

The true way to mourn the dead is to take care of the living who belong to them.
~ Edmund Burke ~

The way in which death comes makes a big difference in the way it is experienced, and how the sorrow it brings is handled. Remember that no matter how death came, the sorrow is always sincere and it takes courage to adapt to life again. This courage we get only from God. His path always leads back to life!

God of life, yesterday there were still tears; today I can smile again. Thank You for leading me to a new daybreak. Amen.

Hope in Times of Sorrow

Rejoice in our confident hope. Be patient in trouble, and keep on praying (Rom.12:12).

Hope is Christian optimism in its purest form. Hope, patience, and perseverance in prayer are gifts of the Holy Spirit to God's believing children. To be patient when trials and sorrow descend on you like a dark cloud, and to place your hope in God despite this, is the revelation of a special relationship with the Father.

The point and meaning of our Christian hope is revealed in a special way in times of deep sorrow and loss caused by death. We don't have to live like those who have no hope left, but in deep-rooted trust and total surrender to God's will.

Through the working of the Holy Spirit we know that without Christ death is a hopeless ending; with Him it is an endless hope. The Holy Spirit enables us to carry on courageously and not to give in under the heavy burden of trials.

He that lives in hope,
dances without music.
~ George Herbert ~

In Jesus Christ we are sure of the final victory. Present sorrow is just mist that will clear, and with hope in our hearts we will walk in the sunshine of God's love again. "Wait patiently for the Lord. Be brave and courageous. Yes, wait patiently for the Lord" (Ps. 27:14).

Spirit of God, keep the hope in my heart burning – even when I am threatened by despair. I praise You for letting hope catch fire in my heart. Amen.

Courage Triumphs over Fear

I am suffering here in prison. But I am not ashamed of it, for I know the one in whom I trust, and I am sure that He is able to guard what I have entrusted to Him until the day of His return (2 Tim. 1:12).

An element of fear is present in most people at the death of a loved one. If it is not controlled, it can paralyze us and poison our thoughts. People always fear radical change: We are afraid of what might happen to us; of the sorrow that will tear us apart; of funeral arrangements – and of that final farewell. Fears hide everywhere and are suddenly let loose in our lives like terrifying phantoms.

During the storm, the wise person doesn't pray for God to calm it, because it is part of the rhythm of nature. He prays for courage and deliverance from paralyzing fear. Inside us, a storm is threatening to paralyze us completely. But we have a Savior who can free us from fear. Jesus often spoke these words in the Bible: "Do not fear!" Fear undermines our faith, but love is the antidote. Love expels fear (see 1 John 4:18). Love strengthens our faith, while fear tries to break it down. God leads us past every dark precipice of fear in His love and through His Spirit.

Nothing in life is to be feared, it is only to be understood.
~ Marie Curie ~

God gives us a recipe through the prophet Isaiah of how to handle fear: "Don't be afraid, for I am with you. Don't be discouraged, for I am your God. I will strengthen you and help you. I will hold you up with My victorious right hand" (Isa. 41:10).

So keep your eyes fixed on Jesus and shake off the chains of fear. In this way, experience deliverance and peace of mind.

Thank You, Father, that Your love drives all fear from our hearts. Give me a sufficient measure of that love every day. Amen.

Helping the Bereaved (1)

Is there any encouragement from belonging to Christ? Any comfort from His love? Any fellowship together in the Spirit? Are your hearts tender and compassionate? (Phil. 2:1).

Draw strength from your faith and accept that God wants only the best for you. Tell God exactly how you feel – He has not abandoned you. He wants to take away your anger and bitterness toward Him. He is waiting for you to bring your heartache to Him. Also, don't neglect the fellowship of believers – it has great therapeutic value.

Don't deny, escape or suppress your emotions. It is not a shame or sin to cry. When memories torment you, when you are part of another's loss, when you don't know where to go with your pain, feel free to cry unashamedly. Tears are love and hope kept alive by memories.

> As gold is purified in the furnace, so the faithful heart is purified by sorrow.
> ~ Guarini ~

Don't isolate yourself. Talk to others and ask for advice. It is essential that people serve as a sounding board for you: people that you can talk to about the questions inside, about your feelings of guilt and especially about your relationship with God.

It is also essential to make time for yourself without isolating yourself. It contributes to the healing of your grief when it is creative isolation. This is what Jesus did in His quiet times with God. At the same time, keep the meaningful relationships in your life strong. Lead your normal life. Maintain a healthy balance between meaningful isolation and participating in life around you.

Holy Spirit of God, help me in my times of sorrow to identify what to avoid and which positive things to do, so that I may be a witness of Your love. Amen.

Helping the Bereaved (2)

The LORD is compassionate and merciful, slow to get angry and filled with unfailing love (Ps. 103:8).

Be careful of making radical changes too soon after someone has died. Don't decide in a blaze of emotion to sell your house or move to a new city. You need time to come to terms with your loss in a familiar and safe place. Guard against turning your home into a museum where you hoard everything that reminds you of the deceased. At the right time, a change of surroundings will possibly be a good idea, but impulsive decisions can stretch out the grieving process.

A very real danger is to neglect yourself during this period. Keep a conscientious check on your health and consult your medical practitioner. Eat regular and balanced meals. Pay attention to your appearance; your morale is closely connected to these aspects.

Sorrow looks back,
worry looks around,
but faith looks up.
~ Anonymous ~

Accept responsibility for your own life. This is important, especially if your spouse carried most of the responsibility. Don't become totally dependent on family and friends. With the input of your heart and mind, and the strong belief that God is with you, you will receive the necessary strength to accept responsibility for yourself and your healing.

Keep inseparable contact with your heavenly Father. Even if it is difficult in the beginning, remember that it is your anchor in this turbulent time. Persevere in prayer and read the Bible. You will find purpose and direction through the Holy Spirit's power. Reflect on what God has to say through what has happened. Be patient with yourself and embrace life every day!

Heavenly Father, let me live with Your covenants in spite of the grief that leaves me totally spent after You have used the pruning shears. Amen.

Hope for the Future

We wait for the blessed hope – the appearing of our great God and Savior, Jesus Christ (Titus 2:13 NIV).

The Christian's hope is not wishful thinking, but concrete reality because Christ is our hope. In Him, we have eternal life (see John 3:36; 5:25; 10:28). It gives the sorrowful person a positive foundation to build on. Sorrow targets believers and unbelievers alike, but there is one big difference: Christians don't grieve like those who have no hope. There is emotion but not panic. There is sorrow, but even in the throes of intense loneliness, believers know that God is with them.

There are those who have died to be with Christ, which is much better than life on earth (see Phil. 1:23). We will be reunited with one another, and Christ will come in glory again one day.

We have many problems and answers that baffle and evade us here on earth.

Once a man is united to God, how could he not live forever?
~ C. S. Lewis ~

Paul gives us the heavenly solution in Thessalonians: "We tell you this directly from the Lord: We who are still living when the Lord returns will not meet Him ahead of those who have died. For the Lord Himself will come down from heaven with a commanding shout, with the voice of the archangel, and with the trumpet call of God. First, the Christians who have died will rise from their graves. Then, together with them, we who are still alive and remain on the earth will be caught up in the clouds to meet the Lord in the air. Then we will be with the Lord forever. So encourage each other with these words" (1 Thess. 4:15-18).

Father God, I see a new heaven coming, and a new and free earth, where God Himself will come and live with us. Amen.

The Pruning Shears

He cuts off every branch of mine that doesn't produce fruit, and He prunes the branches that do bear fruit so they will produce even more (John 15:2).

God often uses sorrow and pain to teach His children important life lessons. In so doing, He strengthens our faith and character and gives us space to grow spiritually. In keeping with His plan, our problems become opportunities to bear more and more fruit, but then we need to accept the pruning shears with the right attitude.

Pain and discomfort make us go to the doctor, and although the treatment is sometimes painful, it brings healing and recovery. It is often our sorrow that drives us to the Great Physician. What a shame if this meeting is in vain.

God is the Great Gardener who prunes our lives with love and tenderness. Our Father is the Master Pruner and He knows where our weaknesses and shortcomings lie. He knows the right time to prune back our lives and His method is always the correct one. If we allow Him to prune in accordance with His plan, He promises fruitfulness and a rich harvest in His kingdom.

In tribulation, immediately draw near to God with confidence, and you will receive strength, enlightenment, and instruction.
~ John of the Cross ~

The wounds caused by the pruning shears are healed by the tender care of the Heavenly Gardener. If we handle affliction with this attitude in our hearts, we can count on God's healing, comfort and liberation. Surrender to God's pruning shears and He will keep His promises.

Heavenly Gardener, thank You that You change the pain of the pruning shears into joy and growth. Amen.

Thankful Despite Loss

The LORD gave me what I had, and the LORD has taken it away. Praise the name of the LORD! (Job 1:21).

George Herbert's prayer is a stirring one: "Thou that has given so much to me, give one thing more – a grateful heart." Job lost everything that was precious to him and yet thankfulness broke through the boundaries of his sorrow in a song of praise to God. Not even Job's overwhelming sorrow could keep him from declaring his thankfulness to God.

It is easy to be thankful when you are riding the wave of prosperity. We all find it much more difficult to give thanks during a raging storm of affliction, or to appreciate our circumstances in times of grief. Paul, who had much experience in handling setbacks, instructs us in 1 Thessalonians 5:18: "Be thankful in all circumstances, for this is God's will for you who belong to Christ Jesus." It is not expected of us to be thankful *for* everything, but *in* everything – in all circumstances, good or bad.

One single grateful thought raised to heaven is the most perfect prayer.
~ G. E. Lessing ~

God certainly doesn't expect us to thank Him for disappointment, sickness and death. But it is particularly in these times that we must focus our thoughts on God's goodness, the support and love of our friends and the many blessings we receive undeservedly. The Lord who takes is also the Lord who gives in abundance.

God will never allow our losses to exceed our gain. If we live from a thankful heart, we gain the peace of God that surpasses all understanding (see Phil. 4:7). This peace brings acceptance and emotional security. It is a life-changing discovery!

I am surrounded by darkness, merciful Father, but in spite of this, please put a song in my heart. Amen.

Death Is Not Final

Thanks be to God! He gives us the victory through our Lord Jesus Christ. (1 Cor. 15:57).

The way in which we experience sorrow and grief will be conditioned by the resources of faith that we as Christians have at our disposal. Christians know and believe that death is not the end of the road. Death is just a turn in the road that leads to that brightly lit glory we call heaven. Those who have died in Christ will rise in glory – this is a great comfort when we've lost a loved one.

Christians know without a doubt that death is not the end. The spirit of those who died in Christ does not die, but moves on to be with Jesus. This, Paul says, is by far the best news on earth. Moreover, Christ is with every believer in their sorrow. As He came to be with Martha and Mary when their brother died, He will come to comfort us.

The seed dies into new life,
and so does man.
~ George MacDonald ~

Everybody who believes in Jesus Christ is strengthened by His presence. He helps them deal with their sorrow. The privilege of loving someone poses the risk of separation, but all the means of grace necessary to help us cope with it are available to us through Jesus Christ.

Jesus' resurrection is our guarantee that because we are believers, we will be raised to a new life. With His help, sorrow that threatens to destroy our lives is gradually transformed into acceptance and the firm hope that we will be reunited with our loved ones one day.

Risen Lord, thank You that Your Holy Spirit planted faith in my heart, so that I know a new and better life awaits. Amen.

The Mystery of Suffering

You have been given not only the privilege of trusting in Christ but also the privilege of suffering for Him (Phil. 1:29).

Paul's pronouncement in today's Scripture is a distinctive revelation. He adds to this, "We can rejoice, too, when we run into problems and trials, for we know that they help us develop endurance. And endurance develops strength of character, and character strengthens our confident hope of salvation. And this hope will not lead to disappointment. For we know how dearly God loves us" (Rom. 5:3-5). Because there is no character development without suffering, suffering is necessary for our spiritual growth to maturity.

God doesn't only want us to go to heaven, He also wants people with character to serve Him here on earth. This is impossible without suffering and trials (see Heb. 12:5-11). Sorrow, suffering and trials are experienced by the believer, not to punish us but to strengthen our faith. It teaches us new things about God all the time and allows us to live closer to Him. Christ's suffering strengthened His human experience and perfected it. If we refuse to suffer and reject the cross, we won't be of much worth to God.

What does anyone know who doesn't know how to suffer for Christ?
~ John of the Cross ~

There is comfort in pain, trial and sorrow. God gives us many blessings in our suffering. Nothing that God allows in His child's life happens by mistake. There is always a higher, holy reason for it. Our faith cannot be built other than through pain and suffering.

Holy Father, I am assured of Your love because You trust me with my portion of suffering. Amen.

Don't Let Your Sorrow Go to Waste

No one is abandoned by the Lord forever. Though He brings grief, He also shows compassion because of the greatness of His unfailing love (Lam. 3:31-32).

It would be an unthinkable loss to emerge from our experience of grief without any lasting gain. Sorrow is an important component of our spiritual growth toward spiritual maturity. It is often the forerunner of a more intense and intimate relationship with our Father.

Those who have suffered most are those who know the Lord best. God turns with tender love to those who cry out to Him in their need. Sorrow is a purifying power: it is like a fire that consumes our weaknesses and at the same time brings refreshing rain and new growth.

Grief is itself a medicine.
~ William Cowper ~

On the one hand, we get to know the warm comfort and all-encompassing love of God through sorrow and suffering. On the other hand, we discover the goodness, compassion and tenderness of those close to us. We can live on the surface for many years and then, suddenly, we are plunged into the darkest depths of sorrow and suffering. There we learn, to our amazement, that new beauty and power are born in our hearts.

There are hidden blessings in every trial. We must just discover those blessings and share them with others. Thus, our own sorrow is tempered and we become instruments of comfort in the hand of the Great Comforter. God sends trials in our lives to bring out the best in us. Satan sends temptations in our lives to bring out the worst in us.

Make good use of your sorrow – through it God is bringing the best in you to the fore: to His honor and glory!

Help me, O Lord, that my sorrow doesn't only bring loss. Amen.

A Witness of God's Grace

He comforts us in all our troubles so that we can comfort others. When they are troubled, we will be able to give them the same comfort God has given us (2 Cor. 1:4).

With God's help and by His grace you have dealt with your sorrow and come out in one piece. Now you are duty-bound to be a witness of God's grace. There is a sea of broken hearts around you; people who are desperate to find a way out of the dark pit of grief and heartache. Your experience will enable you to offer first-hand advice. Only those who have walked this road themselves really know what it entails.

If you have experienced the death of someone close to you and worked through it, and you were blessed by Christ's faithfulness in the process, you are the ideal person to help others. Learn to communicate with others about their loss and give them the opportunity to talk about how they feel. Be a patient listener and a sounding board for broken hearts. Just be yourself and don't prepare a speech. Use your own experiences as a way to start the conversation. Sometimes words are not even necessary.

Let all find compassion in you.
~ John of the Cross ~

Do what you can and don't make promises you can't keep. A prayer, short and to the point, is suitable. A note expressing your condolences is another way that works well. Don't try to avoid the topic of death – that's what the bereaved wants to talk about. The golden rule is: Be sincere, honest and natural. Hospitality and care are also important. These are simple gestures, but they soothe the bereaved emotionally.

Heavenly Comforter, You were patient with me in my sorrow. Help me to treat my grieving fellow humans in the same way.

Amen.

Safe in God's Protection

I prayed to the LORD, and He answered me. He freed me from all my fears (Ps. 34:4).

The person who shoulders his cross without complaint and follows the great Cross-bearer is much like a sailor who weathers raging storms and arrives safely in the harbor. The greatest comfort anyone can experience in their sorrow is the protection of God: "I will comfort you there as a mother comforts her child" (Isa. 66:13).

God's comfort comes to us in various ways – the sympathy of friends, or people who can witness from experience that "weeping may last through the night, but joy comes with the morning" (Ps. 30:5). God also comforts us with His promises in the Bible. Comfort runs like a golden thread throughout Scripture. It tells us that God is the source of all comfort (see 2 Cor. 1:3); that He sent us a Comforter and a Counselor (see John 14:16); that Jesus feels great pity for us (see Matt. 9:36) and; that His Son knew suffering and pain Himself (see Isa. 53:3).

> The opposite of joy is not sorrow. It is unbelief.
> ~ Leslie Weatherhead ~

God comforts us especially through certainty of faith. He tells us through Jesus, "Don't let your hearts be troubled. Trust in God, and trust also in Me" (John 14:1). Faith is our anchor in tribulation. It is the source of our quiet joy under all circumstances.

God's final aim for our lives is for us to be happy. Jesus reassures us about this: "I have told you these things so that you will be filled with My joy. Yes, your joy will overflow" (John 15:11). We are able to emerge from our suffering purified, with Christ's joy in our hearts and protected by God's love.

Holy God, You are my refuge and strong fortress. You are the source of all my joy and gladness. Amen.

A Song of Praise after Suffering!

We were filled with laughter, and we sang for joy. And the other nations said, "What amazing things the LORD has done for them." Yes, the LORD has done amazing things for us! What joy! (Ps. 126:2-3).

In this pilgrim's song, the author sings the praises of the miracle-working and renewing grace of God. Unless we refuse to be comforted, God will always produce gladness and joy from our sorrow and grief. In His supreme wisdom, God varies the experiences in our lives like He varies the seasons.

Sorrow always insists on staying fresh, but we must firmly resist this line of thinking.

When we accept God's comfort, the jubilant sound of a song of thanksgiving bursts from our hearts: "You surround me with songs of victory" (Ps. 32:7). If we have been trained in God's school, showing worthiness and faith, we have the stature of people who have become spiritually mature. Then, in conclusion, we testify with Robert Browning Hamilton:

The sweetest of all sounds is praise.
~ Xenophon ~

I walked a mile with Pleasure, she chattered all the way,
But left me none the wiser for all she had to say.
I walked a mile with Sorrow and ne'er a word said she;
But, O, the things I learned from her, when Sorrow walked with me.

Now our suffering and sorrow are not only loss, but by the grace of God and the Spirit of comfort, spiritual gain. Thus we are prepared to proclaim the glory of God and sing His praises.

You are my God, and I will praise You! You are my God, and I will exalt You! Give thanks to the LORD, for He is good! His faithful love endures forever (Ps. 118:28-29). Amen.

August

His light on my path brings peace.

And just as they were telling about it, Jesus Himself was suddenly standing there among them. "Peace be with you," He said.
~ Luke 24:36 ~

Peace and justice are two sides of the same coin.
~ Dwight D. Eisenhower ~

Holy God and through Jesus Christ, our heavenly Father,
In the midst of chaos, suspicion, hate, selfishness
and confusion, we lift up our hands to You:
Lord, give peace in our time!
We know very well that we cannot live in peace with others
if we have not found peace with You;
that there cannot be peace anywhere
before there is peace everywhere;
that the power of a nation does not lie in its armory,
but in the integrity of its people;
that peace is born in righteousness.
We confess in shame that we are also
responsible for the conditions of conflict and strife:
we have been careless and negligent about our spiritual priorities;
we were selfish and inconsiderate in our daily walk through life;
we were complacent and uninvolved in times of unrest;
we were arrogant and self-satisfied.
Forgive us, Lord our merciful God!
Let Your will for peace on earth be done.
Let Your Word indicate the way to peace.
Give us the love that sets us free from bitterness,
hatred and an unforgiving spirit.
Help us to live together in peace and harmony.
We pray this in the name of
the Prince of Peace, Jesus Christ.

Amen.

God Is the Source of Peace

I pray that God, the source of hope, will fill you completely with joy and peace because you trust in Him. Then you will overflow with confident hope through the power of the Holy Spirit (Rom. 15:13).

Peace is a gift that God gives His children. This is a state of mind which leads us to join David in saying, "In peace I will lie down and sleep, for You alone, O Lord, will keep me safe" (Ps. 4:8). We spend sleepless nights because we seek peace outside of God. We punish ourselves unnecessarily by trying to find tranquility elsewhere. Our reward is inevitable: stress and sleeplessness.

Peace of mind is the quiet but certain knowledge that you are secure in God's care. When I accept God as the Source of my peace and joy, and I become inseparably united with Him, I have taken the first step on the road to peace.

We should have great peace if we did not busy ourselves with what others say and do.
~ Thomas à Kempis ~

When my spirit is in peaceful harmony with God, I live in harmony and peace with my fellow humans. A bad relationship with God makes a good relationship with others impossible. Few things can destroy peace of mind as completely as strife in your relationship with God and those around you. To remedy this situation, our relationship with God needs to be strengthened through Jesus Christ and the Holy Spirit.

The wonder of God's peace is one of the "perks" of a surrendered life. The condition for this is faith.

Merciful Father, my soul yearns for peace. Thank You that I can draw near to You, the source of true peace. Amen.

Christ's Legacy Is Peace

"I am leaving you with a gift – peace of mind and heart. And the peace I give is a gift the world cannot give. So don't be troubled or afraid" (John 14:27).

Peace was Jesus' legacy to His followers. The search for peace is humanity's passion. The peace the world offers is a poor reflection of God's legacy of spiritual peace to His believing disciples of all centuries.

To claim this peace legacy, we must first have a right relationship with God. We must become children of God by accepting Him in faith: "To all who believed Him and accepted Him, He gave the right to become children of God" (John 1:12). We must confess our sins, accept God's forgiveness and be purified of all unrighteousness. Then we must seek His perfect will for our lives.

No God, no peace.
Know God, know peace.
~ Anonymous ~

Following Christ's example, we must say with Him, "Yet I want Your will to be done, not Mine" (Luke 22:42). Christ allots us the highest peace we can imagine: God's peace! Then we live in peace not only with God, but also with ourselves and the world around us.

The peace of Christ has the highest distinction: it is one of a kind and not like the feigned peace the world offers us. It is complete and non-partial and it spans our entire lives. It is constant and doesn't chop and change with our changing moods. It is genuine, and universal, and not limited to certain places and certain privileged people. So, we will not fear, because fear is an enemy of peace, and Jesus Christ overcame fear.

Source of everlasting peace, thank You that I can find a place of peace with You amidst the storms of life. Amen.

Peacemakers for God

"God blesses those who work for peace, for they will be called the children of God" (Matt. 5:9).

Peace is all about a never-ending search that lasts a lifetime. Like the search for truth, the search for peace never ends. The person who seeks permanent peace in this torn world is doomed to be disappointed.

Peace is all about people and not things. Money and weapons don't make war – people do! It is our sinful nature that leads to strife, time and time again. Peace is not found by means of violence, but by honest and sincere dialogue. And peace without righteousness is just another form of tyranny.

Being a peacemaker is a difficult and thankless task, but it remains a God-appointed task. The peacemakers God blesses are people who don't avoid their responsibilities. Our feelings are too changeable to rely on in our search for peace. Only once we are at peace with God, are we able to pray for our enemies.

> I couldn't live in peace if I put the shadow of a willful sin between myself and God.
>
> ~ George Eliot ~

Peace must be shared. Christ's blessing is promised to people who *make* peace – not those who *have* peace. We achieve peace only by working for it and this makes us God's children. As His witnesses, we must persuade the world to receive peace from God's hand.

God of peace, let Your peace become visible in my life so that the world will get to know Your peace through me. Amen.

Shalom!

Unfailing love and truth have met together. Righteousness and peace have kissed! (Ps. 85:10).

The Hebrew word *shalom* conveys the original meaning of well-being. It includes health, welfare and prosperity. When people greeted each other with the words *Jehovah jireh* (the Lord will provide) they confirmed that God is the origin of life. The individual, the family and the nation were involved.

When there was well-being in the religious, social and political field, there was peace in the land. This condition was described as *shalom*: they could plant, sow, harvest and gather. It was founded on orderliness and solid relationships. Without these, there was no *shalom.* Thus it was a condition of order between humans and God, nation and nation, person and person.

In Thy will is our peace!
~ Dante ~

God alone can give this peace. Without God there was no hope of well-being in Israel. But when they served Him in all sincerity and observed the covenant, He gave them peace and rest.

Both true and false prophets could proclaim "peace." Peace and sin can't live together, which is why the false prophets' *shalom* was powerless. The Old Testament *shalom* had more to do with the nation than the individual. It had more to do with law and order.

The predictions of Isaiah, Jeremiah and Ezekiel gave the word *shalom* a new and deeper meaning. It became peace connected with the coming of the Savior and the King called the Prince of Peace. He would maintain and guarantee peace in the land, because this is what He was destined for.

Holy God, You are my peace because I am inseparably bound to You. Let Your Spirit help me to bring peace into Your world.

Amen.

The Fruit of the Holy Spirit

The Holy Spirit produces this kind of fruit in our lives: love, joy, peace, patience, kindness, goodness, faithfulness, gentleness and self-control (Gal. 5:22-23).

Eirene is the Greek word for peace and had two important meanings. It referred to the peace and calm enjoyed when a wise and just emperor reigned. It also referred to the good order in a city or town. The leader of the city or town was the keeper of the *eirene,* or public peace.

It is similar to the Hebrew word *shalom,* and means not only freedom from problems, but also everything that contributes toward bringing about the noblest things in a person's life.

Billy Graham says, "Christ alone can bring lasting peace – peace with God – peace among men and nations – and peace within our hearts" And we read in Ephesians 2:17 NIV, "He came and preached peace to you who were far away and peace to those who were near."

> I smiled to think God's greatness flowed around our incompleteness, round our restlessness His rest.
> ~ Elizabeth Barrett Browning ~

When the long-awaited Messiah came, the earth was filled with the prospect of good relationships, well-being and happiness. In keeping with this, the heavenly message that was heard across the fields of Ephrata on that first Christmas was, "Glory to God in the highest heaven, and peace on earth to those with whom God is pleased" (Luke 2:14). Because we are followers of the Prince of Peace, we must focus our Christian zeal on living in peace, good order and harmony with all people. Where there is faith in God, there is love and where there is love, there is peace. Where there is peace, there is God – and where God is, there are His blessings.

Thank You, Lord Jesus, that You came to our world as the Prince of Peace. Make me a channel of Your peace. Amen.

Peace through Jesus Christ

He came and preached peace to you who were far away and peace to those who were near (Eph. 2:17 NIV).

Christ is the source of our peace. He made peace with God possible for us. "Therefore, since we have been made right in God's sight by faith, we have peace with God because of what Jesus Christ our Lord has done for us" (Rom. 5:1). The unique relationship of peace between Creator and creature became possible through Christ's sacrificial death.

This *eirene* peace enables us to live in peace with our fellow humans (see Rom. 14:19). It brings joy and gladness into the household because it enriches the lives of all family members. It grows in us as a fruit of the Holy Spirit. It creates spiritual unity that inevitably leads to peace (see Eph. 4:3). It forms an integral part of Christ's character (see James 3:17-18). Everything inside us is also in order and our priorities are arranged with Christ at the top. It gives us a foretaste of the heavenly peace and joy that are the end result of *eirene* – peace with God.

My soul can see no other remedy pleasing to God than peace. Peace, peace, therefore, for the love of Christ.
~ Catherine of Siena ~

When it seems as if there is no order in your life, remember that Christ's peace creates order from chaos. Then your peace need not rely on your feelings, emotions or state of mind, but on your relationship with God through Jesus Christ. He is, after all, the source of all genuine and lasting peace.

Holy Lord Jesus, my salvation and peace are found in You alone. Let this certainty remain the mainstay of my peace, calm and undying hope. Amen.

God's Gift

May there be peace within your walls. For the sake of my family and friends, I will say, "May you have peace" (Ps. 122:7-8).

When Christ came into this world, songs of praise were sung to celebrate peace on earth (see Luke 2:14). When He left the world, He left behind a gift of peace (see John 14:27).

Peace of mind and heart is the special gift that God gives His children who surrender their lives to Him. To many He gives talent and beauty. Wealth is commonplace. Fame is not rare. But inner peace is God's final token of approval, the most special sign of His love. He gives it with great discretion. Most people are never blessed with this and others wait a lifetime before it descends on them like dew.

This miraculous gift comes into its own in our lives when we use it for the benefit of others. Accordingly, St. Francis of Assisi prayed:

A great many people are trying to make peace, but that has already been done. God has not left it for us to do; all we have to do is enter into it.
~ Dwight L. Moody ~

Lord, make me an instrument of Your peace. Where there is hatred, let me sow love; where there is injury, pardon; where there is doubt, faith; where there is despair, hope; where there is darkness, light; and where there is sadness, joy. O Divine Master, grant that we may not so much seek to be consoled as to console; to be understood as to understand; to be loved as to love. For it is in giving that we receive; it is in pardoning that we are pardoned, it is in dying that we are born to eternal life. Amen.

God of love and peace, make me willing to share Your gift of peace with others. Amen.

Peace as an Answer to Prayer

Gideon built an altar to the LORD there and named it Yahweh-Shalom (which means "the LORD is peace") (Judg. 6:24).

Peace describes the ideal condition in life. It embraces completeness and harmony along the entire ancestry of life. It symbolizes our spiritual development up until perfect peace of mind and heart is achieved. We must pray continuously and in earnest for this. It is to *be* instead of to *possess*; to be what God meant us to be.

We must pray that peace will also be the distinguishing mark of our family life. It is a tragedy when the family becomes a battlefield of strife and antagonism among members of the household. Every step closer to peace in the world must wait on what is done in the household. If the family can't live under one roof in peace, there will never be peace on earth. Therefore, the whole household must stay on their knees for the sake of receiving God's gift of peace.

> Who except God can give you peace?
> ~ Gerard Majella ~

If you don't have love, you don't have peace either. A famous paediatrician once thoroughly examined a very sick child and then made the following diagnosis: "What this baby needs more than anything else is love." He did not receive it because there was no peace in the home, and there was no peace because there was no love. Therefore, we must pray all the time to God who is the source of love. Let those who yearn for peace seek it on their knees.

Andrew Murray said, "Prayer is the unconditional requirement for everything God wants to bring about in this world." Remember that the things the Holy Spirit is occupied with bring life and peace. And the Spirit is especially occupied with prayer.

O Holy Spirit of God, help me to pray sincerely and faithfully for the peace of God in my heart and in my family. Amen.

Striving for Peace

Let the peace that comes from Christ rule in your hearts. For as members of one body you are called to live in peace (Col. 3:15).

Henry van Dyke writes the following: "The Bible teaches us that there is no lasting foundation for peace on earth, except in righteousness. It is our duty to strive for peace, to take a firm stand on it and to suffer for it if necessary. We are obliged to fight for it if we have the strength. And if God gives us the victory, we must use it for establishing peace through righteousness."

If I could have my life over again, I would strive more for peace and peace of mind. I would relax more often and there are many things I would not take too seriously. I would create more peaceful memories. I would climb more mountains and swim in more rivers. I would walk barefoot at every opportunity. I would not try to achieve so much unless I found joy in working for my achievements.

Until he extends his circle of compassion to include all living things, man will not himself find peace.
~ Albert Schweitzer ~

I would make more friends, go on a merry-go-round and pick more flowers along the road. Peace is something we should diligently strive for along the sidewalks of life. Hear in your spirit, "How beautiful on the mountains are the feet of the messenger who brings good news: the good news of peace and salvation, the news that the God of Israel reigns!" (Isa. 52:7).

I praise and thank You, Father, for the desire You put in my heart to strive for peace. Grant in Your grace that this desire never dies. Amen.

Heavenly Peace

Glory to God in highest heaven, and peace on earth to those with whom God is pleased (Luke 2:14).

Many people's life philosophy is, "What's in it for me?" Children of God, however, ask, "What can I give?" They expect nothing in return and their love has no price tag. They are people with heavenly peace in their hearts.

Kahlil Gibran aptly says in *The Prophet*, "There are those who give and know no pain in giving, nor do they seek joy, nor give with mindfulness to virtue. They give as the flowers spread their fragrance into space. Through the hands of such as these God speaks, and from behind their eyes He smiles upon the earth." They are the true peacemakers who are in touch with heaven.

All men desire peace; few desire the things which make for peace.
~ Anonymous ~

If we see Christianity merely as a matter of something we are given and not what we can give, we have not yet begun to understand the meaning of God's peace. Giving is a godly initiative. God is always giving: He gives us life, strength, forgiveness, His Son, and together with Him, His peace, directly from heaven. In answer to all God's gifts of love, we can devote our lives to Him and become messengers of His peace.

We must praise God for this very special gift from heaven: "Glory to God in the highest heaven!" When we praise God, we are peacemakers and messengers of peace. We can do this only when the Holy Spirit has become a personal reality in our lives.

I praise You, O God, that You sent Christ to our world as the Prince of Peace. Help me to share the glory of Your love and heavenly peace with others. Amen.

War Is Countered by Peace

Come, see the glorious works of the LORD: See how He brings destruction upon the world. He causes wars to end throughout the earth. He breaks the bow and snaps the spear; He burns the shields with fire (Ps. 46:8-9).

Herodotus, a Greek philosopher of old, said, "No one is so foolish to prefer war to peace. Because in peace sons bury their fathers, but in war fathers bury their sons." War is a breach of God's will. He wants us to live in peace with Him, with ourselves and with our fellow humans. War means that meaningful talks have proved futile and thus peace has come to an end.

When Adam and Eve hid from God among the trees in Paradise and didn't want to speak to Him, the peace in their lives changed to fear. When Cain didn't want to speak to Abel, he became a murderer and a fugitive. When God spoke to Moses like a friend in a crisis on the road to Canaan, peace calmed Moses' turbulent heart. This meaningful dialogue led to God's reassuring answer to Moses: "I will personally go with you, Moses, and I will give you rest." Moses answered God, "If You don't personally go with us, don't make us leave this place" (Exod. 33:15).

The past is prophetic in that it asserts loudly that wars are poor chisels for carving out peaceful tomorrows.
~ Martin Luther King, Jr ~

As long as people still talk, war can be warded off. God speaks to us continually through His Word. He speaks of salvation, sorrow, joy, tears, love, and hate, but more importantly of peace for all who persevere in speaking to God.

Open up my heart, Father God, to receive Your Word. Keep me from war inside me that robs me of Your peace. Amen.

ptivated by God's Peace

eace to you from the One who is, who always was, and who is still to come; from the sevenfold Spirit before His throne; and from Jesus Christ. He is the faithful witness to these things, the first to rise from the dead, and the ruler of all the kings of the world (Rev. 1:4-5).

Saint Augustine wrote in his book *Confessions,* "You touched me and I was carried away by Your peace." In *Paradiso,* Dante worships God as follows: "In Thy will is our peace." This timeless exclamation didn't start and end with Dante.

The loftiest human wisdom is the acknowledgement that all genuine peace flows from God. In every successive generation, poets, philosophers, teachers and singers join the uncountable choir that confesses jubilantly with St. Augustine: "We were created for God and we find peace nowhere before we have found peace in God." How fortunate are those that have found their peace in God. These people walk the main road of life light-footedly and with inner calm, peace and admiration. They can only whisper, "O God of love, Your peace fascinates me."

> Peace is not made at the council table or by treaties, but in the hearts of men.
> ~ Herbert Hoover ~

Mordechai Kaplan, a Jewish theologian, describes this fascination: "God is the 'religion' that helps us triumph over the fear of loneliness, helplessness, failure and death. God is the 'hope' that cleaves the dark depths of sin and despair like the light of a torch. God is the 'love' that creates, protects and forgives. He is the Spirit that floats over the chaos created by humankind, and re-creates. In His omnipotence He transforms evil into pure life and creates a new world in which 'peace' reigns."

Thank You, Lord my God, that I yielded to the enchantment of Your peace and that I find safe shelter with You. Amen.

Peace = Responsibility

"Love your enemies! Pray for those who persecute you! In that way, you will be acting like true children of your Father in heaven" (Matt. 5:44-45).

We must be prepared to accept great responsibilities in our quest for peace. We dare not sit back, hands folded. The renowned philosopher Baruch de Spinoza said, "Peace is not the absence of war; it is a virtue, a state of mind, a disposition for benevolence, confidence, and justice."

Peter uses three phrases in connection with the search for peace: "Work," "search" (1 Pet. 3:11) and "make every effort" (2 Pet. 3:14). We are called to work on peace with dogged responsibility.

Christ's coming to this world is a reminder of the true meaning of the message of peace. There can only be peace if it starts in our hearts and lives. Our lives must first be put in order. We must find peace with God through Jesus Christ. We must allow Him to create order in our battered lives, to clear up the mess, to put an end to confusion and chaos in our hearts, to remove the fear, worry and self-reproach once and for all.

The followers of Christ must not only have peace but also make it.
~ Dietrich Bonhoeffer ~

We must also pay personal attention to mutual peace. Broken relationships must be put right. In our country and our time, this is of the utmost importance. We are all affected by the problem of human relationships. We are scattered like a broken pearl necklace because we are in need of a strong cord. Only Christ can bind us together with the cord of love so that we may live together in harmony and peace. But then we must accept and meet the challenges and responsibilities that comes with it.

God of Peace, give me the grace to faithfully meet my responsibilities in my quest for peace. Amen.

Prescription for Peace

"How I wish today that you of all people would understand the way to peace. But now it is too late, and peace is hidden from your eyes" (Luke 19:42).

Our panic-stricken world is heading for self-destruction – a war to end all wars. Weapon arsenals are becoming bigger, more formidable and more sophisticated, with the sole purpose of destroying and eliminating. The world population is living in enmity with one another.

We go through life in a blind rage; we wear blinkers and don't see what leads to our peace. The battle lines are drawn between employers and employees – while in fact they urgently need each other. Neighbors live in enmity. Homes, marriages and hearts are broken by unfaithfulness and uproar.

> God cannot give us happiness and peace apart from Himself, because it is not there. There is no such thing.
> ~ C. S. Lewis ~

The human being is, in his very being, in conflict with himself and with God. And all of this because we do not want to know the things that lead to peace. The more sensitive we become to Christ's voice, the more sensitive we will be to the promptings of the Holy Spirit. He will lead us to peace.

We need to acknowledge God's Kingship and sovereignty and remove the self from the throne in our hearts. We must admit our dependence on one another. Family members must live together in love. We must take Jesus seriously. Our words, thoughts and deeds must be placed under His rule. Peace is within every person's reach. It is not an empty dream ... it's an achievable reality in Christ.

Prince of Peace, open my eyes through the Holy Spirit so that I can see what leads to peace. Amen.

Peace of Mind

I pray that God, the source of hope, will fill you completely with joy and peace as you trust in Him. Then you will overflow with confident hope through the power of the Holy Spirit (Rom. 15:13).

Peace of mind is a gift that God gives His children in abundance. It is a state of mind where we can repeat after David, "In peace I will lie down and sleep, for You alone, O Lord, will keep me safe" (Ps. 4:8). How many sleepless hours do we spend in anxiety because we do not search for God's peace? We punish ourselves unnecessarily by stubbornly looking for calmness and acceptance elsewhere. Our meager reward is tension, sleeplessness and stress.

Peace of mind is the quiet but certain knowledge that I am secure in God's care. Therefore, the opportunities in life are so much more than the cares. When I accept God in my very being as the Source of my peace and joy, and know that I am bound to Him through faith, I have already taken my first important step on the road to peace.

Peace is the power that
comes to souls arriving.
Up to the light where
God Himself appears.
~ G. A. Studdert Kennedy ~

Because my spirit is in harmony with God, I live in harmony and peace with my fellow human beings. A dysfunctional relationship with God makes it impossible to enter into and maintain good relationships with people. To remedy this condition, I need to make a determined effort to put my relationship right with Christ, and to keep it that way.

The wonder of this peace is that it is a byproduct of a surrendered life, where God Himself leads us to green pastures and quiet waters. The only condition is a living faith through Jesus Christ.

Thank You, loving Leader, that I can learn how to find peace of mind and heart from You. Amen.

At Peace with My Memories

I focus on this one thing: Forgetting the past and looking forward to what lies ahead (Phil. 3:13).

Good memories are precious and give us much joy and peace. But there are also bad memories that make us sad and rob us of our peace. Jesus has good advice for this. He can even remedy the problem. By His grace, the Prince of Peace can totally erase it.

To find inner healing from negative memories, the first thing you must do is to go aside and seek God in solitude. Praise Him for His grace and omnipresence. Confess your sins in sincere remorse and plead for His forgiveness. Surrender yourself completely to Him and accept His forgiveness. Remember to also forgive yourself! Resist all negative thoughts and feelings of guilt from Satan. Ask for the support and guidance of the Holy Spirit, and pray in earnest that Christ will free you from the pain of past memories.

Never live in the past,
but always learn from it.
~ Anonymous ~

Then firmly deal with the memories that are behind you and break free from them once and for all. Is it a matter of rejection in your childhood? Is it the separation of your parents or divorce or death? Is it a lack of love on your parents' part that left scars on your heart? Are secret sins from the past tormenting you? God knows all about this – He understands and He can heal. Whether your misery has its origin in your school days, your marriage or your failure as a parent – Christ is able to heal it completely. The psalmist says with good cause, "When doubts filled my mind, Your comfort gave me renewed hope and cheer" (Ps. 94:19).

Thank You, heavenly Comforter, that You set me free from all my painful memories and that I am at peace with myself now.

Amen.

The Fruit of Peace

The Holy Spirit produces this kind of fruit in our lives: love, joy, peace ... (Gal. 5:22).

Peace is love that has come to rest in God. Peace is attributed to all the Persons of the Holy Trinity. God the Father is the God that gives peace. God the Son is the Prince of Peace (see Isa. 9:6). God the Holy Spirit creates peace in our hearts (see Gal. 5:22-23). Peace is the soothing resignation of the soul that has found rest in Christ.

Jesus promised us, "I am leaving you with a gift – peace of mind and heart. And the peace I give is a gift the world cannot give. So don't be troubled or afraid" (John 14:27). Born-again children of God have this peace. In the midst of storms and confusion they have peace which nothing and nobody can take from them.

> The blood of Jesus whispers peace within.
> ~ E. H. Bickersteth ~

On our journey on the sea of life, we sometimes bob up and down on stormy waters. We are attacked by Satan and his evil agents, but still, deep down, there is the peace of God that surpasses all understanding. We find this peace at the foot of the cross. It is there that the love of God is revealed, the price for our sin is paid, and where we are inseparably bound to God.

In both the Old and New Testaments we have ample promises of God's peace. The anarchy of the old sinful life has been broken. We now live in peace with God, with our fellow humans and with ourselves because the Holy Spirit has taken complete control of our lives. Let us hold fast to this peace and let us never stop praising and thanking God for it.

Holy Spirit of God, please bring Your peace into my life so that I can live in peace with everyone. Amen.

Peace Comes with Trust

You will keep in perfect peace all who trust in You, all whose thoughts are fixed on You! (Isa. 26:3).

God's peace is unique in many respects. It is beyond human understanding (see Phil. 4:7). The sinful human being's mind and thoughts are not familiar with it. Jesus said Himself that the peace the world offers is not the same as the peace He gives.

Paul repeatedly states that Christ is our peace (see Eph. 2:11-22). He creates peace and He proclaims peace. God's peace is far beyond our wildest dreams and expectations. The wealth of God's peace is overwhelming (see Eph. 2:11-22). The gospel embraces far more than any of us could ever imagine. It exceeds all our expectations time and again. What the eye has not seen and the ear hasn't heard, this is God's peace. But this peace is subject to specific conditions.

Oh wonderful, wonderful peace, sweet peace, the gift of God's love.
~ Peter P. Bilhorn ~

We must trust God unconditionally. We must do away with self-satisfaction, and trust only in God for our strength and power. We must discipline our thoughts and raise them up to God (see Phil. 2:5; John 17:14).

This means that we must force ourselves to a standstill every now and again and reflect on God's wondrous acts. "Trust in the LORD always" (Isa. 26:4). This is the most important condition for peace, and peace of mind. The writer of Proverbs called on us in his wisdom: "Trust in the LORD with all your heart; do not depend on your own understanding" (Prov. 3:5). If we seek our peace in Jesus Christ, the God-given heavenly peace will not evade us.

Lord, Your Word teaches us that our power lies in being still and in trusting You, but we so easily forget it. Let Your Spirit guide us to lasting peace. Amen.

Peace Calms a Troubled Mind

"Don't let your hearts be troubled. Trust in God, and trust also in Me" (John 14:1).

Jesus assures His disciples that they can trust God to calm their troubled minds. The building of peace and inner calm rests on the foundation of faith – even in the midst of the storm. The Word of God leads us to rest and peace. Like God promised Joshua, He promises to guide each of us who obey His Word (see Josh. 1:8). In addition, God sent the Holy Spirit as a Comforter. He leads us to peace, and this knowledge should fill us with courage and inner peace.

Through prayer we also have an open door to the throne of grace (see Matt. 6:6). We can talk to God in times of trouble because the throne room is never locked. Wherever Christ is, we hear His comforting words, "Peace be with you!" God also gives us fellowship with believers: "Your love for one another will prove to the world that you are My disciples" (John 13:35). We love Jesus because He loved us first. By means of our church membership, worship, Bible study, prayers and songs of praise, we are able to receive the supportive strength of fellow believers that ripples outward to us, and that we then pass on to others. Spending time with other believers can have a calming effect on our turbulent hearts.

May the peace of God, my Father, rule my life in everything.
~ Kate B. Wilkinson ~

God is faithful! He doesn't want us to be in a permanent state of fear. He expects us to experience His peace no matter what happens. Through His Son and the Holy Spirit, He protects us from turmoil and He gives us peace in a sin-torn world.

Lord Jesus, we so easily get upset, but You calm our troubled minds every time. Help us to find peace through the Holy Spirit.

Amen.

The Roots of Peace

Since we have been made right in God's sight by faith, we have peace with God because of what Jesus Christ our Lord has done for us (Rom. 5:1).

At the deepest level, our peace depends on our unconditional faith in God. He is the source of all true peace in life. When God is at the center of our lives and thoughts, we will know true peace. This is why we must resist evil in all its forms. We must stay close to Jesus at all times because He is the guarantee of our peace with God. If we break all ties with Satan, we must accept Christ's dominion absolutely. We live positively and peacefully when we live close to Jesus.

What a treasure I have in this wonderful peace.
~ Warren D. Cornell ~

We must strive for a pure life. After his atrocious sin, David prayed, "Purify me from my sins, and I will be clean. Restore to me the joy of Your salvation" (Ps. 51:7, 12). We must confess our wrongdoings and give them up; we must wrestle with them in Jesus' name and gain the victory, otherwise our search for peace will be in vain.

Our attitudes must also change. Pride and self-righteousness must die. We must become people who humbly reveal the attitude of the Master (see Phil. 2:1-11). Our lives and our witnessing must supplement each other in a meaningful way. We must work and pray faithfully for spiritual growth so that we may reach spiritual maturity with the help of the Holy Spirit.

Peace with God and people is more precious than gold. If we set our minds on heavenly things, then the peace of God will descend on our lives. It is then that we become messengers of His peace.

Holy Spirit of God, inspire me to be disciplined, so that I may know God's perfect peace by virtue of Jesus Christ. Amen.

Messengers of Peace

He came and preached peace to you who were far away and peace to those who were near (Eph. 2:17 NIV). For shoes, put on the peace that comes from the Good News (Eph. 6:15).

The word *peace* appears more than 400 times in the Bible. It is mostly called "God's peace" (Phil. 4:7). This is a gift to us from the God of love: "We have peace with God because of what Jesus Christ our Lord has done for us" (Rom. 5:1). Without the absolution by virtue of Jesus Christ, and our acceptance of it, peace with God is not possible. Our Father is the God of peace and He makes the believers holy so that we can devote ourselves to Him, body and soul (see 1 Thess. 5:23).

Jesus Christ is the Prince of Peace and "the government will rest on His shoulders" (Isa. 9:6). By virtue of His death and resurrection, we share in the peace of God. He came to the world to proclaim God's peace. God the Holy Spirit brings forth the fruit of peace in the believer's life (see Gal. 5:22). He makes the peace grow through our obedience to Jesus Christ and to God the Father. He urges us to be messengers of this wonderful peace: "You will receive power when the Holy Spirit comes upon you. And you will be My witnesses, telling people about Me everywhere" (Acts 1:8).

> We may think God wants actions of a certain kind, but God wants people of a certain kind.
> ~ C. S. Lewis ~

In such a way, we are all able to become messengers of God's peace through the Holy Spirit and Jesus Christ.

Prince of Peace, through the Holy Spirit, make me a faithful messenger of Your peace. Amen.

Peace Tempers Sorrow

You will not grieve like people who have no hope (1 Thess. 4:13).

If we are unshakable in our conviction that we are God's children, this is our guarantee that we can break through the barriers of sorrow and pain. Then we get to the waters where there is peace. It is not God's will for us to be unaffected or dry-eyed when death and sadness cast dark shadows on our path. It isn't a sin to grieve. Christ Himself wept at the tomb of His friend Lazarus. What He means is that we should not allow our sadness to rob us of peace.

There is hopeful joy in the knowledge that our faith and trust in God weathered the test of personal sorrow and loss. The fact that we are children of God, however, does not safeguard us against sorrow. But God does promise us, and very often, is His peace.

In times of affliction we commonly meet with the sweetest experiences of the love of God.
~ John Bunyan ~

Time heals all wounds. God helps His believing children to deal with sorrowful experiences better, and gives us a more mature understanding of these things. This brings us closer to His Father's heart and His peace! The loftiest experience in life is not borne of superficial occurrences, but rather in the hours of our pain and sorrow. It is as if we recognize God better through our tears than in our joy.

Then sorrow serves the purpose of creating peace: "Yet what we suffer now is nothing compared to the glory He will reveal to us later" (Rom. 8:18).

God of peace and grace, I want to be close to You in my sorrow to find peace of mind and tranquility. Amen.

God's Peace Creates Self-Confidence

God Himself has prepared us for this, and as a guarantee He has given us His Holy Spirit. So we are always confident (2 Cor. 5:5-6).

Disobedient people always live in fear of the consequences of their sin, and this undermines their self-confidence. If self-respect is important to you and you are trying to live in peace, it is essential that you obey Christ. It is not a fatalistic, unwilling and sullen acceptance of the unavoidable, but a joyous acceptance of whatever it is that God gives you in His wisdom.

God gives you the gift of His Spirit, and when you accept the Spirit gratefully, your highest purpose is to know and obey God's will. This is the condition, but at the same time, also your guarantee of God's peace in your life. At first it will seem difficult, but because His Spirit lives in you, you will be given the strength that enables you to live a life that pleases God.

This peaceful self-confidence in your life, that creates faith in God as a byproduct, is by no means a matter of overestimating yourself. It simply enables you to work and live without feeling inferior or guilty. Your relationship with God gains meaning and depth. You develop healthy relationships with those around you and have a humble appreciation for your own inherent worth as a unique creation.

What other people think of me is becoming less and less important; what they think of Jesus because of me is critical.
~ Billy Graham ~

You cannot possibly live in harmony and peace with God and still lose confidence in yourself and the future. This peace is the precious gift of God to His believing and obedient children who travel through life with Him.

I kneel before You in thankfulness, my God, because You chose to share Your grace with me. Amen.

Peace Requires Communication

Inside the Tent of Meeting, the LORD would speak to Moses face to face, as one speaks to a friend (Exod. 33:11).

Communication is a very important component in our search for peace. The communication channels in our lives must be kept open, because if there are obstructions, peace disappears. When Adam and Eve stopped communicating with God in Paradise, they had no more peace, and fear entered their lives. Cain didn't want to speak to his brother, Abel, and murdered him instead, becoming a murderer and a fugitive from God and people.

When God and Moses communicated, it brought peace to Moses' heart. As long as we continue communicating with God, we have hope for peace of mind and heart, no matter how dark our circumstances may seem. Just think with what tenacity Abraham kept talking with God for the sake of Sodom and Gomorrah (see Gen. 18:16-33). As a result, Lot and his family reached Zoar safely.

> When God wants to speak and deal with us, He does not avail Himself of an angel but of parents, or the pastor, or of our neighbor.
> ~ Martin Luther ~

God came to speak to us in a perfect way, through Jesus Christ, about everything concerning our peace. When the evil world thought they had at last silenced Him with death on the cross, He started communicating with people in their own languages on the Day of Pentecost.

God speaks to us through the Holy Spirit – if only we would listen for His voice. He speaks of salvation from sin, joy from sorrow, love from hate. Peace has been set aside for each of us who perseveres in speaking with God and obeying Him.

Almighty God, open up my heart to receive Your words and to arrange my life accordingly. Amen.

Patriotism and Peace

Glorify the LORD, O Jerusalem! Praise your God, O Zion! For He has strengthened the bars of your gates and blessed your children within your walls. He sends peace across your nation and satisfies your hunger with the finest wheat (Ps. 147:12-14).

Sincere patriotism is love for your native country that seeks peace for everyone. The peacemaker longs for the day that weapon arsenals won't be necessary anymore and that we will be free from violence. It is the ultimate hope of the patriotic peacemaker that the money spent on weaponry will be used to feed the hungry, fight disease and give the homeless shelter.

The British historian Arnold Toynbee expressed the hope that his generation would be remembered, not for the appalling destruction through sophisticated weapons, but because it was the first generation that firmly believed that peace on earth is possible. This is true patriotism.

If there is order in the nation, there will be peace in the world.
~ Chinese Proverb ~

There are many dedicated patriots who don't march with flags and are not excited by the sound of the drumbeats of war, but who work quietly and unceasingly to bring about peace among people. This is done through righteousness, a spirit of goodwill and showing respect in our everyday relationships. These people pray all the time that the nations will have enough inner strength to choose peace rather than war. To them the Master said, "God blesses those who work for peace, for they will be called the children of God" (Matt. 5:9).

Prince of Peace, thank You that in my everyday life I can make a contribution to peace in the country that I love, and grant that I love You above all. Amen.

Peace During Tension

Think about the things of heaven, not the things of earth (Col. 3:2).

The grueling pace of modern life is accelerating daily. We feel the effects on our bodies and our thoughts. Consequently, tension becomes an integral part of our lives. Our thoughts are often swamped with trivialities, and our spirit is not fed with positive and constructive thoughts. This leads to spiritual malnutrition and robs us of our peace of mind.

It is a matter of urgency that we spend time alone with God to prevent this from happening. Christ is our perfect example of this. In spite of the demands of His ministry, He often withdrew to spend time alone with God to find strength and peace.

> You have created us for Yourself, and our heart cannot be stilled until it finds rest in You.
> ~ St. Augustine ~

When you embark on your daily pilgrimage by regularly spending time with God in solitude, you must be careful not to overestimate your own strength and abilities. Start gradually but determinedly finding your way back to God. It is better to have two minutes of meaningful fellowship with Him, than twenty minutes in which your thoughts wander to the things of the world.

God doesn't evaluate the quality of your time spent with Him by the clock. Read your Bible regularly and take note of the times in the past when God led His children from stressful situations into peace. Don't think of your prayer life as an endurance test, but as the tranquilizer in your busy and rushed life. Allow an unparalleled peace to descend on you and let the stress flow from your life.

Trustworthy Lord of my life, You know how easily I am caught in the grip of this rushed life. Thank You that I can find rest at Your peaceful waters. Amen.

Longing for Peace

"I have told you all this so that you may have peace in Me. Here on earth you will have many trials and sorrows. But take heart, because I have overcome the world" (John 16:33).

We all long for peace: peace with ourselves; peace with our circumstances, people around us, and especially with God! Christ tells us that we can in fact find peace.

In our personal quest for peace, we take heart from the fact that Christ triumphed over this hate-torn world. Our Creator is the God of peace. He is mighty and has the power to end all wars. Not only does He call on us to make peace, He also enables us to do so. Jesus, the wonderful Counselor and Prince of Peace, came from God to lead us on our road of peace. He often says to us, "Peace be with you" (John 20:21).

The Holy Spirit breaks down the dividing walls that cause strife between our fellow humans and us. He builds bridges leading into the hearts of others, and all we need to do is to cross those bridges. In this process we must be the Holy Spirit's active partners. If we follow our Master's example, by willingly forgiving others, we will receive God's gift of peace in abundance. Peace grows in our hearts with every act of mercy we perform in His name.

When we are unable to find tranquility within ourselves, it is useless to seek it elsewhere
~ Fancois La Rochefoucauld ~

We must bring the good news of peace to all people, because we are God's ambassadors. Salvation and peace are inextricably linked. If we call ourselves Christians, we are bound to strive for peace. Then we become true children of God and we receive God's reward – this is the share of those who spread peace in this world.

I praise You, Lord, that no matter how difficult life might be for me, I will always find peace in You. Amen.

The Soft Footsteps of Peace

It is useless for you to work so hard from early morning until late at night, anxiously working for food to eat; for God gives rest to His loved ones (Ps. 127:2).

Peace is like a beautiful butterfly. As long as you chase after it with stamping feet, it will elude you. If, however, you sit, calm and relaxed, it will flutter its wings lightly and come to rest on your shoulder.

Peace does not depend on your outward circumstances, but on your inner attitude toward your Creator and life. The secret of inner peace has nothing to do with what you like to do. Rather, it is about liking what you have to do. It means giving of yourself to the world, and not just trying to get something out of it for your personal benefit.

Lord, make me an instrument of Thy peace.
~ St. Francis of Assisi ~

Thankfulness is the twin brother of peace. Thankful people live in peace with God, with themselves and with people. They live in the knowledge that God is giving them more than they could ever deserve. Their song of life remains, "Let all that I am praise the Lord; with my whole heart, I will praise His holy name. Let all that I am praise the Lord; may I never forget the good things He does for me" (Ps. 103:1-2).

God did not intend us all to be powerful, rich and important, but that we would all be heirs of His peace. For that to happen, we simply need to discover the quiet act of full surrender and obedience to God. After all, our strength lies in quietness and confidence (see Isa. 30:15).

God who gives peace, let Your peace flow quietly through my life.
Amen.

Fake Peace

They give assurance of peace when there is no peace (Jer. 6:14).

In countries where earthquakes occur often, there is always an eerie silence before it strikes. This is obviously an illusion, but it seems as if nature is muted in a mystical way and the earth is holding its breath, awaiting the coming disaster. The air is heavy with an ominous atmosphere and no birdsong is heard. Meanwhile, homes, towns and cities as well as thousands of people are faced with devastating tragedy.

This is like God's silence surrounding the fake peace proclaimed by people in His name. But it will be followed by His devastating judgments. Paul warns the Thessalonians, "When people are saying, 'Everything is peaceful and secure,' then disaster will fall on them." (1 Thess. 5:3).

Fake peace is turned into God's peace only through obedience: "Those who love Your instructions have great peace and do not stumble" (Ps. 119:165). If we stay within God's perfect will, we experience His peace.

There is a fundamental difference between the peace of God and the peace of death. It can be likened to the difference between the peace of a calm sea and the Dead Sea. We find true and genuine peace only with God, because He is our source. When we get to know Him through Christ, we also get to know the meaning of genuine peace. Then we live from that peace daily and can say with all honesty, "All is well with my soul!" We can say this because we are in the right relationship with God and consequently share in genuine peace!

Wish always, and pray, that the will of God may be wholly fulfilled in you. Behold, such a person enters the land of peace and rest.
~ Thomas à Kempis ~

Keep me, O Savior, from becoming part of the fake peace of this sinful world. Bring me to the peace that is found only in You.

Amen.

On My Way with the God of Peace

Don't worry about anything; instead, pray about everything. Tell God what you need, and thank Him for all He has done. Then you will experience God's peace, which exceeds anything we can understand. His peace will guard your hearts and minds as you live in Christ Jesus (Phil. 4:6-7).

Peace with God is the point of departure to peace in your life. Your debt has been paid – the cross on Golgotha is the guarantee. Without it, you can never have lasting peace. "Therefore, since we have been made right in God's sight by faith, we have peace with God" (Rom 5:1).

Trust in God is vital if you want peace. The assurance is given so often in God's Word: "Make them prosper and give them peace, Lord, because they put their trust in You." Peace with God is the result of a personal relationship with Him; the result of experiencing Him first hand.

May the road rise to meet you, may the wind be always at your back, may the sun shine warm upon your face, the rain fall soft upon your fields, and until we meet again, may God hold you in the hollow of His hand.

~ Irish Blessing ~

God's peace is meant for all people and not only for a select few: "'May they have abundant peace, both near and far,' says the LORD, who heals them" (Isa. 57:19). Without that peace we will be driven by restlessness: "But those who still reject Me are like the restless sea which is never still" (Isa. 57:20).

Martin Luther said, "We receive in our hearts, in our entire being, the peace that surpasses all understanding, the peace of reconciliation and justification, at that moment when the soul takes a deep breath and says 'Amen' to everything God has done for us."

Loving Father, help Your struggling child to know Your perfect peace in the midst of the storm. Amen.

Epilogue: Prayer for Peace

May the Lord bless you and protect you. May the Lord smile on you and be gracious to you. May the Lord show you His favor and give you His peace (Num. 6:24-26).

Lord, our Lord, the earth and everything in it belongs to You. Therefore, grant us Your blessings and peace, because we are lost without the good things that come our way from Your loving hand.

Give us spiritual growth, faith, hope and love. Make health, strength, joy, success and peace our undeserved but precious gift. Father, grant us Your protection and keep Your almighty hand on us. Cover us with eagles' wings, be our shelter each day.

Holy God, come to our rescue: You were there when Jesus lay in the crook of His mother's arm. You were there at Golgotha and the empty tomb. Let us not live a single day as if You were dead! Hallelujah, our God lives!

It isn't enough to talk about peace. One must believe in it. And it isn't enough to believe in it. One must work at it.
~ Eleanor Roosevelt ~

Lord, have mercy on us; we so readily mistake stray lights for stars; we unthinkingly drift away from You and our peace is so easily taken from us. Hold us tight in Your mercy, Lord! Lord, hear our prayer for peace: Your *shalom*. Help us to be at peace with You, ourselves and everybody around us.

You are the Creator and Recreator who makes everything new.

Lord, I praise You for the blessings and peace that You bestow on me! Amen.

September

His light on my path lets me grow spiritually.

"Remain in Me, and I will remain in you. For a branch cannot produce fruit if it is severed from the vine, and you cannot be fruitful unless you remain in Me."
~ John 15:4 ~

Growth is the only evidence of life!
~ John H. Newman ~

Living Lord Jesus, we worship You
as the source of life and growth:
We worship You as the God who maintains creation.
Everything in nature is
so breathtakingly lovely that it stirs an almost painful joy inside us.
Touch our hearts and bring new life and
growth in our barren existence.
We feel praises stirring in our deepest being breaking into song:
"Praise the Lord, O my soul, and forget not all His benefits." We
thank You for our senses so we can hear the dove;
the wealth of flowers that we see;
the fragrance of spring that we smell,
and for the surge of life in nature that we feel gushing from
our hearts. Give us hearts that are open to this abundant beauty.
Savior and Redeemer, also bring new life and growth inside us.
Let the grain of wheat that fell to earth and died, sprout and grow
strong and bear fruit, a thousand-fold. We pray also for our youth,
the blossoms of our time – our most precious young ones. Keep
them from ever-changing values and spiritual threats. Help them
in their battle against evil, and let them strive for the preservation
of the good and the noble. Let the older generation be an example
to them of faith, hope and love. Call Christian crusaders from their
generation that will boldly continue Your glorious work here on
earth, wearing the full armor of God.
Let all of us grow to spiritual maturity,
so that we may live victoriously.
This we pray in the name of our Leader to life,
Jesus, our Lord and Master.

Amen.

The Law of Atrophy

Instead, let the Spirit renew your thoughts and attitudes. Put on your new nature, created to be like God – truly righteous and holy (Eph. 4:23-24).

The dictionary defines *atrophy* as the "wasting away of the body or part of it through lack of nourishment or use." It is an unrelenting law for all living beings, but it is also true of our spiritual lives. Growth is crucially important to life, otherwise there is a standstill of all activity, resulting in degeneration and ultimately, death.

According to the Law of Atrophy, everything that is not used or nourished, wastes away and dies. If I keep my arm in a sling for years, I will lose the use of it. Babies bring us incredible joy, but if they don't outgrow babyhood, they cause worry and heartache. This is just as true of the spiritual being.

Don't go through life, grow through life.
~ Eric Butterworth ~

We can't miss the sadness in Paul's words to the Corinthians: "When I was with you I couldn't talk to you as I would to spiritual people. I had to talk as though you belonged to this world or as though you were infants in the Christian life. I had to feed you with milk, not with solid food, because you weren't ready for anything stronger. And you still aren't ready, for you are still controlled by your sinful nature" (1 Cor. 3:1-3). We pick up the same despondency in Hebrews 5:12-13.

This month, God speaks to us about spiritual growth in Jesus Christ through the powerful work of the Holy Spirit. May God Himself walk this stretch of the road with us – so that our spiritual lives will be richly blessed.

Father, I place myself in the competent hands of Your Holy Spirit. Blow like a refreshing breeze through my life and bring spiritual growth that results in fruit-bearing for Your kingdom. Amen.

Behind the Scenes for Christ

Andrew, Simon Peter's brother, was one of these men who had heard what John said and then followed Jesus. Andrew went to find his brother, Simon, and told him, "We have found the Messiah" (which means "Christ") (John 1:40-41).

Before we discuss the dramatic and dynamic growth in Peter's life, we must first meet Andrew. We don't know much about him. He is mentioned only three times in the Bible, but what a well-liked man he must have been. He was a person who wanted to share the glory of the gospel with others.

The source of humility is the habit of realizing the presence of God.
~ William Temple ~

First he brought his brother to Christ – possibly the most difficult ministry by far (see John 1:40-41). Then he led a child to Jesus and became instrumental in the miracle of the bread and the fish (see John 6:7-9). Eventually, he brought the Greeks to Jesus (see John 12:20-22). Andrew was a man with the heart of a missionary.

Andrew is introduced mostly as "Simon Peter's brother." It is clear that he lived in Peter's shadow. He was not one of the inner circle of disciples. He was not taken along to the Mount of Transfiguration, to the house where Jairus's daughter was raised from the dead or, to when Jesus went to pray alone in the Garden of Gethsemane. He could have felt bitter about this because he was after all one of the first disciples. This didn't even occur to him: he allowed his brother to be in the limelight while he worked behind the scenes for Christ. All he wanted was to be Jesus' servant.

It is wonderful to play second fiddle in Jesus' orchestra and to be part of His symphony – to His honor and glory.

Holy Master, I place myself unconditionally in Your hands to be used as Andrew – in honor of Your name. Amen.

Identification

"Your name is Simon, Son of John – but you will be called Cephas" (which means "Peter") (John 1:42).

If there is one person in the Bible the ordinary person can identify with, it is Simon Peter. Not only because he is popular with readers of the Bible, but because we often see ourselves in him. We admire him despite his weaknesses and faults. We see in him our own faults, weaknesses and shortcomings. In his falling-and-getting-up-again life, we see our own stumblings and our own yearning for a deeper and richer spiritual life.

Simon Peter was sincerely human. He didn't hide behind masks. He never pretended to be what he wasn't, especially in his relationship with the Master. He said what he thought, and not what people wanted him to say.

Simon Peter also had the gift of leadership; the quality that is also called charisma. Without this, a witness can be quite ineffective. He was the indisputable leader of the fishermen of Capernaum. Simon Peter also had the ability to give his all for what he believed in. Sometimes he was on the right side of the fence and sometimes on the wrong side, but he was never lukewarm.

If thou desire the love of God and man, be humble, for the proud heart, as it loves none but itself, is beloved of none but itself.
~ Francis Quarles ~

Christ wanted to walk a wonderful road with this truly human, impulsive, arrogant Simon Peter – a road of spiritual growth to maturity. The Holy Spirit would play a powerful role in this. Christ specifically chose him to say to you and me through Him, "Follow Me. I gave My life for you and people like Simon." Open up your heart to Jesus now and follow Him.

Thank You, Living Master, that spiritual growth is meant for ordinary people. I once again surrender to Your Holy Spirit.

Amen.

The Potter's Clay

"Your name is Simon, Son of John – but you will be called Cephas" (which means "Peter") (John 1:42).

When they met, Jesus' first words to Peter were, "Your name is Simon, the Son of John – but you will be called Cephas" (which means "Peter"). And Peter means *rock*. This is how the Master greeted the high-spirited Peter at their first meeting, in this way indicating to him what he was and what he could become in the hands of the Master Potter.

In effect, Christ was saying to Peter, "You will become a man of unshaken character." One could have expected the arrogant Simon to freeze in his tracks: "Me, Lord? This impulsive man, a rock? Impossible!" His friends would have looked at each other with a knowing smile and shaken their heads in disbelief. His enemies would have laughed out loud: if any one of the disciples would become a rock, it could surely not be Simon!

He loved us not because we are lovable, but because He is love.
~ C. S. Lewis ~

Simon was an egoist. His self-confidence was so unrestricted that it was actually quite entertaining.

Simon always had to take first place; failure was not acceptable to him. When the disciples washed each other's feet, he thought nothing of giving Jesus a bit of advice. His feelings ruled his reasoning and not his mind, and he was controlled by his emotions. He was unpredictable and unreliable. Sometimes he spoke wisely and sometimes like an absolute fool. He was a hero and at the same time a coward.

It was with this mixture of weakness and strength that Jesus told Peter to follow Him, and walk the road with Him that would make Peter the rock.

Heavenly Potter, You changed Peter; please change me! Amen.

A Meaningful Name Change

I will write on them the name of my God, and they will be citizens in the city of my God – the new Jerusalem that comes down from heaven from my God. And I will also write on them my new name (Rev. 3:12).

In biblical times, a name change often indicated a change in that person's lifestyle. Jacob wrestled with God during the night at the Jabbok River and he became Israel – the Prince of God! Saul became Paul after his experience with God on the road to Damascus. Simon became Peter – the rock. With this, Jesus gave Peter a vision of his possibilities in Jesus' service. The Lord saw him for what he could be: A person whose weaknesses could be transformed into strengths; whose pride could be changed to humility; whose failure could become triumph. It is as if Christ was saying to him, "This is the type of follower you can be; this is My holy purpose for your life!"

Salvation is God's way of making us real people.
~ St. Augustine ~

Christ says this to each of us through Peter. He sees us as individuals and says, "This is you – and this is what you can be!" When Michelangelo was asked why he used the marble rejected by other sculptors, his answer was, "In every block of marble I see a statue as plain as though it stood before me, shaped and perfect in attitude and action. I have only to hew away the rough walls that imprison the lovely apparition to reveal it to the other eyes as mine see it." This is what God wanted to do with Peter and what He wants to do with you and me. He brings out the noblest and the best in us.

Peter was victorious because he was willing to struggle: when he fell, he just got right back up again. He was unconquerable because he was enabled by the Holy Spirit to endure.

Redeemer and Savior, I place myself in Your hands, with child-like faith. Change not only my name, but my whole life. Amen.

Cooling Down Too Quickly

Stepping into one of the boats, Jesus asked Simon, its owner, to push it out into the water (Luke 5:3).

During an unforgettable visit to a glass factory in Venice, we saw in the foyer two glass statues made of the same exceptional glass. One was particularly beautiful with exquisite engravings and patterns. The texture was sheer like gossamer and the embossed work on it perfect – a masterpiece! The other one was made of the same glass, but unrecognizably marred and distorted: a mockery of what it was meant to be. When we asked the glass blower what caused the difference, he answered: "The failure cooled down too quickly!"

Peter had already taken his first step on the Master's road to fulfillment with the Holy Spirit: A beautiful, promising start. Now, a mere nine months later, we find Peter back at his former life – the fishing boats. Was he not already supposed to be fishing for people?

There is no more urgent and critical question in life than that of your personal relationship with God and your eternal salvation.
~ Billy Graham ~

Not everyone has the faith to go the full distance for God. Terah, on his way to Canaan with Abraham, only got halfway. Lot's wife fled with him from Sodom and Gomorrah. She, however, looked back with longing for her old life, and turned into a pillar of salt. Demas, an enthusiastic young man, risked everything to follow Paul. But the bright lights of the world became too tempting, and he left Paul.

What does your spiritual relationship look like? Where were you and where are you now? Has your love cooled or is it still burning strong.

Keep me, Holy Spirit of God, from cooling down. May the distinguishing mark of my Creator always be visible in my life.

Amen.

Soul-Enriching Advice

"Now go out where it is deeper, and let down your nets to catch some fish" (Luke 5:4).

Jesus wanted to teach Peter a lesson on perseverance and dedication. The Lord, in His grace, did it in surroundings Peter understood best: at the waters of Galilee. When Peter despaired of himself and his task, Jesus came along and taught him the lesson of unconditional obedience. He told them to go out into deep water.

Peter knew the best time to catch fish was at night, and also in the shallower parts of the lake. Now Jesus was saying the direct opposite of what Peter knew about fishing. Peter must have been tempted to teach Jesus a few things about fishing. On top of everything else, Peter was tired and in low spirits. He did, however, obey Jesus and then a great miracle happened: their nets were so full that they began to tear; and Peter was on his knees, back with his Lord. Now he could start fishing for people because he was in the deep water of faith.

When God gives a command or a vision of truth, it is never a question of what He will do, but of what *we* will do.
~ Henrietta Mears ~

At some time or another Jesus steps on board our boat of life and takes control. Otherwise we would flounder in shallow, muddy water for the rest of our lives. Make Christ the captain of your boat of life and take hold of the oars; go where He instructs you – out to the depths of surrender, dedication, faith and love for Him – and in absolute obedience. Let us live through the Holy Spirit from one miracle to the next.

Thank You, Holy Spirit, that You escort me to the depths. Give me faith and courage to follow You fearlessly. Amen.

I Am not Worthy

When Simon Peter realized what had happened, he fell to his knees before Jesus and said, "Oh, Lord, please leave me – I'm too much of a sinner to be around You" (Luke 5:8).

We cannot escape the horror of our sin on our road of spiritual growth. This is a sad fact. The most wonderful thing about Jesus is that although He hates sin, He deeply loves the sinner. He is a God of abundant grace and forgiveness. Sir James Simpson, a great scientific discoverer, said on occasion that the greatest discovery he ever made was the foulness of his own sin.

Peter had to be confronted with his sin when following God on his pilgrimage. This cannot be avoided. The Heidelberg Catechism states this: I need to know the extent of my sin and misery.

Dost thou wish to receive mercy? Show mercy to thy neighbor.
~ John Chrysostom ~

Sin is an outmoded term nowadays: call it an anxiety disorder, a psychological defect, an illness or human weakness – and meanwhile sin mercilessly claims its victims.

Fortunately, Peter's closeness to the Savior brought him to an awareness of his sin. His first reaction was, "Please leave me." How much self-contempt, strife and remorse, failure and shame was locked up in his heart? And where would he go with his sin? What if the Lord had given up on him?

There is only one road: the road to Christ, the man of Sorrows who carried the cross because of my sin: "If we confess our sins to Him, He is faithful and just to forgive us our sins and to cleanse us from all wickedness" (1 John 1:9)

Lord Jesus, cleanse me with Your precious blood. Amen.

A Significant Discovery

When Simon Peter realized what had happened, he fell to his knees before Jesus and said, "Oh, Lord, please leave me – I'm too much of a sinner to be around You" (Luke 5:8).

They were still at the Sea of Galilee when Peter made this discovery. Against his better judgment, he had obeyed Christ's instructions and took the boat out into deep water. Suddenly the nets ballooned out; the fishermen's muscles bulged and the nets were on the verge of tearing.

Suddenly Peter knew: this is the Lord! The Messiah! For nine months he walked with Him and didn't realize it. You can grow up in a Christian home; your parents can teach you to pray and go to church; you can attend Sunday school; and you can serve in the ministries of the church – without knowing Christ personally!

Acute longing must be present or there will be no manifestation of Christ to His people. He waits to be wanted. Too bad that with many of us He waits so long, so very long, in vain.

~ A. W. Tozer ~

The light suddenly dawned on Peter and he saw Christ for who He really was – and himself for who he actually was. It is as if Peter wanted to say, "I will always love You, and always think about You with nostalgia when I put down my nets under the bright stars. It breaks my heart to part from You, Master, but I will only disappoint You. I am a sinful person!" And in his heart he muttered, "But I don't know how I will live without You. Where will I go with this heavy burden of my sin?"

Christ loves you too much to leave you. No one is too sinful for Him. The Lord took you into the deep waters to meet your Savior. He will never leave you. He always says, "Come to Me!" The choice is yours.

Lord Jesus, I left You because I wanted to find You. Thank You for Your love that never leaves. Amen.

Save Me, Lord, I'm Sinking!

So Peter went over the side of the boat and walked on the water toward Jesus. But when he saw the strong wind and the waves, he was terrified and began to sink. "Save me, Lord!" he shouted (Matt. 14:29-30).

After walking on the water for a short while, in close proximity of Christ, Peter started sinking. There were specific reasons for this: He still had the Peter temperament: the impulsive Peter who always allowed his feelings and emotions to dictate to him. He had to learn to first count the cost of his actions before rushing into a situation.

Peter started sinking in familiar waters; but overconfidence caused carelessness. We should never pride ourselves on our own strength and experience. Christ said to Peter, "Come!" (v. 29) He was not on the road of intended disobedience, but responded positively to Christ's invitation. The Christian can fail even on the Christian path. Those who stand must be careful not to fall, and should therefore watch and pray.

Never doubt in the dark what God told you in the light.
~ V. R. Edman ~

Peter sank when he looked away from Jesus. He saw only the waves and threatening dangers around him and his faith failed him. But Jesus' helping hand was already there to save him. Hold on to the courage of your faith and keep your eyes fixed on Jesus, the Leader and Finisher of our faith.

I thank You, Lord and Leader, that You make allowances for my weaknesses and that You are always there when I am in need of You. Let me look past my problems and always see You. Amen.

The Great Desertion

At this point many of His disciples had turned away and deserted Him (John 6:66).

People flocked to Jesus, but mostly for personal gain. They wanted Him to help them shake off the hated Roman yoke; they wanted to live off His miracle-working influence. After all, He did make the blind see, the deaf hear, and yes, He even raised the dead. They saw in Jesus a political leader, a popular doctor and a provider of food.

Jesus talked about suffering and sorrow on the horizon where the cross loomed. He did this so that the work of His salvation could be realized. He set spiritual demands and told the people about the narrow gate and the wide gate. The harsh reality of spiritual growth was explained to them in no uncertain terms.

As well could you expect a plant to grow without air and water as to expect your heart to grow without prayer and faith.
~ Charles H. Spurgeon ~

Naturally, this caused quite a tremendous reaction. In John 6:41 they "began to murmur"; in verse 52 they "began arguing with each other" and in verse 60, even His disciples said that what He expected of them was a bit much. In verse 61, the great desertion began.

Their religion was going to cost them something and they were not prepared to pay the price. They started leaving Him. When the synagogue had practically emptied, Jesus turned to His disciples and asked them if they didn't want to leave as well. He, who always said "Come," was now talking about going away! At this point, the Holy Spirit gave every one of Jesus' disciples a choice – are you leaving or are you staying?

Savior and Friend, protect me against the lure of the world and hold me in the grip of Your love. Amen.

A Decision at the Crossroad

Simon Peter replied, "Lord, to whom would we go? You have the words that give eternal life. We believe, and we know You are the Holy One of God" (John 6:68-69).

A while before the above Scripture verse, Peter said, "O Lord, please leave me!" Today we hear him say, "Lord, to whom would we go?" This was a moving and decisive moment in Peter's spiritual journey. He had come to a crossroad and had to make a choice – walk away into the darkness without Christ, or stay forever in the love of Christ.

> Those who insist upon seeing with perfect clearness before they decide, never decide.
> ~ Henri-Frederic Amiel ~

Christ pertinently asked each of His disciples the question of the open door: "Don't you want to leave too?" With Christ there is no compromise; we follow Him or we desert Him. Peter saw the difficult road ahead. Dare he venture onto the road of faith?

Will you, like the prodigal son, surrender yourself to the world and waste your life in lust and sin? Or will you get up and return to the feast in the Father's house? Only Christ is able to quench the eternal thirst and longing in your soul. He doesn't only talk of eternal life, He *is* eternal life. If you have reached a crossroad in your spiritual life, remember: Jesus is *there*! He is waiting for you with outstretched arms.

When Peter chose Jesus, it was forever. He would still stumble and even fall, but Christ would help him up. When Peter reached spiritual maturity, he would bring others to Jesus to make the same choice and experience the same salvation.

Trusted Master, thank You for the happy day when my heart chose You as King, forever. Amen.

Seeing the Unseen

Faith is the confidence that what we hope for will actually happen; it gives us assurance about things we cannot see (Heb. 11:1).

Just like us, Peter had to learn what faith is. It is one of the most difficult lessons in the Christian's course of growth to spiritual maturity. Faith consists of three very important components:

First, you must *trust* someone you have never seen. You don't know if He exists because you haven't seen Him in the flesh. Faith is to be convinced of the existence of things we cannot see. Therefore, Jesus says in John 20:29, "Blessed are those who believe without seeing Me."

Secondly, you must be daring, even if it means giving up your precious life and existence, not knowing if you will die of thirst along the way. You must take Christ at His Word when He says, "Those who drink the water I give will never be thirsty" (John 4:14).

Faith is not belief without proof, but trusting without reservations.
~ Elton Trueblood ~

The third important component is that you must be willing to work. Faith does not mean a blissful life of doing nothing. There is prayer work, Bible study, meditation, witnessing, church attendance and many other spiritual disciplines that must be followed. You don't earn your salvation with works, but this is the way to show your gratitude for your salvation. James says, and rightly so, "So you see, faith by itself isn't enough. Unless it produces good deeds, it is dead and useless" (James 2:17).

On his way to full Christian discipleship, Peter could not sidestep the lesson in certainty of faith, and neither can you or I.

Gracious Lord Jesus, I desperately want to believe like the biblical heroes. Help me to do so through Your Holy Spirit. Amen.

Confession of Faith

Then He asked them, "But who do you say I am?" (Matt. 16:15).

Peter had to get to that point where the light dawned and he could say with conviction, "You are the Messiah, the Son of the living God" (Matt. 16:16). The Heidelberg Catechism says that I must believe that Christ assures me of eternal life, through His Spirit. To testify to certainty of faith is not pride, it is the humblest form of godliness. There is no evidence of my own virtue or self-righteousness in it. I cast myself exclusively and solely on Christ.

What an incredible privilege to have this undeniable certainty in these uncertain times: Jesus Christ is my Savior and Redeemer! To be able to rejoice in humility but with certainty, "I know for sure that Jesus lives!" The time for insecurity is over. No more "I hope, I guess, I wish, I trust." No, now I proclaim: "I know! I *know* my Savior lives. I *know* I am His child. I *know* He died for me. And I *know* that I will live forever with Him!"

> Faith is not a refuge from reality. It is a demand that we face reality, with all its difficulties, opportunities and implications.
> ~ Evelyn Underhill ~

It was of His own free will that Christ placed Himself before the judicial bench of His followers. They were in Caesarea-Philippi at the time, surrounded by idols of various religions. The disciples had been under Jesus' training for two years and it was a mere six months before His death. Would there be people of faith who would continue with His work and build His church?

Thank You, my Savior, that You have given me the gift of faith through Your Spirit. Let it keep on growing in my life. Amen.

What Is Your Answer?

Then He asked them, "But who do you say I am?" Simon Peter answered, "You are the Messiah, the Son of the living God" (Matt. 16:15-16).

To Jesus the question is not, what do the masses believe and what are the latest acceptable religious trends? He wants to know what you and I personally think of Him. This is the test for Christian discipleship: "Who do you say I am?" Peter sees this question both as a challenge and an opportunity to confess his personal faith. He answers with the jubilant song of the saved through all the centuries, "You are the Messiah, the Son of the living God."

This was an important and irreversible moment in Peter's life: To him Christ was God's Anointed One, the Savior who was sent to make His children holy. This is eternal life: that we acknowledge Him. If you are asked today about your faith in Jesus Christ, would you have an answer?

Faith is not the belief that God will do what you want. Faith is the belief that God will do what is right.
~ Max Lucado ~

The following refrains echo throughout the entire Bible: "It is impossible to please God without faith" (Heb. 11:6). "Your faith has made you well" (Matt. 9:22). "Have faith in God" (Mark 11:22). "Believe in the Lord Jesus and you will be saved" (Acts 16:31). "But to all who believed Him and accepted Him, He gave the right to become children of God" (John 1:12). "He gave His one and only Son, so that everyone who believes in Him will not perish but have eternal life" (John 3:16).

Your answer should be, "I believe You are the Messiah, the Son of the living God."

I praise Your holy name, my Father God, that I may confess that Christ is my Savior and Redeemer. Amen.

Do You Have an Answer?

Jesus replied, "You are blessed, Simon son of John, because My Father in heaven has revealed this to you. You did not learn this from any human being" (Matt. 16:17).

Do you remember the answer the foolish girls were given when they arrived at the feast, standing at the closed door, holding their dead lamps in their shaking hands, and pleading to be let in? "I don't know you!" (Matt. 25:12).

If we should arrive at the heavenly feast holding empty lamps without the oil of faith, we will also hear these words from His mouth. He who always pleaded, "Come to Me!" will then say, "I don't know you!" Not that God doesn't know us – He knows us only too well. But He does not know us as His. You must be very sure of your answer to this question. There cannot be any room for doubt. This life is too short and eternity too long.

What a wonderful thing it is to be sure of one's faith! How wonderful to be a member of the evangelical church which preaches the free grace of God through Christ as the hope of sinners! If we were to rely on our works, what would become of us?

~ G. F. Handel ~

Faith is the axle around which the wheel of your salvation revolves. This is what God will demand from you in the final instance. Then the answer of your heart must be, "You are the Messiah, the Son of the living God!"

Lord Campbell, a Scottish minister, was asked by a friend, "How do I know that I will always hold on to God in faith?" Campbell answered, "How do I know? No, this I don't always know. But what I do know without any doubt is this: He will always hold on to me!" This is faith: the unshakable knowledge that God holds me in His hand and that nothing can pull me away from Him.

God, thank You that I know You are my Savior. Amen.

Take Pride in the Cross

May I never boast about anything except the cross of our Lord Jesus Christ. Because of that cross, my interest in this world has been crucified, and the world's interest in me has also died (Gal. 6:14).

At the time of Christ's death on the cross, a Roman soldier said the following about Christianity: "This religion will never survive. It is built on disaster and tragedy; on the death of its leader on a cursed tree – a cross." Today, twenty centuries later, the mighty Roman Empire is just a historical memory, but Christianity is growing powerfully – the bare cross its inspiring symbol.

On his way to true Christianity, Peter had to learn the lesson of carrying the cross. The glory of doing so is that you are carrying the instrument of your own salvation. Peter had already experienced exciting things under Christ's teaching: a new name; a new direction; a new heart; a new confession. Then Christ asked Peter to carry the cross. This was a shocking disappointment to him. Possibly he still had dreams that Christ would be their political liberator, and now Jesus was talking about suffering, sorrow, carrying a cross and death. Peter said, "Heaven forbid, Lord. This will never happen to You!" (Matt. 16:22).

The cross is God's truth about us, and therefore it is the only power that can make us truthful. When we know the cross we are no longer afraid of the truth.
~ Dietrich Bonhoeffer ~

We so easily accept the easy and pleasant part of our faith, as long as no drastic demands are made on us. You and I will also have to meet this challenge of Christian discipleship, because it is the price of spiritual maturity. When He spoke of carrying the cross, it was not only talk; He demonstrated it in His own life. Dare we, His believing disciples, do less?

Crucified Lord Jesus, give me the strength and grace to carry my cross with dignity like You did. Amen.

Carrying the Cross (1)

Jesus turned to Peter and said, "Get away from Me, Satan! You are a dangerous trap to Me. You are seeing things merely from a human point of view, not from God's" (Matt. 16:23).

One minute we hear Peter confess, "You are the Messiah!" and the next the Master has to reprimand him. Peter was not yet prepared to pay the price of Christian discipleship, of accepting the Holy Spirit. Poor blundering Peter, how we see in you the image of our own laborious path of spiritual growth!

In his rash and misdirected love, he admonished the Master because He spoke of suffering and death. If Christ hadn't died, we would never have known a Savior. How poor this world would be if Peter had had his way.

> By the cross we get to know the gravity of sin, and the greatness of God's love toward us.
> ~ John Chrysostom ~

Christ said that He would build His church on Peter's confession that He is the Messiah. Peter wanted to take over, dictate and rebuke. As Satan tempted the Lord in the desert, he now used Peter for the same purpose. The building block now became a stumbling block. It must have been a hard blow to Peter to be called Satan. It was said to Peter to rescue him, because it was part of God's work of grace in Peter's life. God's fairness demanded that Christ carry the cross: Your sin and mine made it vitally important: "He was beaten so we could be whole" (Isa. 53:5).

By virtue of Jesus carrying the cross and His death, the gates to heaven swung open again and you and I can rejoice, "O God's mercy, rich and free: the gates are open, also for me!" Praise the Lord, O my soul!

Crucified Savior, thank You that You paid the price so that I may be Your cross-bearing disciple. Amen.

Carrying the Cross (2)

"If any of you wants to be My follower, you must turn from your selfish ways, take up your cross, and follow Me" (Matt. 16:24).

Peter's fundamental mistake was that he wanted to avoid the cross: "If your Lord is going to suffer and carry His cross and die, what about you, Peter? Surely you can't be let off." Yes, we all want to be part of His glory – but don't expect us to share in His suffering.

Jesus' cross is carried daily by people just like you and me: a broken body, loss, loneliness and desertion, disappointment and failure, suffering and trials. These crosses we have to carry, whether we are Christians or not. Jesus is talking about carrying a cross *for Him:* Self-denial, dedication, testifying that leads to persecution, losing the world but gaining Jesus as Savior.

Christ's blood
is heaven's key.
~ Thomas Brooks ~

Peter had to learn that carrying a cross makes your shoulders strong. The potter paints the vase black and puts it in the furnace, and when it comes out it has a golden color. The goldsmith heats the gold to melting point and then purifies it. When he can see his own reflection in the gold, he knows it is pure. It is in our moments of cross-bearing that our purest qualities come to the fore. Many of us will say at the end of our pilgrimage that it was carrying the cross that brought me to my Savior and Redeemer.

Our encouragement is that Christ is helping us carry our crosses. He will not allow us to be tempted beyond what we can bear. This was the power of the martyrs. At the height of Roman persecution, Peter went back to Rome to encourage the Christians and to die a martyr's death on a cross himself – but he gained eternal life. Are you willing to carry your cross?

Mighty Savior, help me to carry my cross and follow You in faith.
Amen.

Satan's Plan

"Simon, Simon, Satan has asked to sift each of you like wheat" (Luke 22:31).

There is a difference between trial and temptation. A trial is something the Lord sends on your path to bring out the best in you. Temptation is something Satan sends to bring out the worst in you.

The crosses that we carry for Christ's sake are trials that God sends to purify and strengthen us. Temptations are Satan's subtle sifting plan to sift us like wheat. We are either purified by the fire of the Holy Spirit, or we are burnt in Satan's oven. Peter's arrogance and fall is a warning to all of us that those who stand must watch out that they don't fall. In humility Peter says to Jesus, "Lord, I am ready to go to prison with You, and even to die with You" (Luke 22:33).

Non-chalance in our spiritual development is fatal. It makes the dynamics disappear from our religion. Therefore Jesus warns, "Not everyone who calls out to Me 'Lord! Lord!' will enter the Kingdom of Heaven" (Matt. 7:21).

When led to the Spirit, the child of God must be as ready to wait as to go; as prepared to be as to speak.
~ Lewis S. Chafer ~

The devil lulls us into complacency in his sieve: just stay close to the church; don't be too serious about Christ; don't allow your religion to become too important to you. In this way, the dark cloud of a false sense of security descends ominously on us, and prevents us from growing to spiritual maturity in Jesus Christ.

Lord, my God, I humbly plead that You fill me with Your Spirit, so that I will not only exist, but live my spiritual life to the full.
Amen.

Christ Prays for Us!

"I have pleaded in prayer for you, Simon, that your faith should not fail" (Luke 22:32).

In Satan's sifting plan to reduce us to chaff, there is one great and saving grace: Christ prays for us so that we can stand firm in the faith. Poor terrified Peter. How badly he wanted to die for Christ, and how great was his fear of the world: "I want to do what is good, but I don't. I don't want to do what is wrong, but I do it anyway" (Rom. 7:19). This is Paul's cry, on behalf of Peter, and on behalf of us all.

Peter was warned, but he was too self-assured. Others might stumble – Andrew or John or Judas, but not Peter! He was, after all, the rock. But Jesus knew Peter better than he knew himself. Thank God! There is hope for all of us! *Jesus prays for us!* When Satan messes with us, Christ prays for us.

Our Lord is the ground from whom our prayer grows and in His love and grace He Himself gives us our prayer.
~ Julian of Norwich ~

He has compassion with our weaknesses. When we despair of ourselves; when we shamelessly deny Him; when we follow Him at a distance – then Christ prays for us! He doesn't pray that we are taken from the sieve, but that we stand firm in faith. This is the good news: Christ prays for us! And when Christ prays, Satan is powerless!

Peter received a commission for life: "So when you have repented and turned to Me again, strengthen your brothers" (Luke 22:32). Christ is calling you to be a good Samaritan.

Child of God – Jesus prays for you to be a powerful witness and to strengthen others in Satan's sieve.

Praying Savior, hold my hand because I am weak and helpless. I will venture no farther if You don't go with me. Amen.

Tears of Remorse

Peter left the courtyard, weeping bitterly (Luke 22:62).

Charles H. Spurgeon, the prince of preachers, said that he had a dream in which he saw the devil standing at the gate of heaven. Resentment and fury were visible in his eyes while he watched Christians streaming into heaven. His rage reached its peak when he saw people who were once evil sinners entering heaven, singing and rejoicing, and he asked Peter, "How can you allow all the sinners in while I have to stay outside?" Peter's answer to Satan was, "The difference is that you never repented; that you didn't shed a single tear about your sin."

What soap is to the body, tears are for the soul.
~ Jewish Proverb ~

People show up at funerals wearing sunglasses to hide the "shame" of tears. Our children, especially boys, are taught not to cry. "Cowboys don't cry" has become the slogan of our time. It must have been touching to see a big, strong fisherman like Peter crying bitterly. But he was crying about something everyone should cry about: He was crying over his sin! Remorse made him cry, and they were liberating tears.

Aren't we perhaps paying a price for our tearless eyes? Could depression, neuroses and complexes not be traced back to this? Jesus says in Matthew 5:4, "God blesses those who mourn, for they will be comforted." Tears prevent sorrow from turning into despair. Peter cried and he was saved.

Let us thank God for the healing, liberating and purifying power of tears. The soul would have known no rainbow if the eyes knew no tears.

Thank You, Lord Jesus, for that day when You will wipe the last tear from our eyes. Make my tears of remorse holy, genuine and sincere. Amen.

The Eyes of Jesus

At that moment the Lord turned and looked at Peter (Luke 22:61).

Peter slipped into the courtyard of Caiaphas's palace and tried to hide in the shadows. It was after midnight and suddenly the clanging sound of weapons and the voices of soldiers could be heard. A prisoner had just been brought in: Jesus of Nazareth.

One of the servant girls said that Peter had also been with Jesus. Embarrassed and afraid, Peter stammered and stuttered and denied that he knew Jesus. He denied it, three times, even with an oath – and then a rooster crowed. Peter leaned against the cold stone wall in the dark, and cried bitterly.

His tears were also a declaration of love. His tears were already saying what his mouth would later say: "Lord, You know everything. You know that I love You" (John 21:17). Peter's tears were the turning point in his life. Have you ever cried about your sin? Cried because you love Jesus passionately and are full of remorse for what your sins are doing to Him? When someone cries about sin, the merciful feeling of liberation and peace follows.

The confession of evil works is the first beginning of good works.
~ St. Augustine ~

Peter looked into Jesus' eyes and saw only love. What unleashed his stream of tears? The rooster that crowed? The mocking of the bystanders? No, Christ looked at him with compassion, pity and love. The worst thing about sin is not the wrath of God, but the sadness and pain in the eyes of Christ when He looks at us, with love.

O Holy Spirit, Comforter sent by God, give me a heart soft enough to cry, and strong enough to resist sin. Amen.

You Can't Go Without It

If I didn't love others, I would be nothing (1 Cor. 13:2).

There is absolutely *no* substitute for love. Not languages, faith, knowledge or education. This is confirmed in 1 Corinthians 13. Therefore, it is a meaningful question that Jesus asked Peter at this stage on the way to a Spirit-filled life: "Simon son of John, do you love Me?" (John 21:16). This question goes to the roots of our faith: to the essence of our discipleship. It asks of our relationship with our Creator. Christ doesn't ask: Do you believe in Me? Do you understand Me? Do you confess My name? Are you obedient and do you serve Me? Do you love My Word? Do you love My work and My children? All this is secondary. The primary question is, "Do you love *Me*?" If our answer to this question is yes, we can approach the future without fear.

The love of Christ is like the blue sky into which you may see clearly, but the real vastness of which you cannot measure.
~ Robert M. McCheyne ~

Jesus asked Peter the question three times. Jesus didn't reprimand him, didn't ask for a guarantee that Peter would never do it again. Jesus asked only about his love for Him! It was a reasonable question. He was under Jesus' training for three years. Even when Peter disappointed Christ, He did not leave him to fend for himself. Jesus saw all the possibilities borne of pure love.

Peter knew how empty life could be without Christ. "There is no greater love than to lay down one's life for one's friends" (John 15:13). Against the backdrop of this loving involvement in Peter's spiritual growth, Jesus' question to Peter was within reason: and it would be a reasonable question to ask of us.

Spirit of God, awaken so much pure love in my heart that it will be revealed in my everyday life. Amen.

A Meaningful Question

"Simon son of John, do you love Me?" (John 21:16).

We reasoned that Jesus asked Peter a fair question. It was, however, also an intimate and very personal one. All classifications and comparisons were now stopped. The essential question was: Do you love Me? There comes a time when your faith can no longer be something impersonal. Eventually, you cannot deny your uniqueness and individuality before God; when you have to stand alone before God and answer this question: "Do you love Me?"

The question was razor-sharp and penetrating. The masks were down now. It was as if the Lord wanted to say to him, "Simon, you should have been Peter long ago. Where do you stand now after all the years of grace in the discipleship school of your Master? Shouldn't you be much farther along the road of spiritual growth? Do you still warm yourself at enemy fires? You say you love Me, but don't you love yourself more?"

> Every Christian would agree that a man's spiritual health is directly proportional to his love for God.
> ~ C. S. Lewis ~

The Savior had to be sure of Peter's love: The church had to be established; the gospel had to be spread all over the world; a mammoth task had to be performed; history had to be written.

Where did the short circuit lie? In sin, superstition, unbelief, worldly interests? Is Christ visible only on the fringes of our lives and not at the center? The answer and the solution are obvious: confess that you love Christ – and mean it with your entire being!

Father God, I thank You for the privilege to love, and to confirm it with my love for my fellow humans. Amen.

A Confession that Sets You Free

"Lord, You know everything. You know that I love You" (John 21:17).

Only our very best, our noblest and our most precious are good enough for God. Peter was given an opportunity for spiritual stocktaking: to confess his faith; to declare his love, the greatest confession of his entire life: "You know that I love You!" This brought glorious freedom to his heart. He had become part of God's salvation plan with this world and could rejoice with Paul: "Thank God! He has made us His captives and continues to lead us along in Christ's triumphal procession" (2 Cor. 2:14).

Peter's declaration of love to Christ did not bring him a life of blissful rest. On the contrary, it brought him an important and lofty task. He had to take care of the Lord's flock. In implementing his duty of loving others, Peter was fulfilling his commitment of love to Christ. The thought of getting anything in return didn't even occur to him – as if it could contribute to his own salvation or holiness! It was purely his thankfulness for the grace and love of the Lord that set him free and saved him.

> He who loves God with all his heart dreads neither death, torment, judgment or hell, for perfect love opens a sure passage to God.
> ~ Thomas à Kempis ~

Love is our most precious possession, but it also brings great responsibilities for the Christian. Peter's love brought him a task, but also a cross. God's love culminated in a cross on Golgotha. The way a life is lived shows where love lies – Peter's life would have to become a testimony to where His love lay.

This is one of the greatest challenges in our spiritual development: that the quality of our love distinguish us as Jesus' followers. Would you be able to repeat after Peter, "Lord, You know everything. You know that I love You"?

You know that I love You, Lord. Purify my love for You every day through the Holy Spirit. Amen.

Exam Results

Then Jesus told him, "Follow Me" (John 21:19).

For three years Peter was trained by the greatest Teacher who ever lived. He learnt to become a devoted, Spirit-filled follower of Christ. While he was attending classes, he had to take tests from time to time. Some he failed and others he passed.

Peter failed geography because the rock often crumbled. He failed seamanship, because when he was supposed to be in deep waters he wasted his time in dangerous shallow waters. When he wanted to walk to Jesus on the water, he sank in unbelief. He failed agriculture, because he couldn't separate the wheat from the chaff. He failed human relationships, because he followed his best Friend at a distance and denied Him at the fires of the enemy. He failed theology, because when he was expected to be growing spiritually. The Master had to say to him, "Get away from Me, Satan!" (Matt. 16:23).

We turn to God for help when our foundations are shaking, only to learn that it is God shaking them.
~ Charles C. West ~

It was time for the final examination. The paper could include questions like: What are the dangers of pride? What happens if you put your trust in yourself? Why do you sink if you want to walk on water? What makes you so fearful that you deny Jesus? All difficult but justified questions. But there was only one question to answer: "Simon son of John, do you love Me?" There it was, three times, and three times Peter answered correctly.

Peter passed the Christian discipleship exam because he loved the Lord unconditionally. Now he was ready for the path of discipleship that Christ outlined for him. He heard the Master's command: "Follow Me" (John 21:19).

Gracious Teacher, thank You for hours, months and years of tuition in Your classes on loving. Amen.

The Master Potter

Jesus replied, "If I want him to remain alive until I return, what is that to you? As for you, follow Me" (John 21:22).

The Lord changed Peter's life completely. At first Peter was, to all outward appearances, a very successful man. He was a big, strong man, very knowledgeable about the sea and fishing; he had much influence among the fishermen of Capernaum. But in Jesus' school he had to learn that inner strength was more important than brute strength. Peter had to learn that his knowledge was limited and that he couldn't fix his own life like he fixed fishnets. Only the great Artist of life could repair his life. His leadership characteristics and pride had to be changed to make him humble. While he used to be the influential leader, he had to learn to become a follower.

No sacrifice can be too great to make for Him who gave His life for me.
~ C. T. Studd ~

Peter was in fact a man with great inner weakness. When Christ talked of suffering and death, he shied away, terrified. At the great catch, he realized his own sinfulness and pleaded with the Lord to leave him. When he wanted to walk on the sea toward Jesus, his faith failed him and he started sinking. At the gate of Gethsemane, he fled with the other disciples. In Caiaphas's courtyard, he denied his Savior three times.

But take heart, poor sinner! Peter's inner weaknesses were transformed into spiritual power when he was filled with the Holy Spirit. The Peter who failed his Master brought thousands into the kingdom at Pentecost. The man who fled at Gethsemane was now willing to be a martyr for Christ. Peter got his marching orders: "Follow Me!" And so did you and I – what will we do about it?

Living Lord Jesus, thank You that You hold my hand. I will faithfully follow wherever You lead. Amen.

The Test of Solitude

Before daybreak the next morning, Jesus got up and went out to an isolated place to pray (Mark 1:35).

The Master had a very busy ministry. The crowds followed Him wherever He went. He was aware that healing power flowed from Him. The only way He could maintain and replenish His spiritual strength was to guard His valuable relationship with His heavenly Father. To do this, He had to spend time alone with God. He got up early, before dawn, and spent time in fellowship with God in the silence of daybreak.

Many people today find it difficult to separate themselves from others and be alone. They have to be part of a crowd. This is true of religious people too. They are strong when they are involved in an emotional act of worship, but when the excitement of the moment has passed, they stand alone. What then? Many become so frantically active in the service of God that they lose sight of the God they are serving.

Language has created the word 'loneliness' to express the pain of being alone. And it has created the word 'solitude' to express the glory of being alone.
~ Paul Tillich ~

Christianity flourishes in fellowship, and sharing in Christian brotherhood is essential to spiritual growth. But it is when you are alone that your faith is tested. When you stand alone and God calls you into fellowship with Himself – then the true quality of your faith is revealed. While you spend time in God's presence, these moments become times of spiritual strength and renewal.

Gracious Master, grant me the desire and determination to regularly spend time in solitude with You. Amen.

Prayer for Pentecostal Fullness

"But you will receive power when the Holy Spirit comes upon you. And you will be My witnesses, telling people about Me everywhere" (Acts 1:8).

Blessed God and Father of our Lord Jesus Christ, You who existed from the very beginning and sent Your Spirit to Your children, let Your Spirit also work powerfully in me so that He will lead my thoughts in truth; cleanse my heart of every sin; keep my lips from impure words; keep my eyes from looking at what displeases You; make my hands zealous in Your holy service! Send Your Spirit to cleanse and purify me of all wrong motives, envy and an unforgiving spirit.

Let Your Spirit blow through my life and bring new life and growth. Send Your Spirit as a dove to bring me the peace that surpasses all understanding. Allow Your Spirit to wash me whiter than snow, so that I will bear fruit. Send Your Spirit as dew to refresh me and nourish me with power from heaven. God, make me receptive to new truths; encourage me to action in Your kingdom.

Make me a powerful witness of truth and a willing bearer of Your good news. I surrender myself to You unconditionally, so that You can equip me for the task You call me for. Grant that I will work without reservation for Your kingdom. Let the world know through my witnessing that God saves sinners and can make them children of God. In Jesus' holy name.

True discrimination between right and wrong does not then depend on the acuteness of our intelligence, but on the wisdom of the Spirit.
~ John Calvin ~

Lord, I praise You for the blessings and peace that You bestow on me! Amen.

October

His light on my path teaches me about the fruit of the Spirit.

"Remain in Me, and I will remain in you. For a branch cannot produce fruit if it is severed from the vine, and you cannot be fruitful unless you remain in Me."
~ John 15:4 ~

The only saving faith is that which casts itself on God for life or death.
~ Martin Luther ~

God of unfathomable grace and love,
all the riches of wisdom, truth and holiness
are inherent in Your being. Grant that,
through ongoing fellowship with You,
the fruits of a Christian character may
keep on growing in me and ripen in my soul.
The fruit of a thankful and contented heart;
of waiting patiently and answering Your call without delay.
The fruit of courage in suffering and danger;
enduring problems like a warrior of God;
fearlessly standing up for what is right and
being prepared for every temptation.
Loving Father, give me a peaceful heart.
Let me not brood over the little things
in life and allow them to get me down.
Banish all uneasiness from my heart and life.
Refresh me through Your Holy Spirit
so that I will live to Your honor.
In the name of Jesus Christ, my Redeemer and Savior.

Amen.

What Is the Fruit of the Spirit?

"I am the vine; you are the branches. Those who remain in Me, and I in them, will produce much fruit. For apart from Me you can do nothing" (John 15:5).

Fruit is a word used in the Bible to indicate what God expects from His children. The basic necessity of producing fruit is described in three fundamental parts in the Bible.

John 15:1-8 describes unity with Christ; without it, bearing fruit is impossible.

Psalm 1 emphasizes the connection between bearing fruit and the Word of God.

Galatians 5:22-23 proves that bearing fruit is the spontaneous result of the indwelling Holy Spirit.

God wants fruit in the lives of those who love His name (see Isa. 5:1-2). We are united with Christ in order to bear fruit (see Rom. 7:4). The Gardener prunes the branches so that they will bear more fruit (see John 15:2). He will patiently wait for fruit (see James 5:7). He is pleased when the fruit starts appearing (see Song of Sol. 4:13-16). Paul prays that fruit will be visible in the lives of young converts (see Phil. 1:9-11; Col. 1:9-10).

Just as important as knowing what gift God has given you is knowing which gifts He hasn't given you.
~ C. P. Wagner ~

We must consider what the fruit of the Spirit is. Winter storms, spring rains and the scorching heat of summer are all instrumental in producing the best in us. It is the same with the fruit of the Spirit. The Father's pruning shears that are like the farmer's plow, are used in one of the processes by which the fruit is produced and through which the hungry heart is satisfied (see Heb. 12:11; Matt. 5:6).

Loving God, I willingly submit myself to Your pruning shears so that I will bear the fruit of the Spirit according to Your will.

Amen.

Spiritual Fruit

"Still other seeds fell on fertile soil, and they produced a crop that was thirty, sixty, and even a hundred times as much as had been planted!" (Matt. 13:8).

The fruits of the Spirit must be clearly distinguished from the gifts of the Spirit. Fruit consists of moral qualities that are the result of being born again and the work of the indwelling of the Holy Spirit. Gifts are miracle-working "awards" that are allotted to certain individuals. Fruit is for everybody; God gives gifts to individuals as something separate.

The fruit of the Spirit sanctifies the nature or temperament of a person. Gifts come on the basis that something is given to an individual for free. Fruit is the perfection of grace in the heart and life of a person. It grows by means of virtue and is perfected without worry or care. Christ tells us what the stumbling blocks are in the process of growing this kind of fruit. Of four kinds of seed, the first falls on dry ground. The second penetrates the soil, but doesn't go down deep enough. The third goes down deep enough, but never germinates. The fourth falls to the ground, penetrates the soil, produces new growth and brings forth fruit (see Matt. 13:3-8).

I was baptized with the Holy Spirit when I took Him by simple faith in the Word of God.
~ R. A. Torrey ~

The spiritual explanation is found in Matthew 13:18-23. The respective stumbling blocks are the enemy (Matt. 13:9), persecution and problems (vv. 20-21), the cares of the world and the lure of wealth (v. 22). The only ones who bear fruit are the ones who hear, and are able, through the Holy Spirit, to understand and do it.

Holy Spirit, make me obedient to Your promptings and faithful to Your eternal Word. Amen.

Growth Is Imperative

"The earth produces the crops on its own. First a leaf blade pushes through, then the heads of wheat are formed, and finally the grain ripens" (Mark 4:28).

Human beings are created to grow. The Creator made you for creative growth. The alternative is stagnation, degeneration and death. It is a law of nature that the body will gradually stop growing, no matter how hard you try to delay it.

People's bodies can become so important to them that aging can cause the stagnation of their entire being. If you live only for the comfort and convenience of the body, you might discover too late that your soul has become entangled with it. The greatest tragedy of life is to see a person's body, soul and spirit stop growing and eventually die. This lack of growth is the core reason for the deepest unhappiness in a human life. It is because you know that the central and all-important purpose of your life stays unfulfilled – but even worse: that it was deliberately violated by you.

> If we're not growing, we must feel guilty, because we are not fulfilling Christ's command.
> ~ Evan Burrows ~

On the other hand, if you fulfill the purpose of your life by acknowledging the law of growth and applying it, the essence of happiness spreads to all the other areas of your life. Even areas in your life that make you unhappy are positively affected. Complete happiness in life is a fringe benefit of a growing, creative personality.

Father God, help me to nourish and develop the wonderful possibilities of spiritual growth. Amen.

God Enables Us to Grow

My servant grew up in the LORD's presence like a tender green shoot, like a root in dry ground (Isa. 53:2).

There are people who say that God brought an imperfect creation into being: there are earthquakes, tornadoes, droughts, floods, snakes, scorpions, germs, disease, suffering and death. Within all these imperfections, God concealed the solutions. We just need to discover them.

There is material to make cement and steel so that we can build tornado-resistant homes, there are antidotes to certain snakebite, there is a way to heal the sick – and thanks to Jesus' resurrection, there is even a solution to death.

Be not afraid of growing slowly, be afraid only of standing still.
~ Chinese Proverb ~

The story is told of a man whose every wish was granted. He wanted a house – and there it was, servants and all! He wanted a classy car – and there it was, chauffeur and all! At first he was ecstatic about this marvelous state of affairs, but gradually his joy faded, until one day when he said to his personal servant, "I want to get out of this situation. I want to create something, I want to suffer a bit ... I would rather be in hell than to carry on with this kind of life." The servant politely replied, "So where do you think you are?"

If our way of life is hostile toward our growth as moral beings, God has provided us with help to grow in all circumstances and surroundings. All this has been made possible for us by Jesus Christ. He is the door to all the wealth and grace of God that enables us to grow spiritually.

Thank You, God of love, that You provide all the means for my spiritual growth. Thank You that You change the difficulties in my life into opportunities. Amen.

An Open Secret

Oh, the joys of those who do not follow the advice of the wicked, or stand around with sinners, or join in with mockers. But they delight in the law of the LORD; meditating on it day and night (Psalm 1:1-2).

Every time we face an obstacle in our quest for spiritual growth, God provides for us in the most wonderful way. He simply waits for us to discover the solutions. That discovery comes when we accept Jesus as our Savior and Redeemer. He came from an obscure country as a member of an ordinary family. He worked as a carpenter, a humble trade. Without any sign of self-importance, His message found its way into the hearts of people – mostly fishermen and ordinary people. God's spiritual provision for our spiritual growth was revealed in the heart of Jesus, broken on the cross for people like you and me.

The more we grow in grace, the more we shall flourish in glory. Though every vessel of glory shall be full, yet some vessels hold more.
~ Thomas Watson ~

God provides all we need to grow and become the person God wanted us to be. "Dear friends, we are already God's children, but He has not yet shown us what we will be like when Christ appears. But we do know that we will be like Him, for we will see Him as He really is. And all who have this eager expectation will keep themselves pure, just as He is pure" (1 John 3:2-3). We are moving toward a breathtaking final destination: to grow in the perfect image of Christ.

This makes us humble, yet also self-assured. We are on our way to great and glorious things: to become more like Christ. This turns our faces away from the past and directs us to the future. Christ makes it possible and He is the open secret of the way to that possibility.

Gracious God, we plead in joyous anticipation for this glory in our lives. Amen.

The Aim of Spiritual Growth

"You are to be perfect, even as your Father in heaven is perfect" (Matt. 5:48).

We must know the road we are traveling in order to grow spiritually, so that we can bear the fruit of the Spirit. Paul Harnack says, "Christianity doesn't offer solutions, it sets goals and then gives us the strength to move toward those goals."

In the Sermon on the Mount, Christ says that we must be perfect as our Father in heaven is perfect. These words place the entire Sermon on the Mount in perspective. Christ expects practical characteristics from us. We must strive for perfection of character. We cannot be perfect in this life, but we must try to be like God as best we possibly can, by striving for moral perfection.

If we don't change,
we don't grow.
If we don't grow,
we are not really living.
~ Gail Sheehy ~

We must strive to live holy lives and turn our backs on the sinful values of the world. We must devote ourselves to the things of God's kingdom and doing God's will. We must crucify our own desires and put His love and grace into practice in the world. Our deeds must supplement our words meaningfully. We must also *grow* to maturity. We can't become instant Christians, develop a Christian character and live holy lives straightaway. We must grow spiritually all the time and always move closer to perfection. We must keep on growing until we reach maturity.

There is always room for growth. The fact that we still stumble dare not keep us from trying to be like Jesus. Those who persevere in the quest for perfection will be perfect one day, just as their Savior is perfect (see 1 John 3:2).

Holy God, You have amazing prospects for me and You enable me through the Holy Spirit to realize them. I praise and thank You for this. Amen.

Growing in Grace

Grow in the grace and knowledge of our Lord and Savior Jesus Christ (2 Pet. 3:18 NIV).

If you see your life as holding the promise of ongoing growth according to God's plan, you can face the future confidently. If this is the purpose of your life, where do you start? And how? The answer to this question lies in the message of 2 Peter 3:18. You must make sure you grow in the knowledge and grace of the Lord Jesus Christ.

The point of departure for this growth is precisely where you are right now. You don't grow *toward* grace, you grow *in* grace. The question is: How do you know you are "in" grace? This happens through a new life, a born-again life, by moving the focal point in your life from yourself to God. You do this by surrendering to Him.

If you are planted in the soil of self-interest, you simply cannot grow. If you try to grow in your own soil through your own work, you will soon realize that you live in a desert. Micah puts it like this: "The land will become empty and desolate because of the wickedness of those who live there" (Mic. 7:13). As long as you live for yourself and your own selfish purposes, the ground you grow in will be desert sand. The universe is God's flower garden because it is subject to God and obeys Him.

It is the laden bough that hangs low, and the most fruitful Christian who is the most humble.

~ Anonymous ~

It is only by the grace of God, through Jesus Christ, that you are transplanted from the soil of sin and to the fertile soil where you will be able to bear the fruit of the Spirit.

Thank You, Father God, that You called me to grow in kingdom soil. Help me stand firm in this soil. Amen.

Blistered Hands

They have lost connection with the Head, from whom the whole body, supported and held together by its ligaments and sinews, grows as God causes it to grow (Col. 2:19 NIV).

Before we can grow in grace and bear the fruit of the Spirit, we must get "in" the grace of God by faith and surrender to Him. Isaiah first had to fall to the ground before God in brokenness and call out, "I am doomed, for I am a sinful man. I have filthy lips, and I live among a people with filthy lips" (Isa. 6:5).

But God doesn't break just for the sake of breaking; He breaks to build. That is why he let the seraph purify Isaiah with a burning coal from the altar – in the New Testament this is symbolic of the Holy Spirit. Thus, Isaiah was freed from his sinful past and he met the future with an answer to God's call: "Here I am! Send me" (Isa. 6:8). Broken, purified, sent ... this is always God's plan for His children.

Great peace is with the humble man, but in the heart of a proud man are always envy and anger.
~ Thomas à Kempis ~

On occasion a lady wrote to me, saying, "My hands are blistered by my efforts to serve the Lord and do good deeds." She was looking at her own hands and trusting them, instead of looking at the pierced hands of Christ. We must always remember, "God makes it grow!" Growing to spiritual fruit-bearing is not the result of human effort, but of a personal and total surrender to the grace of God. It teaches us humility, but also leads to victory – humility because we know it's not because we are so good, and victory because we are saved by grace.

Don't get the idea that grace costs nothing. It will cost us sacrifice. But it is the only way that we can grow and bear the fruit of the Spirit.

Lord Jesus, You opened the door to growth for us at a tremendous price. Please help me to surrender to You. Amen.

To Whom Do I Belong?

You are included among those Gentiles who have been called to belong to Jesus Christ (Rom. 1:6).

We cannot walk the road of spiritual growth before we are able to give an answer to the question, "Who do I belong to – myself or God?" We are not primarily called to "do" or to "be," but to belong.

Where will we find the strength to conquer self-obsession? "Oh, what a miserable person I am! Who will free me from this life that is dominated by sin and death? Thank God! The answer is in Jesus Christ our Lord" (Rom. 7:24-25).

The purpose of our salvation is threefold: "May God our Father and the Lord Jesus Christ give you grace and peace. Jesus gave His life for our sins [*past*], just as God our Father planned, in order to rescue us from this evil world in which we live [*present*]. All glory to God forever and ever!" [*future*] (Gal. 1:3-5).

> When Christ's hands were nailed to the cross, He also nailed your sins to the cross.
> ~ Bernard of Clairvaux ~

Thus the purpose of our salvation is to free us from the power of sin to protect us at all times from the sinful world, and to save us from ourselves. Christ lays His hands on our past, on the surrounding present, and our unreliable inner person.

Can we be freed from this threefold slavery? A boy was told to hammer a nail into a piece of wood every time he sinned, and then to take it out again when he had confessed and asked forgiveness. "All the nails are out!" he called out triumphantly. "Yes," his dad answered, "but all the marks the nails made in the wood are still there." The Carpenter of Nazareth not only pulls out the nails, but He also makes the marks disappear!

Lord Jesus, thank You that You forgive and erase the past. I want to belong to You forever. Amen.

Christ Cultivates the Ground

As you endure this divine discipline, remember that God is treating you as His own children (Heb. 12:7).

In Luke 13:6-9, the owner of a fig tree comes looking for fruit after three years, but finds nothing. He says to the gardener, "Cut it down!" But the gardener pleads, "Give it one more chance. Leave it another year, and I'll give it special attention and plenty of fertilizer. If we get figs next year, fine. If not, you can cut it down."

The fig tree is often used in the Old Testament as a symbol of a life that has been made holy. But God will not tolerate our lack of growth and productivity forever. We must respond to the Gardener's care. We must grow and bear fruit for His glory.

Spiritual growth consists most in the growth of the root, which is out of sight.
~ Matthew Henry ~

God reprimands us through our conscience, His Word and our fellow believers. When Peter denied his Master three times, Jesus did not condemn him. After Jesus' resurrection, He asked Peter three times, "Do you love Me?" Jesus was preparing the ground of Peter's soul. With his threefold confession that he loved Jesus, his threefold denial was erased (see John 21:15-19). In Peter's life, the work of the heavenly Gardener bore rich fruit.

Father God, I know that You love me because You are always working in my life through Jesus Christ. Thank You for not giving up on me. Amen.

Fear Delays Growth

The wicked writhe in pain throughout their lives. The sound of terror rings in their ears, and even on good days they fear the attack of the destroyer (Job 15:20-21).

Otto Rank claims that there are two kinds of fear: fear of living and fear of dying. The first is the fear of living as an isolated person: the fear of not moving ahead and becoming a full-fledged individual. The fear of death is the fear of deterioration, losing your individuality. The human being is tossed to and fro between these two poles of fear.

The fear of life is clearly illustrated by the boy who gave an answer to a question in an exam paper on the phenomenon of twins: "I think the reason for twins is that little children don't like coming into the world alone." The individual doesn't only fear being born alone, but also dying alone.

> The fear of God kills all other fears.
> ~ Hugh Black ~

Living means responsibility and humans fear this. This is the root cause of our inability to grow, as well as many of our other spiritual problems. We don't want to get involved and give ourselves to others. Consequently, we can't grow to spiritual maturity.

Many of us suffer from a fear of living with all the consequences it may bring about. Instead of living and growing, we would rather stagnate and die. The difference is Christ! He gives us the courage to live and die because His Spirit constantly encourages us with the words, "Do not fear!"

Lord, I don't want to live in constant fear. Thank You for Your assurance that takes away my fear. Amen.

Escape from Fear

"I am leaving you with a gift – peace of mind and heart. And the peace I give is a gift the world cannot give. So don't be troubled or afraid" (John 14:27).

A few steps can be followed to keep fear in check. Firstly, if there is a secret fear in your life you wish to escape from, don't be afraid to admit it. Trying to hide it only makes matters worse. Bring it out into the open in the right way and you will prevent it from coming out badly. If you have a hidden fear it will haunt you. Admit it, and take a critical and balanced look at it. The Holy Spirit will support you in this.

Courage faces fear and thereby masters it; cowardice represses fear and is thereby mastered by it.
~ Martin Luther King, Jr ~

Secondly, don't try to justify your anxiety or fear. "I thought it was a Christian's duty to be worried," a depressed lady once confessed. A Christian's faith is supposed to set you free from your fears, not justify them. As long as you are held captive by fear, anxiety and worry, it is impossible to grow and bear the fruit God expects you to.

Fear and worry are Satan's way of sabotaging your life. In this way, he disrupts your spiritual life. Christ expects us to be courageous in our faith. Paul says in Philippians 4:13, " I can do everything through Christ who gives me strength."

Lord Jesus, You came to give us peace and courage. Let me live from Your abundance without fear. Amen.

Perfect Love Expels All Fear

There is no fear in love. But perfect love drives out fear, because fear has to do with punishment. The one who fears is not made perfect in love (1 John 4:18 NIV).

It would be good to repeat the words of today's Scripture to yourself regularly, because these words are crucially important. If there is no fear in love, then the obvious thing to do is to love everything and everybody. Fear can only exist and thrive where there is no love. The more love you give, the more you receive. That is the law of love.

Albert Schweitzer's philosophy in life was, "Respect everything that lives." In other words, nurture an attitude of love toward every living being.

> Whatever a person may be like, we must still love them because we love God.
> ~ John Calvin ~

The residents of a hotel in Estes Park, Colorado, were terrified of a big St. Bernard dog. When Schweitzer arrived there, the dog wound its way through the crowds and put his head on Schweitzer's lap. The dog followed him wherever he went. Love breaks down the barriers of fear between people and humans and animals. "There is no fear in love."

It is said that Helen Keller wanted to meet a lion. The warden reluctantly allowed her to enter the lion's cage after he had taken all the necessary precautions. No such measures were necessary. She started stroking the lion with loving hands and the animal allowed her to do it because she had a loving and caring touch. There is no fear in love. Without the soil of love there can be no spiritual growth or fruit.

Savior and Redeemer, You won our hearts with Your love.

Amen.

The Danger of the Rut

Jesus told him, "Anyone who puts a hand to the plow and then looks back is not fit for the Kingdom of God" (Luke 9:62).

If there is one thing in life that stunts growth, it is to get stuck in a rut – physically, mentally or spiritually. An elderly lady started painting as a hobby and at the age of eighty-eight, she said, "Anyone can paint. All you do is take paint and a brush and start." Someone once said of a friend that he had died at fifty but was only buried at eighty-one. The only difference between a rut and a grave is the depth.

Many people get stuck in a spiritual rut. There is a stretch of road in Canada with a signpost that reads, "Choose your rut. You're going to be in it for the following ten kilometers."

When a new phase dawns in some people's lives, they choose a rut and stick to it. For them, life has lost its excitement and adventure and consequently nothing surprises them anymore. Life becomes dull and boring. Fruit does not grow in barren ruts.

> Mere change is not growth. Growth is the synthesis of change and continuity, and where there is no continuity, there is no growth.
> ~ C. S. Lewis ~

Many people are like the man in H. G. Wells' *The Croquet Player* who calls out, "I am willing to fall in with everything good, but if I must *think* it's too much for me!" Or as a leader once said, "Great thoughts make me sleepy."

Falling asleep mentally, physically or spiritually robs us of the ability to bear fruit in the kingdom of God. Lot's wife "looked back," and she changed into a pillar of salt – forever in a rut!

Loving Savior, help me through Your Spirit to soar on eagles' wings and to undertake the flight of faith. Amen.

Positive Thinking

For I can do everything through Christ, who gives me strength (Phil. 4:13).

It is essential that we think positively if we want to produce the fruit of the Spirit. To shift from the negative to the positive, we must take certain steps. Firstly, prayerfully meditate on your life and determine if there are areas that are dominated by negative thoughts. It isn't easy, because we all have blind spots where our faults lie. But with a positive approach, you will overcome all the stumbling blocks: Ask God, fellow believers and yourself what they are, and lay them before the Spirit.

Secondly, replace the negative things in your life with positives. If you simply fight the negative, you are merely opposing a negative with a negative. Replace hate with love; strife with peace; unfaithfulness with faithfulness. It is the only way to overcome negativity. If you find it difficult to like certain people, make an effort to get to know them. You'll be surprised!

The Holy Spirit is the secret of the power in my life. All I have to do is to surrender my life to Him.
~ Kathryn Kuhlman ~

Lastly, find the positive in every negative situation. Jesus did it. The Pharisees criticized Him because He mingled with tax collectors and sinners; insinuating that He was just like His friends. But Jesus didn't oppose the negative with a negative. On the contrary, He told them the parable of the lost sheep, the lost coin and the Prodigal Son. It was a positive pointer to make them see the love of God.

Paul also did it, making progress for lost souls in his hardship: "But thank God! He has made us His captives and continues lead us along in Christ's triumphal procession" (2 Cor. 2:14).

Loving Teacher, help me to rule out what You ruled out and to confirm what You confirmed. Amen.

The Fruit of the Spirit

The Holy Spirit produces this kind of fruit in our lives: love, joy, peace, patience, kindness, goodness, faithfulness, gentleness, and self-control (Gal. 5:22-23).

Each fruit of the Spirit is a moral quality and not a supernatural power. The perception often exists that being filled with the Spirit makes one a miracle-worker who can bring about signs and wonders. Miracles do happen through Christians, but this is not the main focus.

The real product is a life that is characterized by the fruits of the Spirit. All of them are moral qualities. Not one is a miracle. Therefore, the emphasis is quite rightly placed on the spiritual and moral, and not on the supernatural and miraculous. And this is healthy because it keeps the character healthy, apart from the manifestation of miracles. This is in line with what Paul says about his ministry. In 2 Corinthians 6:4-10, he mentions things that make him a true servant of God. Each of them is a moral quality of life and a specific action. He doesn't mention miracles once. They happened around him, but he knew that the greatest miracle was happening inside him.

> If you are looking for painless ways to grow toward each other and toward maturity, call off the search.
> ~ J. G. Howard ~

In Galatians 5:19, Paul talks about the acts of the sinful nature, and in verses 22-23, about the effect of the Holy Spirit in our lives. Fruit is a natural manifestation of the Holy Spirit's presence in our lives and this is what God wants to see in us.

Holy Father God, thank You for allowing me to bear the fruit of the Spirit. Amen.

The First Fruit: Love

If I could speak all the languages of earth and of angels, but didn't love others, I would only be a noisy gong or a clanging cymbal (1 Cor. 13:1).

Paul quite rightly mentions love as the first fruit of the Holy Spirit. This emphasis on love links with Paul's hymn to love in 1 Corinthians 13, which ends with the words, "the greatest of these is love."

The importance of love in our spiritual lives is not a coincidence or artificial condition: it is inherent. If you are filled with God's Spirit, you have love. If you lack love, you don't have the Spirit. It's as simple as that. It is not a coincidental attitude toward those who love you, but a characteristic attitude of love. If love is lacking, all the other fruits of the Spirit will be lacking, too.

Take away love and our earth is a tomb.
~ Robert Browning ~

Joy is jubilant love; peace is love that has found rest; patience is love that waits out the storm; friendliness is love that spreads a godly fragrance; kindness is love manifested in good works; faithfulness is love that trusts at all times; humility is love carrying a cross; self-control is love that crucifies the flesh. The primary characteristic of Christianity is love. All the fruits of the Spirit originate in it.

Jesus Christ is the personification of love. He demonstrated to everyone the tender, deep, forgiving love of God. In so doing, He gained their trust, their hearts and their lives for the kingdom of God. One Corinthians 13 is a full-length portrait of Jesus Christ and should be closely studied. To ponder it, strive for it and pray for it to manifest in our lives is the duty of every Christian.

Dearest Master, You who are love grant that I will always take the trouble to develop the primary fruit of love so that it will be the main aim of my life. Amen.

The Second Fruit: Joy

Always be full of joy in the Lord. I say it again – rejoice! (Phil. 4:4).

Joy is love rejoicing! It is the blessed and uplifting experience of rejoicing because Christ saved us. When the heart loves, God gives joy. Joy is rooted in our relationship with Christ. Joy flows from God and takes shape in our lives.

Christian joy enables us to rejoice in serving God – no matter how difficult this might be. It originates from the realization of what is good, and the knowledge that our salvation in Christ is certain and will last forever. Because we belong to God, "we rejoice with a glorious, inexpressible joy" (1 Pet. 1:8). "So now we can rejoice in our wonderful new relationship with God because our Lord Jesus Christ has made us friends of God" (Rom. 5:11).

To be simply ensconced in God is true joy.
~ C. C. Colton ~

The presence of the Holy Spirit in our lives also brings joy to the believer's heart: "The Kingdom of God is not a matter of what we eat or drink, but of living a life of goodness and peace and joy in the Holy Spirit" (Rom. 14:17). Doing God's will brings joy to the soul and makes us cheerful and happy. Sincere service to God and our fellow humans is inspired by the Holy Spirit. Accordingly, love and acts of love lead to joy.

The saved child of God understands what Paul means when he says, "Always be full of joy in the Lord" (Phil. 4:4). Christ sent them this message: "I have told you these things so that you will be filled with My joy. Yes, your joy will overflow!" (John 15:11). A joyful person always walks in the light of a merciful God and says with the psalmist, "You will show me the way of life, granting me the joy of Your presence and the pleasures of living with You forever" (Ps. 16:11).

Jesus Christ, You are the source of all joy. May my gladness be visible because I am grateful for my salvation. Amen.

The Third Fruit: Peace

"I am leaving you with a gift – peace of mind and heart. And the peace I give is a gift the world cannot give. So don't be troubled or afraid" (John 14:27).

Peace is love that has found rest in God. Peace is attributed to all the Persons of the Holy Trinity: God the Father gives peace (see 1 Thess. 5:23); God the Son is the Prince of Peace (see Isa. 9:6); and God the Holy Spirit creates peace in the human heart (see Gal. 5:22).

Peace is the sweet acceptance of the soul that has found rest in Jesus Christ. When Jesus had to leave His disciples, He gave them their inheritance of peace: "I am leaving you with a gift – peace of mind and heart." The believing children of God have this peace. They might often be tried, become confused and face trials and temptations, but deep in their souls they have peace which the world can't give.

There is never any peace for those who resist God.
~ Francois Fénélon ~

This peace is the privilege of God's children. As Job's friend, Bildad said to him, "God is powerful and dreadful. He enforces peace in the heavens" (Job 25:2). At last, Job found his peace in submission to God's will and providence.

The human heart finds peace at the foot of the cross. There the love of God is revealed, righteousness comes into its own, the debt of sin is paid and the human heart becomes inseparable from Christ's salvation. The outcome is peace in the heart of the believer (see Rom. 5:1). The greatest promise of the Old Testament, and the richest blessing of the New Testament, is peace.

Holy Heavenly Father, grant that I will pursue peace all the days of my life through obedience to the Holy Spirit. Amen.

The Fourth Fruit: Patience

Dear brothers and sisters, be patient as you wait for the Lord's return. Consider the farmers who patiently wait for the rains in the fall and in the spring. They eagerly look for the valuable harvest to ripen (James 5:7).

Patience is love that waits out the storm. To the natural human being, revenge is sweet. One of the first things the Holy Spirit does is to us rid of all hatred and revenge. There isn't a more blessed or more difficult ideal than to let the heart rise above insults and suffering. To endure wrongs with patience is to be like Christ. We can carry this cross only by the grace of Christ. In the training school of Christian discipline, patience is one of the lessons we *must* learn. We often fail because we want to manage in our own strength. When God revealed Himself to Moses, He described Himself as, among other things, "slow to anger" (see Exod. 34:6-7).

Faith takes up the cross, love binds it to the soul, patience bears it to the end.
~ Horatius Bonar ~

When we think of Christ's patience toward those who harmed Him, can any of us still pay back evil with evil? Romans 12:19, says "Dear friends, never take revenge. Leave that to the righteous anger of God." We can obtain a patient disposition through prayer and by following the Master's example.

Patience also teaches us to endure hardship. We can repeat what Job said, "The LORD gave me what I had, and the LORD has taken it away. Praise the name of the LORD!" (Job 1:21). Jesus prayed in Gethsemane: "Your will be done." James can be called the patient apostle with reason – especially when you read James 5:7-11. Patience can be achieved through the power of the Holy Spirit. Because God is love, He is patient with us.

Holy Spirit of God, daily grant me patience and allow me to bend under the hand of Your love. Amen.

The Fifth Fruit: Kindness

Instead, be kind to each other, tenderhearted, forgiving one another, just as God through Christ has forgiven you (Eph. 4:32).

Kindness is love that spreads a godly fragrance. It is the nobility of the heart. It comes from the Latin word *gens*, from which the word *gentleman* originates. Kindness is goodness that is gentle; a virtue equipped with tenderness. Paul says to the Romans, "I am fully convinced, my dear brothers and sisters, that you are full of goodness" (Rom. 15:14). Kindness can be both soft and firm at the same time.

The greatest thing a man can do for His heavenly Father is to be kind to some of His other children."
~ Henry Drummond ~

The kind person surrendered to the Holy Spirit is calm and treats all people with respect. Christ cleansed the temple to the glory of God, but He was also kind to the sinful woman who anointed His feet. Kindness is not a passive tolerance. True kindness is a special relationship with God and people. The kind heart is quick to forgive and has compassion with suffering. That is why Paul says in 1 Corinthians 13:4, "Love is patient and kind."

Christian kindness does not arouse anger. It is tender behavior and unselfish in action. It is never arrogant in a position of authority and does not abuse power.

Kindness admonishes gently and never forces an opinion on others; it does not accuse impulsively and is careful to contradict. It cannot prevent tears, but will comfort a sad heart. Kindness follows Christ's example in everything. Therefore Paul says in 2 Corinthians 10:1, "I appeal to you with the gentleness and kindness of Christ."

Enable me, O Holy Spirit of God, to pursue the virtue of kindness under all circumstances so that the Master will be glorified.

Amen.

The Sixth Fruit: Goodness

We are God's masterpiece. He has created us anew in Christ Jesus, so that we can do the good things He planned for us long ago" (Eph. 2:10).

Goodness is love in work clothes. It is an active virtue. Being kind is being like God. To bear the fruit of goodness and kindness is to rejoice in works that glorify God: works of love, mercy, compassion and tolerance. Goodness brings sunshine to the lives of others and originates in our relationship with God.

A compassionate person always remembers how infinitely good God is. Goodness drives us to do good to others and is the fruit of a devoted life. It ministers to the body and the soul. Our whole Christian experience sets us free to be kindhearted.

> You can never do a kindness too soon because you never know how soon it will be too late.
> ~ Ralph Waldo Emerson ~

How are we enabled to do good? By firstly being good: "A good person produces good things from the treasury of a good heart" (Matt. 12:35).

The Holy Spirit gives all of us ample opportunity to practice the virtue of goodness. We must use them conscientiously. "Then Jesus went around doing good and healing all who were oppressed by the devil, for God was with Him" (Acts 10:38).

O Holy Spirit of God, enable me to follow Christ's example and make use of every opportunity to do good. Amen.

The Seventh Fruit: Faithfulness

"Remain faithful even when facing death, I will give you the crown of life" (Rev. 2:10).

Faithfulness is love that stands firm. The person who is faithful is trustworthy. It is important to be faithful in all the big things in life, but also in the small and insignificant things; to be faithful when all is well, but also, and especially, when all is not well; to be faithful in prosperity but also in adversity; to be faithful when people are watching you, but also when no one (but God!) sees you.

It is being faithful in the secular things in life, like faithfulness to your family, your spouse, your job and your friends. It is being faithful in the loftiest and noblest things that God has called you to, and to be what He meant you to be.

> The faithful person lives constantly with God.
> ~ Clement of Alexandria ~

It also means being faithful on a spiritual level: to fulfill your spiritual calling; to be faithful in your Bible study, prayer, churchgoing and *koinonia*; being faithful in witnessing in all the fields of life.

If you have faith, your life will show faithfulness. You will honor your promises and vows, even if it is to your disadvantage and you can be trusted at all times with all things. True service to God makes a person faithful.

In the end, God will judge: not on the grounds of other people's opinions or our own opinion of ourselves, but according to our faithfulness and our loyal acceptance of Jesus as our Savior.

Holy Spirit of God, help me to strive to remain faithful to my Savior until the very end. Amen.

The Eighth Fruit: Gentleness

All of you, serve each other in humility, for "God opposes the proud but favors the humble" (1 Pet. 5:5).

Gentleness is love that carries the cross. The alternative words given for gentleness in the Amplified Bible are *meekness* and *humility*. In Matthew 5:5 (NIV), the Lord says, "Blessed are the meek, for they will inherit the earth." Those who are gentle already enjoy this blessing because it is their Father's earth and He makes it new and beautiful for them.

There is resignation in humility. The humble person trusts God absolutely and therefore is granted godly peace. They gratefully receive everything God gives them, with patience and in faith.

Humility is not grace that can be acquired in a few months: it is the work of a lifetime.
~ Francois Fénélon ~

We can only have the right approach to God and others through a humble attitude. With this attitude, we will not overestimate ourselves or think that God has forgotten us. Humility enables us to work for the glory of God, not people.

Humility enables us to deal with disappointment in a dignified way. Humility is not cowardice; on the contrary, it bears evidence to boldness. The humble heart waits in faith. Problems, carrying the cross and trials, are nothing in comparison with God's reward. The qualities that are of great importance to the world is a noble spirit. The wisdom of the humble is based on honest knowledge of themselves and their weaknesses. Their nobility is sustained by God in His grace. Their power lies in their trust in Him.

Holy God, enable me through Your Spirit to walk in humility and always submit myself to Your will. Amen.

The Ninth Fruit: Self-Control

All athletes are disciplined in their training. They do it to win a prize that will fade away, but we do it for an eternal prize (1 Cor. 9:25).

Self-control is love in training. Everything done in excess is a sign of a lack of self-control, even things that are justified like eating, sleeping and playing. It is not in using things, but in abusing them that results in a lack of self-control.

Uncontrolled use of the tongue can destroy character and torture the heart. It is wrong to be quick-tempered and allow your short temper to gain the upper hand. Then you are used by Satan to hurt others. Self-control is a fruit of the Spirit that enables you to master yourself, to such an extent that you can be the servant of others.

A lack of self-control can even be revealed in your religious views. As the writer to the Romans says, "I know what enthusiasm they have for God, but it is misdirected zeal" (Rom. 10:2). You need to live a self-controlled life to keep both your body and soul fit. Through the work of the Holy Spirit, you are enabled to exercise control over every bad quality in your life.

> Self-control is the mother of spiritual health.
> ~ John Climacus ~

A lack of self-control will let love weep, joy change into grief and peace flee. Patience will hang her head in shame, kindness will not be able to do what she does best, goodness will die, faithfulness will be impossible and humility will pine away.

All the other fruits of the Spirit are banned from the heart when there is no self-control. Self-control is the golden cord that binds everything together in unity.

Lord Jesus, strengthen me through the Spirit in my quest for self-control. Amen.

The Value of the Fruit of the Spirit

The Holy Spirit produces this kind of fruit in our lives: love, joy, peace, patience, kindness, goodness, faithfulness, gentleness, and self-control (Gal. 5:22-23).

In retrospect, it becomes clear that the fruit of the Spirit can be divided into three distinguishing groups:

The first three are about our relationship with God: love, joy and peace. Love is the fruit of the knowledge of God, joy is the fruit of our salvation and peace is the fruit of our reconciliation.

The second group teaches us about our relationship with others: patience, kindness and goodness. Patience teaches us to tolerate others, kindness makes us care for them and goodness inspires us to be good to them.

Let us thank God heartily as often as we pray that we have His Spirit in us to teach us to pray.
~ Andrew Murray ~

The last three have a bearing on our relationship with ourselves: faithfulness, gentleness and self-control. We should be faithful in what has been entrusted to us, gentle in our attitudes, and self-controlled in all our duties and problems in life.

To bear the fruit of the Spirit can make you seem like a weakling or a coward. But this perspective is so wrong! It takes courage to be on the side of God and the truth. It takes heroism to submit yourself to God's will and to control yourself. Any coward can be a sinner, but real courage is fighting on God's side against sin.

Armed with the power of the Holy Spirit, you can face temptations and oppose them in the name of the Savior. Then you are dressed in the armor of the Spirit and you conquer in the name of Christ. "Despite all these things, overwhelming victory is ours through Christ, who loved us" (Rom. 8:37).

Savior and Redeemer, through Your power I will fight sin. Amen.

Live Through the Spirit

Since we died with Christ, we know we will also live with Him (Rom. 6:8).

Paul believed and had first-hand experience of the fact that Christians died with Christ and were raised again to a new life – washed clean by the blood of the Lamb. This is a new life in which the former things of the "I" have passed away, and beautiful new things come into existence as fruit of the Spirit. Remember that the fruit of the Spirit grows through prayer, meditation and praise. Andrew Murray said, "Prayer is the unconditional requirement for everything God wants to accomplish in this world."

> There is no human power that can replace the power of the Spirit.
> ~ Lewi Pethrus ~

The soil in which the fruit of the Spirit sprouts and grows is humility. The work must go on while it is still light, but when ominous clouds gather and it gets dark, the fruit will carry on growing in silence. Also remember the unchanging promise of our Master: "God blesses those who hunger and thirst for justice, for they will be satisfied" (Matt. 5:6).

If the Holy Spirit lets this fruit grow in your life, it is never meant for you alone. Like a flare, you must never just burn for yourself, but rather bring light to others. The Holy Spirit brings this fruit in the lives of those who obey God. The lives of the people who bear this nine-fold fruit spreads a pleasing fragrance in the world. They become an inspiration and benediction wherever they go. It can be the case with all of us, through the grace of Jesus Christ and the blessed work of the Holy Spirit.

Holy Spirit of God, I give my life to You unconditionally so that the fruit of the Spirit will grow abundantly in my life. Amen.

The Secret of Fruit-Bearing (1)

"Remain in Me, and I will remain in you" (John 15:4).

The sinner is saved because Jesus died in their place. Jesus is punished and the sinner set free. Christ, however, doesn't leave it there. He orders the saved to follow Him, to remain in Him just as He wants to remain in the lost.

What does it mean to remain in Jesus as He remains in us? Jesus' definition is, "Anyone who eats My flesh and drinks My blood remains in Me, and I in him" (John 6:56). John also very clearly says what it means to remain in Christ: "Those who obey God's commandments remain in fellowship with Him, and He with them" (1 John 3:24). "No one has ever seen God. But if we love each other, God lives in us, and His love is brought to full expression in us. And God has given us His Spirit as proof that we live in Him and He in us" (1 John 4:12-13). "All who confess that Jesus is the Son of God have God living in them, and they live in God. God is love, and all who live in love live in God, and God lives in them" (1 John 4:15-16).

> We do not need to wait for the Holy Spirit to come: He came on the Day of Pentecost. He has never left the church.
> ~ John Stott ~

To live in Jesus means to identify with Him so that our whole lives are fulfilled by Him. It happens when we meditate on Him in faith and stay occupied with Him. Then we spiritually eat His body and drink from His fullness.

Father God, in prayer I aim to remain in You, just as the Holy Spirit remains in me. Amen.

The Secret of Fruit-Bearing (2)

Fix your thoughts on what is true, and honorable, and right (Phil. 4:8).

Love and faith are the most important qualities of a life in Christ. It is a life that is always open to God and that draws strength and grace from Him. It is a life that overflows with love. Obedience is a result of this love.

If we truly love someone, we think about that person constantly. We live where our thoughts are. Jesus says we must think about Him, concentrate and focus on Him and not ourselves. We must live in His love.

The more we think of His heavenly love, the more we will become part of His love. Thus, our thoughts remain in His joy, peace, victorious faith, strength, success, health and purity. In so doing, we grow in Him more.

Remember sinner, it is not your hold of Christ that saves you – it is Christ.
~ Charles H. Spurgeon ~

By virtue of our second birth, we are already in Jesus Christ as believers, and He is in us. We must not think of ourselves as outside Jesus anymore. What is still outside Christ is the old life that we must die to. Every time the old life seeks expression through us, we must reject it. We must draw a final line across the "I" and take up the cross of self-denial. This we can only do if we are controlled by the Holy Spirit.

The new person is under the total control of the Holy Spirit. As we identify with Christ, we will experience this indwelling in our spiritual lives and we will bear the fruit that is appropriate to our conversion.

Savior and Friend, thank You for the privilege of remaining in You and You in me. Through the strength of the Holy Spirit, I will bear my cross. Amen.

The Unavoidable Condition

"A branch cannot produce fruit if it is severed from the vine, and you cannot be fruitful unless you remain in Me" (John 15:4).

To be able to bear the fruit of the Spirit, we must remain in Jesus Christ. Without Him, we have no spiritual life and we will never know the privilege of bearing fruit, with the result that we cannot glorify God.

The Spirit is essential for spiritual growth. Like water is the vital domain for fish to survive; the good earth for plants to grow; the air we breathe for life – such, and infinitely more, is Jesus Christ to our spiritual life and growth toward fruit-bearing. He must become more until He is absolutely *all*.

If we withdraw certain parts of our lives from God's dominion, we have divided hearts and divided loyalty. This creates tension. If we stay in Christ consciously, we will become aware of the indwelling Spirit in us.

> Every time we say, "I believe in the Holy Spirit," we mean that we believe that there is a living God who is able and willing to enter human personality and to change it.
> ~ J. B. Phillips ~

Thus, the main aim of a Christian's life is to consciously remain in Jesus. The crucial connection with Him must be sustained. Therefore, we must become all the more aware of our oneness with the risen Christ.

We must walk in His presence every moment of every day. Daily quiet time with Him in solitude promotes, strengthens and maintains this consciousness of oneness. Where the bond with Christ is strong and powerful, it leads to a fruitful life – a branch that bears the fruit of the Spirit in abundance.

Living Lord Jesus, let me remain in You, the True Vine. Flow through me, inspire me and bless me so that I will always remain fruitful. Amen.

Fruitful Abundance

They are like trees planted along the riverbank, bearing fruit each season. Their leaves never wither, and they prosper in all they do (Ps. 1:3).

The exceptional qualities of character in Galatians 5:22-23 don't grow naturally in the soil of the human heart: They appear only in the lives of those who are controlled by the Holy Spirit. This is clearly revealed in Galatians 5 from verse 19, where the most serious sins are listed. Contrary to this it says in verse 22, "When the Holy Spirit controls our lives ..." and then follows with a list of the most beautiful attributes.

The sins mentioned in Galatians (vv. 19-21) are the consequences of deliberate actions. The fruit of the Spirit, however, is evidence of a life controlled by the Holy Spirit. These are the fruits of a spontaneous life!

All growth that is not toward God is growing to decay.
~ George MacDonald ~

The difference between the "evil results" of the flesh and the fruit of the Spirit is the same as heavy machinery, endless toil and deafening noise of a landscape compared with a garden with of sparkling sunshine, soundless dew, the absence of effort and unbroken peace. Fruit is not artificially manufactured – it grows!

The words that describe the admirable qualities mentioned in Galatians are only different forms of love. Joy is jubilant love; peace is acquiescent love; patience is love that sways with the storm; kindness is the pleasant flavor of love; goodness is love revealed in good deeds; faithfulness is love in the arena; humility is love that carries the cross; self-control is love in training.

May the source of true love, through the work of Jesus Christ and the Holy Spirit, make each of us a fruit-bearing disciple.

Lord, You are the True Vine. Grant that I will always be fruitful and that You will be glorified in me. Amen.

November

His light on my path lets me live with hope for the future.

Jesus has been taken from you into heaven, but someday He will return from heaven in the same way you saw Him go!
~ Acts 1:11 ~

We must never speak to simple, excitable and emotional people about "the Day!" without emphasizing again and again the utter impossibility of prediction.
~ C. S. Lewis ~

We're waiting on You, O Son of God;
we're waiting for You to come!
The fig trees are already in bud; winter is on the run!
Those who believe in You and place their hope in You,
seek no form of escapism – "Come, Lord," is our expectation;
"Come, Lord," is our hope and plea.
I see a new heaven; an earth new and free;
the sea and everything that separates will disappear.
God Himself is coming to live with us. Drink from the fountain of
the water of life, glorious and pure.
As conquerors we inherit all;
and God will shine on us.
When the Lord was here on earth, He promised to come again,
but first He left for His Father's house
to prepare a dwelling place there.
And for us on earth new hope was born.
The godly future is approaching, for us to enter forever.
A wedding table is already prepared in a manner fit for a king.
Wake up, watch constantly – the end has already begun;
endeavor to work for God's cause – we're running out of time!
In the name of Him who is and was and will come again,
Jesus the Living Savior.

Amen.

En Route to the Feast

"The Kingdom of Heaven will be like ten bridesmaids who took their lamps and went to meet the bridegroom" (Matt. 25:1).

This is one of Jesus' parables of the Kingdom. No less a person than Christ Himself emphasizes the urgency of being ready for His Second Coming; that we should yearn for it and keep on praying and watching.

On the day of Jesus' resurrection, the heavenly messengers said to the disciples, "Jesus has been taken from you into heaven. Someday He will return from heaven in the same way you saw Him go!" (Acts 1:11). In this parable, the church of Christ is compared to a joyful wedding procession on their way to meet the Bridegroom. They are carrying torches and lamps. The background of the parable is taken from the Eastern marriage custom of the time. Before the ceremony the bridegroom and his friends – between thirty and sixty of them – would set off for the bride's home to escort her to the bridegroom's home where the marriage feast would take place.

The great thing is to be found at one's post as a child of God, living each day as though it were our last, but planning as though our world might last another hundred years.
~ C. S. Lewis

All along the way, friends would wait for them and the bridal couple would take the longest route to include as many people as possible. This was truly a feast! It lasted up to a week.

The procession usually took place at night and each person had to carry a lamp, contributing to the festive atmosphere. To be without a lamp was an insult to the bridegroom. When the bride and groom arrived at the venue, they were heartily welcomed. Then the doors were locked. Latecomers missed the feast!

Thank You, living Savior, that You, the Bridegroom, will come to fetch us so that we may celebrate with You forever. Amen.

The Final Drama

"Do wedding guests fast while celebrating with the groom? Of course not. They can't fast while the groom is with them" (Mark 2:19).

Allow me to introduce you to the characters in the drama of the end times. The Bridegroom is Jesus. The guests are Christ's followers. The bride is Christ's church on earth, the real church – whose members belong to God. The real church is not made of bricks and mortar; there are no books, registers or pamphlets. The church is made up of people. God's people.

What is the wedding ceremony? Let us be glad and rejoice, and let us give honor to Him. For the time has come for the wedding feast of the Lamb, and His bride has prepared herself" (Rev. 19:6-7). This wedding feast will be the greatest celebration of all time! The will be the day that Christ will come in all His glory to fetch His bride.

The Father has uttered only one word, and this word was His Son; He still utters it in eternal silence, and it is in silence that the soul should listen to it.
~ John of the Cross ~

The ten girls are those who take their lamps and go out to meet the Bridegroom: those who know about Christ and His return; those who claim to be friends of the Groom; those who want to share in the joy of the wedding feast; those who belong to the visible church of Christ on earth and who regularly hear the gospel.

Five of these girls were wise (see Matt. 25:2). What is meant by this? Simply this: that being prepared and ready for this great event is essential. What is meant by the foolishness of the five other girls? These are the people who don't plan ahead and are foolish in spiritual matters. Ask the Holy Spirit to work in your heart daily so that you will be ready when Christ returns.

With my lamp, filled and bright, I wait on Your Second Coming, O Lord. Keep me watching and praying at all times. Amen.

The Message Is Unmistakable

"Keep watch! For you do not know the day or hour of My return" (Matt. 25:13).

The message that Christ gives here is that He will certainly return. His Second Coming is the great event that all of creation is waiting for. It could be at any moment – nobody knows, except God Himself. The question is: Are you ready? Many people, even churchgoers, are caught unawares. Distressful questions are draped like a heavy cloak over the festive tables of this world: projectiles and rockets; terrorism and family murders; Satanism and sexual promiscuity; HIV/Aids and drug addiction.

The dishes of this feast have become bitter. The festive songs have become a funeral march. With His holy finger, God has written on the walls of this world's feast: Weighed and found lacking (see Dan. 5:27)! This world offers no feast, rather a dance of death.

Sin has the devil for its father, shame for its companion and death for its wages.
~ Thomas Watson ~

The world anxiously asks, "Where are things heading?" The children of God know exactly where. We are on our way to the wedding; we are on our way to meet the Bridegroom! We who are part of the festive procession, all look the same outwardly. We all have lamps, are appropriately dressed, and are on our way to meet the Bridegroom. Yet, Christ makes a division. Five are wise and five are foolish; five have oil and five don't; five are ready and five aren't; five will be allowed to attend the marriage feast and five will come up against a closed door. Are you wise or are you foolish? Are you saved – or lost?

Holy God, grant that I heed Your warning and respond to it with determination. Amen.

A Jarring Note in the Festive Song

"Five of them were foolish, and five were wise" (Matt. 25:2).

Does this also sound like a death-knell to you: "Five of them were foolish," and that while the wedding bells are ringing? Or are we just being spoilsports? The wedding procession sounds so festive – so why this jarring note? But this is Christ speaking and we dare not ignore it. If we could choose, we would want it to be different, and not spoil this idyllic picture.

We try all kinds of things to keep up the pretence of perfection. We don't want anyone to be left out, we want to include all. We want to see all ten as wise, even if it means providing bandages, ointment and crutches.

I can contribute nothing to my own salvation, except the sin from which I need to be redeemed.
~ William Temple ~

But Christ separated them. It would have been easier to just keep quiet about this part, but we dare not. Soft healers make stinking wounds. Every church that truly wants to be a church of Christ, and feels strongly about not distorting God's Word, must humbly confess its own brokenness. The church of Christ is on its way. There are ten girls with burning lamps, all of them excited and cheerful. Songs of praise resound in the night sky, accompanied by tambourines. They are calling out to one another, "We are going to celebrate! We are going to the wedding feast of the Lamb."

Everything is so sacred, so beautiful and so secure; everything is organized with precision. But amidst these joyous celebrations, a jarring note is suddenly heard in the song: "Five of them were foolish."

Redeemer and Lord, give me spiritual insight so that it will never be said of me that I am spiritually foolish. Amen.

The Difference as God Sees It

"Not everyone who calls out to Me, 'Lord! Lord!' will enter the Kingdom of Heaven. Only those who actually do the will of My Father in Heaven will enter" (Matt. 7:21).

Not all people who walk in the wedding procession of the church, who work together and join in the singing, will necessarily gain entrance to the feast. It is not so much what people say, but what they do and whether it is the Father's will – this is the essential difference.

A very real danger threatens the church: Some people simply imitate religious words and are satisfied with second-hand Christianity, without having experienced a personal and intimate relationship with Christ.

Religiously saying, "Lord! Lord!" is merely a title that a slave uses when addressing his master. It is an expression of respect or dependence, but not necessarily of love. It is an outward form of respect that has nothing to do with the heart and life.

The end of life is not to deny self, not to be true, not to keep the Ten Commandments – it is simply to do God's will.
~ Henry Drummond ~

We know the Lord, we know all the clichés, we cover all the requirements of church membership. But there hasn't been a first-hand meeting with Christ yet. Christ says a terrible thing about such people: They are fools! It has nothing to do with their minds, but with the attitude of the heart.

It is not God's will that any of us stray. God wants us to be saved and enjoy life in abundance. It is all about our relationship with the living God: about remorse for our sins, genuine rebirth and conversion to God, as well as accepting salvation through the blood of the Lamb – this is God's will.

Holy Father God, thank You for a time of grace in which we can do something about Your serious warning. Amen.

A Dangerous Mistake

"You also must be ready all the time, for the Son of Man will come when least expected" (Matt. 24:44).

It is quite scary and disturbing when you think how much the foolish girls did right: They were on their way to the banquet hall; they were not far from the open door. We could think they would all have been allowed in. They accepted the invitation, their lamps were burning; they were in the company of the wise; they joined in the talking and singing in anticipation of the Bridegroom's arrival.

They are like the people in the wedding procession of the church: in their hands they carry the lamps of a Christian upbringing, religious parents, a rich cultural inheritance. Proudly they swing their lamps of formal church membership. It certainly appears that they have every right to take part in the festivities. Who would dare call them fools? For a while their lamps burnt well. It was only when the Groom arrived that their lamps failed. In the eyes of people the lamps showed no defects; in fact, they were quite brilliant. But they were burning on the oil of the moment.

The wise Christian will not let his assurance depend upon his powers of imagination
~ A. W. Tozer ~

Yet they say so religiously, "Lord! Lord!" These foolish girls lacked nothing – except oil. And there you have the dangerous mistake made by thousands: the jarring note in the festive song!

The question God asks you personally is, are you wise or are you foolish? Are you saved or are you lost? Are you ready to enter the banquet hall or will you remain outside? Do you have the faith oil of salvation? The Spirit of God pleads with you: Make sure you have oil in your lamp. Make sure you are saved.

Thank You, mighty Savior, that You have put a new song in my heart and that I am on my way to the feast of the Lamb. Amen.

No Oil at Midnight

"Now learn a lesson from the fig tree. When its branches bud and its leaves begin to sprout, you know that summer is near" (Matt. 24:32).

One of the most dangerous sins is that of omission. People aren't always punished because of their terrible wrong-doing, but because they are guilty of the sin of omission: failing to do the good they could have done.

The Bible pronounces judgment on people guilty of omission. The man with the one talent didn't squander it or misuse it. He lost everything through omission. The barren fig tree was cut down and thrown into the fire – not because it bore bad figs, but because it didn't bear any figs at all.

In the parable of the rich man and Lazarus, the rich man's sin was not that he was rich or that he ill-treated Lazarus. He simply did not do anything to help. He didn't show mercy or compassion.

Putting off an easy thing makes it hard, and putting off a hard one makes it impossible.
~ George H. Lonmer ~

In the parable of the wise and foolish girls, Christ teaches us that the foolish girls omitted to take enough oil with them on their journey to meet the Bridegroom. Thus, their foolishness is about oil. They had lamps, but no oil. This omission was their destruction.

When the midnight hour strikes, when eternity comes or your dying hour, what is the oil you should have? Sincere, genuine faith! Only this makes you ready to meet God; it gives you access to the celebration hall and it makes sure that your lamp is burning when it should be.

Grant in Your grace, Lord Jesus, that my faith lamp will be filled and ready to burn at midnight. Amen.

Useless Lamps in the Dark of Night

"You believe because you have seen Me. Blessed are those who believe without seeing Me" (John 20:29).

Faith is the oil that provides light at midnight when the Son of God comes again in all His glory. Christ warns us in this parable that many people have beautiful lamps that make an excellent outward display, that burn brightly for a while – but fades at the crucial moment. A lamp without oil at midnight means only one thing: darkness.

Does this mean certainty of faith is a relentless precondition for our salvation? Won't I be able to slip in through a back door in the banquet hall – through church membership, or baptism, Holy Communion, good works? Faith is the oil through which the righteousness of God flows into our hearts and lives. It gives us the light by which we find the way to eternity. Throughout the entire Bible, the refrain resounds: If you don't believe, it is impossible to please God. "To all who believed Him and accepted Him, He gave the right to become children of God" (John 1:12). "So we are made right with God through faith and not by obeying the law" (Rom. 3:28).

Faith is from God, not man. Man can do nothing to earn or receive it. We are right with God by faith alone.
~ Martin Luther ~

Faith is spiritual insight. It is the eye of the soul that sees the unseen. It is the connecting line between Creator and creation. "Faith is the confidence that what we hope for will actually happen; it gives us assurance about things we cannot see" (Heb. 11:1).

Holy Spirit of God, strengthen my faith continuously until Jesus comes again. Amen.

Check Your Oil

Anyone who wants to come to Him [God] must believe that God exists and that He rewards those who sincerely seek Him (Heb. 11:6).

So who are the ones saved by Jesus? Who has saving faith? Who has oil in their lamps? To answer this question, we must first distinguish between true and false faith; between foolish and wise girls.

Misleading faith can be categorized as follows: Historical faith, when someone agrees with the historical aspects of the Bible. Yes, someone like Jesus did live; He was a good man; He died. All of this is acceptable, proven history. But it means nothing to me personally.

Intellectual faith: Agreeing with the concepts in the Bible: that the Bible is God's Word; that Jesus is the Savior; that there is eternal life. But I have never personally surrendered my life to Him. I say, "Lord! Lord!" but this is as far as it goes.

Feed your faith and starve your doubts to death!
~ Andrew Murray ~

Then there is feigned faith and emotional faith. You hear the Word of God, gladly accept it, but as soon as you get caught in the crossfire, it dies like the seed that fell on rocky ground.

Sincere faith has three essential elements: knowledge, permission and trust. God does not leave the human mind out of the equation: "You must love the LORD your God with all your heart, all your soul, and all your mind" (Matt. 22:37). To believe sincerely, you must accept that the godly truth as God revealed it in His Word is the truth, the whole truth and nothing but the truth. Then there must be trust: childlike trust that God has given His gifts and promises to you and your salvation is part of His plan. This is quiet, unshakable trust: knowing that you belong to God.

I praise and thank You, Father, that Your Holy Spirit guides me through Your Son to true, sincere faith. Amen.

A Rich Spiritual Oil Source

For His Spirit joins with our spirit to affirm that we are God's children (Rom. 8:16).

The Holy Spirit places knowledge and trust in our hearts. He is the source of our faith oil and we *must* have this oil: "For all who are led by the Spirit of God are children of God" (Rom. 8:14). The wise girls took oil with them. This good example could, however, not influence the other five girls to do the same. They knew that they didn't have the light of sincere faith; they knew that their hearts were not yet made right with God. But they neglected to give God a final yes! They were gambling with their lives and eternity, and risked losing everything.

> If the blind put their hands in God's hands, they find their way more surely than those who see but have no faith or purpose.
> ~ Helen Keller ~

God made a rich source of oil available to them, but in the end they walked in the dark because they refused God's supply of oil.

There are certain things in life that cannot be borrowed, bought or stolen. We cannot "borrow" a relationship with God; we must acquire it first hand. We cannot live on other people's spiritual capital either – we must have our own.

Sincere faith in the living Christ and His Second Coming is a personal asset that you can borrow from no one else. If you don't have it, it means that ultimately, when it really matters, you will walk in darkness.

With my lamp filled and bright, I am waiting on Your future, Savior, where I know I'll find great joy. Amen.

Sleeping Party-Goers

"When the bridegroom was delayed, they all became drowsy and fell asleep" (Matt. 25:5).

In the writings of Alfred the Wise there is a word of warning: A poor man waited a thousand years at the gate of Paradise. And then, while he dozed off, the gate opened ... and closed." Jesus Christ warns us, "Keep watch and pray, so that you will not give in to temptation. For the Spirit is willing, but the body is weak!" (Matt. 26:41).

Back to our parable: The Bridegroom and His companions are expected at any moment. No one knows exactly when, but He can come any moment.

But this is where the problem occurs: The Bridegroom is late and things start going wrong. The tension and expectation start waning and even disappear in some people. This is how it was in the early church of Christ. They were expecting the Second Coming any day. There was a pulsating excitement and a spirit of holy expectation.

> Procrastination is my sin. It brings me naught but sorrow. I know that I should stop it. In fact, I will – tomorrow!
> ~ Gloria Pitzer ~

More than 2,000 years later, the Second Coming has not yet taken place. Some people have become cynical and ask the question in 2 Peter 3:4, "What happened to the promise that Jesus is coming again? From before the times of our ancestors, everything has remained exactly the same since the world was first created."

God, however, has His own time. Some mock, but even more are asleep! This is the great danger of our times – also for you and for me. Only those who are ready and awake at His Second Coming may enter with Him!

Lord Jesus, I wait upon Your return, in prayer and expectation.

Amen.

Satan's Sabotage

You know how late it is; time is running out. Wake up, for our salvation is nearer now than when we first believed (Rom. 13:11).

Satan sabotages Christ's followers by lulling us to sleep. It is tragic that so many unconverted people carry on sleeping in their lost state – and that many Christian disciples do the same. Christ is on His way and the day of reckoning is close. Don't be caught sleeping. The Holy Spirit wants to wake you up.

Unfortunately, this parable is also an image of the sleeping church. The wise girls fell asleep, contributing to the undoing of the foolish girls. They were not supposed to sleep because they had work to do: They had to warn people and witness. You are a believer and have oil in your lamp, but are you still as vigilant as when you were first born again? Are you vigilant in Bible study, prayer life, churchgoing, offerings and witnessing?

I am to become a Christ to my neighbor and be for him what Christ is for me.
~ Martin Luther ~

Have church members not fallen asleep? Downcast, we ask one another, "Why is He taking so long?" Then we doze off and fall asleep. Every Sunday we confess that we believe Christ will come again, but there is a notable slump in our Maranatha expectations.

How will the foolish become wise if the wise are asleep? If the church dozes off while waiting for her festive future, the foolish die in their need. Come, let's proclaim the resurrection and the Second Coming of Jesus Christ with conviction until He returns!

O Holy Spirit of God, make me a faithful witness of the glorious message that my Lord and Master is coming again. Amen.

The Wake-Up Call

"At midnight they were roused by the shout, 'Look, the bridegroom is coming! Come out and meet him!'" (Matt. 25:6).

In this parable, Jesus illustrates the very real danger of "sleeping feast-goers." Peter warns us in 1 Peter 5:8: "Stay alert! Watch out for your great enemy, the devil. He prowls around like a roaring lion, looking for someone to devour."

He often devours us by making us self-satisfied and letting us fall sleep. We dare not fall asleep, *and* we must wake up from our slumber! We must be thoroughly aware of the fact that Christ is coming again! He said it often and with emphasis.

No one who really wants to count for God can afford to play at Christianity.
~ H. A. Ironside ~

The warning that Christ gives us is to stay awake; to be alert and to pray, otherwise this glorious event will come upon us unexpectedly and suddenly. It can bring us everlasting happiness or eternal misery.

The Lord comes in the silence of the night – unnoticed. He comes at midnight, when most people are in a deep sleep; when the Second Coming has been dismissed and is no longer expected; when even some of His children are asleep in church and enjoy the peace and quiet of the graveyard.

The church of Christ is not a place to sleep. It is a workshop, a factory buzzing with alert activity; watching and praying. Because suddenly, unexpectedly, like a lightning bolt, a call will resound: "The Bridegroom is here! Go and welcome Him!"

Come, Lord Jesus, come quickly! Amen.

The Messenger's Warning

"At midnight they were roused by the shout, 'Look the bridegroom is coming! Come out and meet him!'" (Matt. 25:6).

The Bridegroom's arrival is heralded by a cry. A messenger warns that He is on His way. Every time you read the Bible, you hear that cry; every time you attend a church service and every time you partake of Communion, you hear God's messenger. For the sake of your soul, listen to the message.

Each cry might just be God's last warning. He is already on His way, almost in the streets of our towns and cities. The pace will be fast because the Bridegroom is on His messenger's heels.

> Not knowing when
> the dawn will come,
> I open every door.
> ~ Emily Dickinson ~

The word *midnight* appears in the Bible fourteen times. Each time it tells of God's omnipotence to save or to judge. At the exodus from Egypt, the firstborn of all the Egyptians died, but the angel of death passed the Israelites' homes where blood was smeared on the doorframes. It was at midnight that the Philistines captured Samson in Gaza. It was at midnight when Paul and Silas sang songs of praise in prison. It was at midnight when Eutychus fell three stories to his death below because he sank into a deep sleep while Paul was preaching. Paul brought him back to life in the name of the Lord.

In the Bible, midnight always has a message of either salvation or judgment. It is always the most wonderful moment for God's children or the most horrific for God's enemies. In this world it is almost midnight. The world looks at the church for guidance and calls out for revival – and the church is sleeping! When everyone is asleep, the message comes: "Here comes the Bridegroom!" When the night is at its darkest, the Lord is near!

Holy God, thank You that You perform miracles at midnight. Grant that we will always be ready. Amen.

Comfort in Dark Times

He will wipe every tear from their eyes. There will be no more death or mourning or crying or pain, for the old order of things has passed away (Rev. 21:4 NIV).

Midnight is the time when God comforts His children. You who are in the midnight of sorrow and loss: God comes to comfort you, to change your night of sorrow into a bright day of gladness. Just trust Him, and watch and pray.

If you are in the dark night of debt and sadness, or of despair because of your spiritual life; if you yearn for deeper devotion, more holiness, more of the Spirit of God in your life; if you want to be ready for the arrival of the Bridegroom; He says to you, "Don't be afraid, for I am with you. Don't be discouraged, for I am your God. I will strengthen you and help you. I will hold you up with My victorious right hand" (Isa. 41:10).

For the fools that refuse to admit that it is almost midnight, a horrific discovery is waiting for you! You will see your lamp going out and it will become pitch-dark. In your anxiety, you will plead with the wise for oil, but to no avail! "People will beg the mountains 'Fall on us', and plead with the hills, 'Bury us'" (Luke 23:30).

The mark of a saint is not perfection, but consecration. A saint is not a man without faults, but a man who has given himself without reserve to God.

~ W. T. Richardson ~

Because of God's love, we have been given a period of grace. For how long? Nobody knows, except the Father in heaven. But what we do know is this: The Bridegroom is on His way. There is still time to fill your lamp with the oil of true faith; to wake up from your sleep. Don't delay!

Redeemer and Savior, You are the source of my joy and I devote my life to You anew. Amen.

A Tragic Oversight

"The five foolish ones asked the others, 'Please give us some of your oil because our lamps are going out.' But the others replied, 'We don't have enough for all of us. Go to a shop and buy some for yourselves'" (Matt. 25:8-9).

We can so easily miscalculate in life, and it always ends in tragedy. Human tragedy, however, is never as painful as where our spiritual welfare and final destination are concerned. The worst thing that can happen to us is to think that we are saved and to find out too late that we are lost.

"Our lamps are going out." This is a cry of disillusionment from the hearts of the foolish girls. They were sleeping peacefully, expecting to enter the banquet hall. Then they suddenly realized that they had misjudged their position. Jesus warned against this: "On judgment day many will say to Me, 'Lord! Lord! We prophesied in Your name and cast out demons in Your name and performed many miracles in Your name.' But I will reply, 'I never knew you. Get away from Me, you who break God's laws'" (Matt. 7:22-23).

Conscience is the perfect interpreter of life.
~ Karl Barth ~

At the arrival of the bridegroom, the foolish girls first had to go and buy oil. The wise girls only had enough for themselves. Each person is saved by his or her own faith. There are people who die in blessed peace because they accepted Christ in faith, and were looking forward to the day that He would return.

Living Savior, thank You that I may look forward with joyful anticipation to the day that You will come and fetch me for the bridal feast of the Lamb. Amen.

Faith Cannot Be Borrowed

"And then at last, the sign that the Son of Man is coming will appear in the heavens, and there will be deep mourning among all the peoples of the earth. And they will see the Son of Man coming on the clouds of heaven with power and great glory" (Matt. 24:30).

There are people who have walked in the bridal procession of the church of Christ all their lives. Their hands are calloused from working and their feet blistered from walking, all for the sake of worldly things. Yet their hearts have never really lived a life with Christ and His church. They don't have the oil of true faith in their hearts.

There are things no person can do for another. Accordingly, our Savior's warning is serious. What father or mother would not pay the highest price to ensure eternal salvation for their children? And how many parents have had to say, in their sorrow and helplessness, what David said at the death of a rebellious child: "O my son Absalom! My son, my son Absalom! If only I had died instead of you!" (2 Sam. 18:33).

It is not the going out of the port, but the coming in, that determines the success of a voyage.
~ Henry Ward Beecher ~

Moses wanted to die for his people; Paul wanted to die for his people; David wanted to die for his friend Jonathan. But they couldn't. There are certain things you cannot borrow from another: Grace cannot be divided up and it isn't transferable. Each of us needs our own faith oil to be saved, and be allowed to take part in the wedding feast of the Lamb.

This is why this warning of the Master is so important: Watch and pray! Be ready when the Bridegroom comes. Otherwise, you will plead in vain when you find at midnight that you don't have oil in your lamp.

Thank You, O Source of mercy and life, that I found You and received enough oil to keep my lamp burning. Amen.

Buy Oil for Yourself

We are each responsible for our own conduct (Gal. 6:5).

Each person can burn only their own spiritual oil in their own spiritual lamp. You must have personal, first-hand faith in Jesus Christ as your Savior and Redeemer. You must belong to Him through faith and by being born again. Parents cannot believe on behalf of their children; children cannot believe on behalf of their parents. God demands that we have a personal relationship with Him.

Christian church members must not be slow to witness: "Go to a shop and buy some for yourselves" (Matt. 25:9). Here the human being is cast back on themselves; on their own religious experience; on first-hand knowledge of salvation and faith.

We must be willing to give up everything to get hold of the faith oil. There must be a holy concern inside us until we have found it. We must say, and mean it, "Oh, what a miserable person I am! Who will free me from this life that is dominated by sin and death?" (Rom. 7:24).

Live in such a manner that death may not find you unprepared.
~ Thomas à Kempis ~

We must confess ourselves, "My Lord and my God!" This means we must be converted to God with a sincere heart; discover it in the Bible ourselves; hear it in our own churchgoing; confess it in our own prayers. All of this must be a personal act, an answer each person gives to God. Here, no one on earth can take our place. They can help by their testimony, but we must perform the act of faith ourselves.

Lord Jesus, make me faithful in my witnessing to those who are still in the dark. Amen.

The Shop Is Still Open

"Is anyone thirsty? Come and drink – even if you have no money! Come, take your choice of wine or milk – it's all free!" (Isa. 55:1).

At first the foolish girls were left to fend for themselves, but in the end God was their only refuge. He was the only one who could give them the faith oil. God's shop of grace has no business hours: It is always open! God's shop doesn't have any price tags either, because the price was already paid on the cross at Golgotha. God invites everyone, "Come, buy!" So is it a cheap religion? No! A thousand times, no! It cost an incredible price.

Christ had to come and live in this sin-torn world, suffer and die here. This is why Paul says, "You do not belong to yourself, for God bought you with a high price. So you must honor God with your body" (1 Cor. 6:19-20). All we need do is to accept, in faith, that which was secured for us at such a high price.

The devil's favorite tool is tricking people to put things off. Outsmart him. Do it now.
~ Anonymous ~

In the final chapter of Revelation it is written, "The Spirit and the bride say, 'Come.' Let anyone who hears this say, 'Come.' Let anyone who is thirsty come. Let anyone who desires drink freely from the water of life" (Rev. 22:17).

The only price tag God puts on His oil is this: "But to all who believed Him and accepted Him, He gave the right to become children of God" (John 1:12). If you have already bought the faith oil, praise God and don't forget to testify in time. If you are not quite sure of your oil supply, if your lamp is burning low or dying, the shop is open and God is waiting for you. The price has been paid in full. Awake, those who sleep, arise from the "dead" and Christ will light up your life!

Savior and Master, once again I praise You for Your saving grace.
Amen.

Foolishness in the Wise

"You will receive power when the Holy Spirit comes upon you. And you will be My witnesses, telling people about Me everywhere" (Acts 1:8).

In the parable of the ten bridesmaids, God gives His children a serious warning: Those who accept Him in true faith and follow Him with dedication; those who wish to be ready when He comes and who strive for a holy life, but have gradually become weak in their spiritual lives, must wake up! Wake up, because God urgently needs you to save the lost.

To follow the Savior is to participate in salvation, to follow the light is to perceive the light.
~ Irenaeus ~

Light is important throughout creation. Where there is light, there is life and growth. God is where the light is! But we take it for granted. What would happen if the stars in heaven appeared only every fifty years? Everyone would go outside at night to admire the beauty of the stars. When last did you look in wonderment at the night sky? When last did you introduce the Light of the world to someone? If you are only concerned about your own lamp, you have become foolish. The decisive moment on which the suspense line of this parable rests, suddenly reaches a climax. Someone is calling out, "The Bridegroom is coming!" All who were asleep are alarmed by this call. The great moment came unexpectedly.

Now everyone wakes up, grabbing their lamps. We cannot go out to meet the Bridegroom at midnight without light. Where are our lamps? Do we have enough oil? The foolish girls are upset when they discover their lamps are dying. "How is it possible? Why didn't anybody tell us?"

Thank You, Master, that I am not only my brother's keeper, but that I am my brother's brother. Make me a faithful witness.

Amen.

When the Oil Runs Out

"But while they were gone to buy oil, the bridegroom came" (Matt. 25:10).

How is it possible? Why didn't anybody tell us? We read the Bible; we were baptized in church, confirmed and married; we prophesied in the name of the Lord; cast out demons and did powerful things; we tithed faithfully. And now our lamps are going out! It's not fair. How can a God of love allow it?" But that is precisely what He will do. He will allow it because it is our own fault.

It must have been just as painful an experience for the wise girls as the foolish ones. You often talk about things in life: sport and politics, hobbies and issues of life. But suddenly you realize that you never talked about the most important things in life: salvation and eternal judgment! And about your relationship with God and Christ, your Savior!

He does not believe that does not live according to his belief.
~ Thomas Fuller ~

It's strange how difficult it is to speak to your own family about spiritual matters. We sometimes ask the Lord, "Am I my brother's keeper?" But you are your brother's brother! You dare not keep your witnessing from him.

Christ regards each person as so precious that He was willing to die for them. Dare we, His followers, be slack in our witnessing while it is almost midnight?

Loving Christ, You laid down Your life for me so that I would bring the good news of Your saving grace to others. Help me, through Your Spirit, to do it faithfully and cheerfully. Amen.

A Critical Oil Crisis

"But while they were gone to buy oil, the bridegroom came" (Matt. 25:10).

It is significant that the lamps of the foolish girls went out just as the Bridegroom arrived. Up until that moment, their lamps were burning fine. When we sat together in the church pews, worked together with the members of the congregation and had a good relationship with them; when we were part of the wedding procession, listening and singing together as we walked, our lamps still burnt brightly. But when the wake-up call sounded, "The Bridegroom is here!" the lamps of the foolish went out.

The cross is both proof of the immense love of God and the profound wickedness of sin.
~ John MacArthur ~

At that moment, we need oil of a different nature: true rebirth and faith in Jesus Christ. In the darkness that we find ourselves in, we cry out in despair, "Help us! Give us some of your oil. Where will we find oil? How will we be saved?"

At Golgotha, my friend, at the cross; this is the display window of God's "shop." There it overflows – not with oil, but with blood. Once it was also pitch-dark for Him who hung there, so that we could walk in the light forever. Come and kneel at the cross with your burden of sin, with your unbelief and worries, with your feigned religion. Pray while there is still time. Give yourself to God unconditionally, before it's too late.

When you get up from your knees there at the cross, and without your burden of sin, you'll sing joyful hymns of deliverance. Then the light becomes radiant in your life and your lamp will never go out again.

I didn't always wish for You to lead me, Lord; at first I wanted to control my own life, but now You lead me. I was foolish; please forgive me, Lord. Amen.

Doors Opened and Closed

"Those who were ready went in with him to the marriage feast, and the door was locked" (Matt. 25:10).

Open doors: a wonderful and reassuring feeling. The open door of our parents' home, where we know we are always welcome, is also a symbol of hearts that are open to us. The open church door is where God waits for us to shower us with spiritual blessings. This is the open door of heaven.

The gates of Paradise swung shut because of Adam and Eve's sin, but through the death and resurrection of Jesus Christ those gates swung wide open again so that repentant sinners could pass through.

It is frustrating to arrive at a closed door: the post office, the library, the bank or a shop. Think of the door of your parents' home. When they die, you will drive past that door, but be unable to enter because it belongs to someone else. Revelation 3:20 tells us about a "closed door." "Look! I stand at the door and knock. If you hear My voice and open the door, I will come in, and we will share a meal together as friends."

My heaven is to please God and glorify Him, and to give all to Him, and to be wholly devoted to His glory; that is the heaven I long for.
~ David Brainerd ~

The doors of many human hearts are still closed to Christ. His children want to open the door for Him, but as long as evil rules in that heart, it remains closed! We must open the door for Christ ourselves – He doesn't force entry.

Christ gives all of us this warning: As long as the door of our hearts is closed to Him, the door of heaven will remain locked for us. When we open our hearts to Christ and allow Him to change our lives – the gates of heaven will open.

Lord Jesus, through Your grace, I am in the Father's house again.
Amen.

A Warning from the Bridegroom

"Keep watch! For you do not know the day or hour of My return" (Matt. 25:13).

The parable of the arrival of the Bridegroom contains vital truths that Christ wants us to understand. The custom at the time was that if a couple wanted to get married, the bridegroom had to fetch the bride at her parents' home. Then he and his bride and all their friends would travel to the groom's house in a cheerful wedding procession where a feast awaited them. All along the way, invited guests and friends joined the couple. It became a merry, singing, lantern-swinging procession. They walked jubilantly through the night with their own lamp and oil.

> Entrance into heaven is not at the hour of our death, but at the moment of conversion.
> ~ Benjamin Whichcote ~

Everyone could join in the festivities but there were two conditions: They had to have burning lamps and they had to be on time. They were given a warm welcome at the groom's house. Then the festivities began and lasted for seven days. As soon as all the guests were let in, the door was locked. Then you were either inside or outside! Christ is the Bridegroom and His church, the bride. The guests are all His children on earth.

At midnight, when everybody is asleep, Christ will come. Then we must be ready, our lamps burning brightly. It's too late then to look for oil, because by then the wedding procession is entering heaven and we come up against a closed door. At present, the gates of heaven are still open to everyone. We read in Isaiah, "Let the wicked change their ways and banish the very thought of doing wrong. Let them turn to the LORD that He may have mercy on them" (Isa. 55:7).

See me coming close to You, O Lord. Let the door be opened to me. Amen.

Separated by a Locked Door

"Those who were ready went in with him to the marriage feast, and the door was locked" (Matt. 25:10).

A closed door separates: It not only shuts out, but also shuts in! Inside the banquet hall are the Lord's children. They are celebrating, and live with God in heavenly glory. Paul sees it as follows: "No eye has seen, no ear has heard, and no mind has imagined what God has prepared for those who love Him" (1 Cor. 2:9). What a wonderful privilege to celebrate with the Father and the Son and the Holy Spirit forever!

And "outside" that locked door? There it is as dark as the darkest night – eternal darkness, because it is separation from God.

If there are children that are roaming around somewhere outside in the night, far from their parents' home, the parents' hearts are deeply troubled. Your heavenly Father is also deeply worried about your spiritual welfare and He wants you to come home. He keeps calling you softly and tenderly, all the time; He stands and waits at the door of your heart.

Absence from Christ is hell; but the presence of Jesus is heaven.
~ Charles H. Spurgeon ~

Don't you hear Him knocking? Won't you open the door and let Him in, before it's too late? Otherwise, you'll have to stand outside a locked door forever. Make sure you are inside for all eternity – at the marriage feast of the Bridegroom.

Risen and Living Savior, thank You that You unblocked my ears through the Spirit so that I longingly look forward to Your Second Coming. Amen.

Your Time of Grace Passes

"Later, when the other five bridesmaids returned, they stood outside, calling, 'Lord! Lord! Open the door for us!' But he called back, 'Believe me, I don't know you!'" (Matt. 25:11-12).

God calls us and searches for us, day after day, year after year. But finally the time of grace passes. No one knows when that day will be; that is why we must be ready when the Bridegroom comes.

The foolish girls kept on putting off what they had to do and the result was disastrous. It's not that they were "bad;" they were probably no worse than the wise girls. But they weren't willing to go to any trouble to be prepared: "There's still time! I'm young!"

While we are postponing, life speeds by.
~ Seneca ~

But no one can open that closed door, because God Himself will close it. The foolish girls are standing outside that locked door. Their lamps are burning! No, this isn't a mistake. They have oil and they believe now, but it is too late. Therefore, Christ warns all of us, "Blessed are those who believe without seeing Me" (John 20:29).

What can we do now? Organize a prayer meeting? Christ predicted this last prayer meeting on earth: No church bells will ring and it won't be held in a church. But they will pray like never before, "Sir, open the door for us!" It is then that "people will beg the mountains 'fall on us,' and plead with the hills, 'bury us.' " (Luke 23:30). This is because they will see the terrible wrath of God. This is why we daren't make light of Christ's warning and must be alert and pray so that we will be ready when He comes again.

I devote myself to You anew, O Master. Make me Your instrument.

Amen.

Go Away!

"Later, when the other five bridesmaids returned, they stood outside, calling, 'Lord! Lord! Open the door for us!' But he called back, 'Believe me, I don't know you!'" (Matt. 25:11-12).

So it came about that the foolish girls were standing outside a locked door. But this is not the worst part of the tragedy at the end of time: "Oh, perhaps it was just a misunderstanding. The Bridegroom knows us. He will have the door unlocked as soon as He knows who we are. Let's pray – you'll see, now the door will open. After all, five of our friends are inside; surely they are pleading for us. The door simply must open. A God of love will never leave us standing outside. It would not be fair."

But this is the problem: Love has nothing to do with it. It is a matter of justice and we can't play the two off against each other. No, the warning is clear and final: He who was your Advocate is now your Judge.

Thus, the foolish girls stand, hoping against hope, despair gnawing at their hearts. The closed door is not the worst; a voice is still to come. God will speak the last word. This is the worst of this parable: this scathing word from eternity. Many parts of the Bible are written to comfort us and that is why it is called the Good News. But this part was written to serve as a warning.

Has this world been so kind to you that you should leave with regret? There are better things ahead than any we leave behind.
~ C. S. Lewis ~

Have you heard God's pleading voice lately and did you obey it? Or did you fall asleep without enough oil for the dark road ahead? Then you are sure to hear God's stern voice pronouncing judgment. Your Advocate is now your Judge!

O God of mercy, protect me. I want to be with You forever.

Amen.

I Don't Know You!

Having chosen them, He called them to come to Him. And having called them, He gave them right standing with Himself. And having given them right standing, He gave them His glory (Rom. 8:30).

What is the answer that the relentless voice of the Bridegroom calls out in our parable? "I don't know you!" See the foolish girls there at the locked door, in the depths of despair, their useless lamps clanging in their hands. Eternal darkness is descending on them. They were on their way to the feast and now they are overcome with disappointment. Christ is not talking to the heathens, but to His followers, and says, "I don't know you!"

Obedience is the only virtue that plants all the other virtues in the heart and preserves them after they have been planted.
~ Gregory the Great ~

But surely this is impossible, Lord? We are invited guests, part of Your congregation, of Your church. Ask our five friends inside – they will vouch for us. We just quickly went to buy oil, Sir. We didn't think You would come so soon!

"I don't know you!" Stinging words. When God says, "I don't know you!" it doesn't mean He knows nothing about you. He knows you only too well. He stood knocking at the door of your heart a long time. But He doesn't know you as His; not as someone ready for the feast. He doesn't know you as prayerfully longing for His Second Coming.

Thus, this parable ends with, "Then the King will turn to those on the left and say, 'Away with you, you cursed ones, into the eternal fire prepared for the devil and his demons!'" (Matt. 25:41). God's warning is His pure loving grace because He doesn't want one sinner to be lost.

Lord Jesus, I heard Your voice and responded, confessed my sin and received forgiveness. Praise the Lord! Amen.

The Door Is Still Open!

"The master said, 'Well done my good and faithful servant. You have been faithful in handling this small amount, so now I will give you many more responsibilities. Let's celebrate together!'" (Matt. 25:23).

Today we proclaim in the name of the Lord Jesus Christ, our Savior and Redeemer, the door is still open! God has not yet spoken His final word. He is still saying, "Come!" In His love, Christ wants to wake up those who are asleep. He wants us to enter the banquet hall with Him. He finds no pleasure in the death of the sinner, but hopes that sinners will repent and live. He would like to see us arrive with burning lamps and songs of praise and deliverance as we leave the darkness of this torn world to enter the brightly lit glory of the heavenly banquet hall.

God's letter has been delivered to you. You can accept it or reject it. "We are Christ's ambassadors; God is making His appeal through us. We speak for Christ when we plead, 'Come back to God!' For God made Christ, who never sinned, to be the offering for our sin, so that we could be made right with God through Christ" (2 Cor. 5:20-21).

Every virtue is a form of obedience to God. Every evil word or act is a form of rebellion against Him.
~ Stephen Neill ~

This devotional will probably soon be history to you and find its place among other books on your shelf. But you will have to make a decision: for Christ or against! Making no decision is deciding against Christ. May the Holy Spirit of God bring you to an unmistakable decision for Christ, before it is too late and you find yourself on the outside of a locked door!

Lord Jesus, You took my hand when I was still a sinner and gave me the eternal blessing of becoming Your child. Hold me tight, O Lord, in the glory of Your grace. Amen.

Maranatha! The Lord Is Coming!

He came to His own people, and even they rejected Him. But to all who believed Him, he gave the right to become children of God (John 1:11-12).

This past month we discussed a parable that ends with the words: "Keep watch! For you do not know the day or hour of My return" (Matt. 25:13). It is an urgent warning from the mouth of our Lord. The first time, He came to the world to grant us salvation. The second time, He will come in glory to judge the living and the dead and to reign as King forever. When He came the first time, His own people did not accept Him. Will we be ready when He comes again?

Everything that was predicted about the Messiah in the Old Testament has been fulfilled to the letter. Everything that is predicted in the New Testament about His Second Coming will also be fulfilled.

God has promised forgiveness to your repentance, but He has not promised tomorrow to your procrastination.
~ St. Augustine ~

At Christ's resurrection, the angel said to His disciples, "Jesus has been taken from you into heaven, but someday He will return from heaven in the same way you saw Him go" (Acts 1:11). One out of every thirty Scripture verses in the Bible has a bearing on Christ's Second Coming. For every one occurrence where His first coming is mentioned, His Second Coming is mentioned eight times.

Every Sunday we confess in church, "I believe in Jesus Christ ... from where He will come again." Do we really believe it? He promised that He would come again and His Word is truth. Will we be prepared for the Lord's Second Coming? Maranatha! The Lord is coming!

With my lamp filled and burning bright, I wait on Your Second Coming, Lord. Amen.

December

His light on my path lets me grow in faith.

The apostles said to the Lord, "Show us how to increase our faith."
~ Luke 17:5 ~

Faith is not the holding of correct doctrines, but personal fellowship with the Living God.
~ William Temple ~

Resurrected and transfigured Savior,
You who defeated death and will live forever,
help me never to question Your presence. Grant that it will be the
source of growth and point of departure in my everyday life.
Make me unshakable in my conviction that You are always with me:
guide me and steer my course in every moment of uncertainty;
help me to stand firm in every moment of temptation;
reassure me in every moment of loneliness –
yes, until death – when You carry me to God's eternal dwelling.
Assure me that there is nothing in time or eternity
that can separate me from Your love.
Once again give me the blessed assurance
that You have saved me;
that I became a child of God by virtue of Your sacrifice.
Thank You that Your love sustains me from day to day
so that I am able to meet the challenges of this life in faith.
Thank You for assuring me of victory over evil.
Daily build my love, hope and faith.
I bring You the offering of my life and love anew,
my obedience and trust, my prayers and my witnessing.
I do this in Your victorious name, Jesus my Lord!

Amen.

The Anatomy of Faith

Faith is the confidence that what we hope for will actually happen, it gives us assurance about things we cannot see (Heb. 11:1).

Faith is not to believe something we are unsure of, or think is impossible. Faith is being certain, confident and convinced. When faith is at work, even the impossible becomes possible. Faith is a principle we live by daily. We accept some things as a matter of course, like crossing a bridge. We believe in banks, in postal services, in airplanes and in breathing. If we are sure of something, we don't really pay attention to it; we simply accept it.

We can have faith in our emotions and then our emotions control us. We can believe in fear and this can force us into inactivity. We can believe in a political philosophy and allow it to rule our lives. We can have faith in other people and be disappointed time after time. We can have faith in God and find that He will never fail us.

> Faith is the power that moves our ship through the raging sea of this world.
> ~ Bishoy Kamel ~

In the New Testament, different kinds of faith are discussed:

Faith that justifies: This is faith that brings us into a living relationship with God by virtue of Jesus Christ's sacrifice. This faith justifies us and through it we have the right relationship with God.

Dogmatic faith: This includes everything we believe about God. The Bible reveals God's nature and being to us. He is Lord. He is love. He is almighty, omnipotent, omnipresent and holy.

Living or dynamic faith: It is according to this faith that we live day by day.

Christ, my Lord, I want to believe absolutely and fully. Help me in my unbelief and place my faith in the Rock. Amen.

Faith that Justifies (1)

"The Kingdom of God is near! Repent of your sins and believe the Good News!" (Mark 1:15).

The gospel of Jesus Christ is good news. There is obviously also bad news: "Everyone has sinned; we all fall short of God's glorious standard" (Rom. 3:23). We are born with a sinful nature and a tendency toward the wicked. Contrary to this, God is holy, just and perfect in everything He does. So it stands to reason that an unholy, imperfect and sinful person cannot be in a right relationship with a holy, righteous and perfect God.

Something must happen to a person before they can have a holy, righteous and living relationship with God. Their sins must be forgiven and they need to be justified in the eyes of God and have the assurance that He has accepted them completely.

Christians are not men and women who are hoping for salvation, but those who have experienced it.
~ M. L. Jones ~

This is made possible only because of what Jesus Christ did on the cross. God became human in Jesus Christ and came to teach people about the kingdom of God so that it could become a reality to them, both in life and in death. This is why Jesus started His public ministry with a call for conversion. This means turning away from our sinful path and turning back to God. Then we receive forgiveness and are accepted by God as His child: "But if we confess our sins to Him, He is faithful and just to forgive us our sins and to cleanse us from all wickedness" (1 John 1:9).

We can enter the kingdom of God only if we surrender our lives to God and put our trust in what Jesus did for us on the cross. He did not only speak about the kingdom, but also made it possible for us to enter into it.

I bow down in worship, Lord Jesus, because You suffered on the cross for my sake. Amen.

Faith that Justifies (2)

He was pierced for our rebellion, crushed for our sins. He was beaten so we could be whole. He was whipped so we could be healed (Isa. 53:5).

Jesus had to sacrifice Himself on the cross so that we could be forgiven. God's judgment of sin was that the sinner had to die and be removed from God forever. Heaven is a place for believers and not for sinners. No one can declare themselves righteous before God and no one can earn the kingdom of God by their own works. Someone had to take the punishment that each of us deserves. And so Christ died on our behalf. He is our Substitute who stood before God in our place and took our sins. This perfect sacrifice complied with God's righteousness.

To believe in what Jesus accomplished on the cross is to accept that He did these things for us. We are saved and given the gift of everlasting life. Thus, we become children of God's kingdom and live in a loving relationship with God, aware of the fact that He is our Father. "For all who are led by the Spirit of God are children of God" (Rom. 8:14).

Is it not wonderful news to believe that salvation lies outside ourselves?
~ Martin Luther ~

In order to be forgiven, we must confess our sins in true remorse and surrender our lives to God. Then He gives us new life through Jesus Christ. Giving our lives to God is an act of faith that leads to a new birth. He will never turn away those who come to Him. A person can only become a Christian through an act of faith. In reply to that faith, God does His work of grace and gives believers everything He wishes them to receive.

Lord Jesus, I know from experience that Yours is the ultimate salvation. Praise the Lord! Amen.

Faith that Justifies (3)

And now you have also heard the truth, the Good News that God saves you. And when you believed in Christ, He identified you as His own by giving you the Holy Spirit, whom He promised long ago (Eph. 1:13).

If you repent of your sins, confess them before God and establish your faith in Jesus Christ, God does amazing things in your life. Your sins have been forgiven; your former life is over; you become a new creation in Christ and you are given eternal life.

Christ is the only road to justification and you are saved only by faith in Him. Salvation is purely God's grace, and grace means that God gives everything to those who deserve nothing. But He gives His grace in answer to our faith. There is no other name under the sun by which we can be saved; no other savior who can put us in the right relationship with God. "I am the way, the truth, and the life. No one can come to the Father except through Me" (John 14:6).

All I have seen teaches me to trust the Creator for all I have not seen.
~ Ralph Waldo Emerson ~

We are called to live by faith as Christians. Faith is unshakable trust in God and in His promises. Faith is the experience of rebirth and discipleship. Being born again visibly changes our lives, our character and our priorities. Jesus stressed the fact that if we love Him we will keep His commandments and live in an intimate relationship with Him. Salvation and justification are a process that starts with our rebirth and continues all through our lives. It is the unceasing work of God's grace in our lives – in answer to the faith we placed in Jesus Christ.

Redeemer and Savior, continuously do the work of justification in my life through the Holy Spirit and strengthen my faith daily.
Amen.

Dogmatic Faith (1)

"For My thoughts are not your thoughts, neither are your ways My ways," declares the LORD (Isa. 55:8 NIV).

The Bible reveals to us who God really is: His character, His nature, His personality. Many people claim to have their own view of God, but they are in fact creating a god of their own making. Such a god cannot save us or answer our prayers. This is why it is of the utmost importance that we test our ideas about God by comparing them with the Bible.

God is not an idea. He is not a reason; no one can start a relationship with Him through rational thinking. Because He is infinitely greater than us, His thoughts are so much loftier than ours. It is only possible to get to know Him through the Bible. We cannot live by faith if we don't know who we believe in. God acts true to His nature, and that is why it is important to know Him.

God is not in need of anything, but all things are in need of Him.
~ Arcus Aristides ~

God is holy: That is inevitably His nature. We will never be able to describe His holiness; the closest we can get to it per definition is to say that He is complete and perfect in Himself. Therefore, He alone is worthy of our worship and praise.

God is righteous: He always does what is right. Righteousness can only truly be understood in relation to God. He is the criterion by which all our actions are judged. He cannot make a mistake, because He cannot act against His nature. If we live in harmony with Him, we are on the path of righteousness.

God is love: Even if God is always right, He always remains loving. He loves all His creations, even those who reject His love. He treats those who come to Him with tender care, and gives them the rich inheritance of His kingdom, "for God is love" (1 John 4:8).

Holy God, I live in awed thankfulness of Your love. Amen.

Dogmatic Faith (2)

The LORD is compassionate and merciful, slow to get angry and filled with unfailing love (Ps. 103:8).

God is gracious: God's forgiveness is confirmation of this. He doesn't treat us according to merit and the extent of our sin. His grace gave us Christ as a sacrifice for our sin. We can never earn anything God gives us; this He does as a revelation of His amazing grace.

God is our Judge: A time will come when we will all stand before God to be judged. Those who put their faith in Jesus Christ needn't fear, because their guarantee is in Christ who gave His life for them. Those who rejected Christ, however, have every reason to be afraid. The question is whether Christ will find faith in our hearts when He comes again: "So now there is no condemnation for those who belong to Christ Jesus" (Rom. 8:1).

> The life of faith is a continually renewed victory over doubt, a continually renewed grasp of meaning in the midst of meaninglessness.
> ~ L. Newbigin ~

Christians believe that there is a God – but the devil also believes it, and he shudders. It's not so much a matter of whether we believe, but what we believe about God, that will be the deciding factor. We know that: He is the Creator and the Maintainer of His creation. He is not an impersonal power, but someone we can get to know as a father. He revealed His character and nature to us through His Son, Jesus Christ. He is love. He is gracious. He forgives and saves those who place their trust and faith in Him. He gives those who believe in Him eternal life. He answers the prayers of His believing children.

I know for sure that Christ lives; He forgave my sins in His love. I was lost, but by His blood I now have peace of mind. Amen.

Dynamic Faith

When you ask Him [pray], be sure that your faith is in God alone. Do not waver, for a person with divided loyalty is as unsettled as a wave of the sea that is blown and tossed by the wind (James 1:6).

Jesus spent three and a half years teaching His disciples about faith. He constantly called on them to believe in God's omnipotence. Faith in the true God releases His power in our lives. His power is mightier than natural powers or energy. He is able to intervene in our daily circumstances and change situations. He is able to heal people's bodies because He is greater than anything He created.

There is a special dimension of faith that many Christians never experience, even if they are born again. Those who are filled with the Holy Spirit experience the deep inner working of God in their lives. Still, this doesn't necessarily mean that they trust the Word of God completely.

People who do not live in faith try to obtain it when they find themselves in difficult circumstances. They are often disappointed and complain. They admit that nothing is impossible to God, but don't trust Him enough to answer a personal need with a miracle. "Such people should not expect to receive anything from the Lord" (James 1:7). God expects steadfast trust from us that is not influenced by external circumstances.

Faith is not something we can achieve; it is something achieved within us by God.
~ Alister McGrath ~

There is a very definite dimension of faith that God wishes all believers to enjoy. According to the Scriptures this faith comes in two ways: (a) By hearing the Word of God; and (b) as a gift from the Holy Spirit. If you want to live in this faith dimension, you will have to accept the authority of God's Word unconditionally.

Gracious God, grant me dynamic faith through the power of the Holy Spirit. Amen.

Faith in the Word of God

"Heaven and earth will disappear, but My words will never disappear" (Matt. 24:35).

Faith is a matter of choice. It is a lie to say you cannot believe. You can choose to believe the revelation of the truth, or you can doubt it and fear. The choice is yours. When you learn to live by faith, you learn to make the right choices: to believe God no matter what.

Believers are positive. They don't despair, even in difficult circumstances, because they trust that God will act in His own time and way. People who don't put their faith in God think negatively about themselves, their circumstances and others. They can be freed from this through the Word of God. You have the choice to focus your thinking on God; to think like He does; agree with His Word, thus finding peace of mind and heart. "Think about the things of heaven, not the things of earth" (Col. 3:2).

We must allow the Word of God to confront us, to disturb our security, to undermine our complacency and to overthrow our patterns of thought and behavior.
~ John Stott ~

God doesn't want you to lead a life of defeat and failure, but rather a life of faith in Christ, so that His Spirit will influence your life. This is a liberating experience, because God's Word reveals to us what He did in Christ and what He expects from us.

Faith is a matter of choice. If the Spirit speaks a word of faith in your heart, you have the choice to accept or reject it. The Christian living in dynamic faith accepts the truth as God reveals it and applies it to his own life. "Faith comes from hearing, that is, hearing the Good News about Christ" (Rom. 10:17).

Loving Father God, I thank and praise You for the eternal Word that is the light on my path and the lamp for my feet. Amen.

Hear and Believe!

Clearly, God's promise to give the whole earth to Abraham and his descendants was not based on obedience to God's law, but on a right relationship with God that comes by faith (Rom. 4:13).

The Bible is filled with wonders of people who heard God's voice and believed what He said. Moses heard God's voice at the Red Sea. He believed and acted on the word of God and his people walked through the Red Sea on dry ground. This miracle happened because Moses chose not to be put off by the circumstances, but to believe God's revelation.

There are two important ways in which God speaks to us.

Through the Bible: Ask the Holy Spirit to explain the Word of God. Then Bible verses will be placed in your heart in a special way. Then you know that God has spoken to you.

Through the Holy Spirit: The Spirit can either speak directly to your heart or through someone else. Whereas God's Word is infallible, we must test the word of prophesy in the light of the Bible. What is not in line with God's Word can certainly not come from Him: "But one who prophesies strengthens others, encourages them, and comforts them" (1 Cor. 14:3).

> I know that the Bible is inspired because it finds me at a greater depth of my being than any other book.
> ~ Samuel T. Coleridge ~

When you believe God's Word, regardless of the circumstances, then you truly live in faith. Faith trusts God in all circumstances. It is not only important to hear God's Word, but also to respond to it: "Don't just listen to God's word. You must do what it says. Otherwise, you are only fooling yourselves" (James 1:22). If we have heard the truth and believe it, we must act on what has been said if we want to see it bear fruit.

Lord, I believe Your promises and hold on to them. Make me fruitful in Your service. Amen.

I Know for Certain

All who confess that Jesus is the Son of God have God living in them, and they live in God. We know how much God loves us, and we have put our trust in His love (1 John 4:15-16).

When you have put your faith in Jesus Christ, God makes you His child. You are in Christ and Christ is in you; you live in God and God in you; you live in the Spirit and the Spirit lives in you. Once you believe this truth about yourself, you won't need to try to believe – you *will* believe!

One can be a Christian for a long time without understanding what it means to live *in* Christ. In Greek the word *live* is in the continuous tense. It literally means "to continue living in Christ." This is what Christ expects you to do: "Remain in Me, and I will remain in you. For a branch cannot produce fruit if it is severed from the vine" (John 15:4).

Christ has transformed all our sunsets into dawn.
~ Clement of Alexandria ~

The Holy Spirit enables you to live "in Christ." It is made possible by the grace of God. You can receive nothing from God if you are separated from Christ. "In Christ" you already receive your inheritance from God's treasury. God wants you to take hold of it as your own: "We now have this light shining in our hearts, but we ourselves are like fragile clay jars containing this great treasure. This makes it clear that our great power is from God, not from ourselves" (2 Cor. 4:7). Because you are "in Christ," you have the key to this treasure house.

God's purpose is to meet your every need. According to Ephesians 1:4-5, God had you in mind when He created the world. When you heard and believed the gospel of Christ, He put His stamp of ownership on your life and gave you the Holy Spirit as a guarantee of your inheritance! What an amazing truth.

Thank You, Father God, for the wonderful inheritance You prepared for me. Amen.

Crucified with Christ

My old self has been crucified with Christ. It is no longer I who live, but Christ who lives in me (Gal. 2:20).

What is true of Paul is also true of you and me. We were crucified with Christ. At the time of the crucifixion, Paul was not on good terms with Christ. Despite this, Paul realized that when Christ died, the old Saul of Tarsus died with Him. It makes no difference who or what you were before. The old life has been crucified; Christ took you with Him to the cross and you died there with Him. God's evaluation of your old self was that it couldn't be repaired, improved, healed or made acceptable to God. There was only one alternative – it had to die!

> Crucified inwardly and outwardly with Christ, you will live in this life with fullness and satisfaction of soul, and possess your soul in patience.
> ~ John of the Cross ~

The cross was God's way of bringing this about. You were crucified with Christ so that your old life could pass away. The person you are now is not the person you were before. Your new identity is in Christ, who lives in you. Your former life could never have survived the cross. The life you live now is the life of Jesus who lives in your body. "As for me, may I never boast about anything except the cross of our Lord Jesus Christ. Because of that cross, my interest in this world has been crucified, and the world's interest in me has also died" (Gal. 6:14).

Because your former self died, you don't fit into the pattern of the world anymore; your thinking has been renewed. By believing His Word, you are enabled to know God's perfect will. God empowers you to live a new life in Christ.

I praise and thank You, Lord Jesus, that I was crucified with You and that I may live a new life in You. Amen.

Set Free from Sin

Our old sinful selves were crucified with Christ so that sin might lose its power in our lives. We are no longer slaves to sin (Rom. 6:6).

Your old self was crucified with Christ. The person you were before was nailed with Him to a rugged cross. You are inseparably bound to Christ; of this you can be very sure. You know it, not because of your feelings or emotions, but because God says it in His Word. Make up your mind never to forget this truth of salvation and to consciously live in the certainty that your old life was nailed to the cross with Christ.

Because Jesus took you to the cross with Him, you shared in His death on the cross. When He died, you died. That former life has no hold on you. You are no longer enslaved by that person. Sin is your master no more and your body is not an instrument of sin anymore: "And since we died with Christ, we know we will also live with Him" (Rom. 6:8).

The cross is seen as the saving act of Christ, but even more than this, it is seen as the final place of reconciliation between God and humanity.
~ Calvin Miller ~

"For you died to this life, and your real life is hidden with Christ in God" (Col. 3:3). Now you live in Him, and through Him you are united with God. You no longer strive to get closer to God; you already live in Him because you are united with His Son.

"He died once to break the power of sin. But now that He lives, He lives for the glory of God. So you also should consider yourselves to be dead to the power of sin and alive to God through Christ Jesus" (Rom. 6:10-11).

Lord Jesus, let me live the new life only to Your honor and glory.
Amen.

You Died with Christ

For we died and were buried with Christ by baptism. And just as Christ was raised from the dead by the glorious power of the Father, now we also may live new lives (Rom. 6:4).

Because you died with Christ, you are dead to the things that Christ opposed. You live according to the reality of this truth. You can regard yourself as dead to the power of sin. Your body no longer serves sin and the pleasure of sin will be gone.

You can now live like someone who has passed from death into life and devote your body as offering to God, because you have been freed from sin. Assure yourself often of this wonderful truth: I am dead to sin! Sin doesn't rule my life anymore!

Your former life died with Christ on the cross. Your baptism confirms that you were buried with Him. Thus, because you died and were buried with Christ, you were also raised to a new triumphant life: "Since we have been united with Him in His death, we will also be raised to life as He was" (Rom. 6:5).

Justification is an act of God by which He declares sinners to be righteous by grace alone through faith alone because of Christ alone.
~ R. C. Sproul ~

You are identified with Jesus in totality in His plan of salvation. When He died, you died. When He was buried, your old life was buried with Him. When He was raised from the dead, you were raised with Him. It is not your life anymore, but Christ living in you.

Thank You, gracious Father God, that my life is hidden in You through Christ and that Your Holy Spirit teaches me how to live this new life. Amen.

Power from on High

Since you have been raised to new life with Christ, set your sights on the realities of heaven, where Christ sits in the place of honor at God's right hand (Col. 3:1).

Christ has triumphed over all the powers of darkness. He has disarmed them and they are powerless, because He lives in you, and you in Him! His victory over demonic powers is also your victory. Because Christ defeated Satan, he is your defeated enemy. He has no hold over your life.

If you firmly believe this, you will see proof of it: "I also pray that you will understand the incredible greatness of God's power for us who believe Him. This is the same mighty power that raised Christ from the dead and seated Him in the place of honor at God's right hand in the heavenly realms. Now He is far above any ruler or authority or power or leader or anything else – not only in this world but also in the world to come" (Eph. 1:19-21).

He conquers who overcomes himself.
~ Latin Proverb ~

The same power that raised Jesus from the dead is also at work in you. It is a power so tremendous that nothing can be compared to it. It has no limits and cannot be measured. It is the power that triumphed over both death and the powers of darkness. This power works in you as a believing Christian every day: "Together as one body, Christ reconciled both groups to God by means of His death on the cross, and our hostility toward each other was put to death" (Eph. 2:16).

You are already raised to the position of victor. Because you have a part in Christ's heavenly authority, you can rule over all your circumstances and temptation, and over every evil power, through faith in Jesus Christ.

Thank You, Lord Jesus, that I may lead a life of victory through my faith. Amen.

Relationships and Achievements

Now may the God of peace make you holy in every way, and may your whole spirit and soul and body be kept blameless until our Lord Jesus Christ comes again. God will make this happen, for He who calls you is faithful (1 Thess. 5:23-24).

Those who wish to live according to faith, learn to live in line with their relationships rather than their achievements. Your achievements do not always correspond with the relationship you have with Christ. You still do the wrong things at times; you often fail in your thoughts, words and actions. This is contradictory to the type of relationship you have with Christ.

God does not ban you from His kingdom because of this. He has a plan for your life and gradually wants to lead you to a life of sanctification. God never starts something He cannot complete. While you walk the road with Him, He completes this work in you. You can believe and trust God. Even if your achievements are not as good as He expects from you, He keeps loving and encouraging you: "My sheep listen to My voice; I know them and they follow Me. I give them eternal life, and they will never perish. No one can snatch them away from Me" (John 10:27-28).

> You can never establish a personal relationship without opening up your own heart.
> ~ Paul Tournier ~

As soon as you are ready to turn back to Him in remorse, He is ready to forgive you. But the more you put your faith in the revelation of who you are in Christ, the less you will dread fear and failure. You can live as a new creation and enter into God's presence with confidence, because your heart is sincere and your faith complete.

Keep me, Lord Jesus, from counting on my achievements and neglecting my relationship with You. Amen.

Forgiven and Accepted

So now there is no condemnation for those who belong to Christ Jesus (Rom. 8:1).

God's attitude toward you is one of total acceptance, forgiveness and sincere love. Don't listen to the enemy, who falsely accuses you of mistakes and failure. This is His plan: Because you don't reflect Christ's life perfectly, Satan tries to make you feel like a condemned person – someone who has failed completely.

But there is no condemnation for those who are in Christ. You don't need to torture yourself with thoughts of unworthiness. You now live according to the truths in the Word of God, and nothing else. You daren't give way to a negative spirit: "No, despite all these things, overwhelming victory is ours through Christ, who loved us" (Rom. 8:37).

> I was not born to be free. I was born to adore and to obey.
> ~ C. S. Lewis ~

You don't need to be defeated by fear, problems or circumstances. Of all people, Paul knew what it was like to battle with problems and still rejoice in the end: we are busy gaining an overwhelming victory! "I am convinced that nothing can ever separate us from God's love" (Rom. 8:38).

God expects you to believe His Word about yourself. Lead a life controlled by the Spirit, resist sin and walk in righteousness. Live in His power and victory; know His love, acceptance and forgiveness. Look at others and yourself through His eyes.

Lord, I have received forgiveness, and in gratitude, I sing a song of salvation. Amen.

Accountability

"And I tell you this, you must give an account on judgment day of every idle word you speak. The words you say will either acquit you or condemn you" (Matt. 12:36-37).

Jesus says in today's Scripture that your words are meaningful and important. If you, for example, use words of defeat and failure about a situation, you cannot at the same time have faith in the power of victory through Jesus to change those circumstances. If you say, "I fear the worst is going to happen," you don't believe the Word that says, "We know that God causes everything to work together for the good of those who love God and are called according to His purpose for them" (Rom. 8:28).

Every time you speak negatively about fear and defeat, you are not speaking in faith: "A tree is identified by its fruit. If a tree is good, its fruit will be good. If a tree is bad, its fruit will be bad" (Matt. 12:33). See yourself as a tree. He took possession of your life, placed you in His Son and gave you His Holy Spirit. Therefore He expects you to bear good fruit. Faith originates in the heart: "Whatever is in your heart determines what you say" (Matt. 12:34).

Words without actions are the assassins of idealism.
~ Herbert Hoover ~

What kind of fruit do you bear? It originates in the condition of your heart. The good person bears good fruit from the overflow of good things in their heart, and in the same way, an evil person produces evil things from an evil heart (see Matt. 12:35).

Faith must begin in your heart and influence your words and deeds. If your heart is filled with love, you will speak words of love. If your heart is filled with hope, you will speak words of encouragement. If your heart is filled with faith, you will speak the truth about yourself.

Savior, grant that I will speak good words and that my actions will complement those words. Amen.

Things that Resist Faith (1)

You stubborn people! You are heathen at heart and deaf to the truth. Must you forever resist the Holy Spirit? That's what your ancestors did, and so do you! (Acts 7:51).

God gave you intellectual abilities. You have the ability to reason, but your thoughts are sometimes contrary to the Word of God. "'My thoughts are nothing like your thoughts,' says the LORD. 'And My ways are far beyond anything you could imagine. For just as the heavens are higher than the earth, so My ways are higher than your ways and My thoughts higher than your thoughts'" (Isa. 55:8-9).

Your feelings will often contradict what God wants to say to you in His Word, and you will have to choose between what you feel and what God says to you. Once you have learnt to subject your feelings to the truth, your feelings will change. Before you accepted Christ as Savior, your feelings dictated the way you lived: This is to walk in the flesh and not through the Spirit. Your faith must be constant because it is based on God and His Word, and not feelings. "The sinful nature wants to do evil, which is just opposite of what the Spirit wants. And the Spirit gives us desires that are opposite from what the sinful nature desires. These two forces are constantly fighting each other, so you are not free to carry out your good intentions" (Gal. 5:17-18).

Faith is never identical with piety.
~ Karl Barth ~

Heavenly Father, help me to walk in faith. Amen.

Things That Resist Faith (2)

That is why we never give up. Though our bodies are dying, our spirits are being renewed every day (2 Cor. 4:16).

Your circumstances often seem complicated and difficult to handle. Sometimes you may even feel that it's impossible to cope. If your faith is in circumstances, you will ignore the Word of God and His promises. This leads to a futile struggle and, in the end, failure. As a child of God, you must be in control of your circumstances, in Jesus' name.

The devil is God's enemy, and also yours. He is against the Word of God and will try to undermine your faith. He is the father of the lie that kills, steals and destroys. You have the power and authority of Jesus to resist him. Learn to rebuke him and reject every thought that he places in your mind to undo God's promises in your life. God is truth. Satan is a liar. Who will you believe? "For you are the children of your father the devil, and you love to do the evil things he does. He was a murderer from the beginning. He has always hated the truth" (John 8:44).

> A general rule for the good use of time is to accustom oneself to live in a continual dependence on the Spirit of God.
> ~ Francois Fénélon ~

Your feelings often contradict your faith in God's Word. But you have the inner testimony of the Spirit. No one can teach you this – you must experience it for yourself. It is far-removed from emotional feelings. Very little, if any, emotion is involved. You are just convinced that you know. You merely know that God has said something or that He is going to take action. God has everything under control, of this you can be sure.

Thank You, Lord, that You made it possible for my spirit to testify with the Holy Spirit. Amen.

Victory Over the Enemy

We use God's mighty weapons, not worldly weapons, to knock down the strongholds of human reasoning and to destroy false arguments. We destroy every proud obstacle that keeps people from knowing God (2 Cor. 10:4-5).

When you have dynamic faith it is possible for you to maintain effective authority over Satan. He cannot rob you like before. He is a thief who wants to undermine your joy, peace and faith by questioning your relationship with Christ. Learn to reject all his accusations. Stand firm against the thoughts he tries to plant in your mind. Take every thought captive and make it obedient to Christ.

Never talk defeat.
Use words like hope,
belief, faith, victory.
~ Norman V. Peale ~

You have the spiritual authority to destroy all the strongholds of negative thinking that are not in line with the Word of God – and every area in which the enemy still has a hold on your life. Pray that the Holy Spirit will indicate these areas to you and then advance on them with all the spiritual authority of Christ. After you have defeated the negative things, fill your thoughts with positives. "Be strong in the Lord and in His mighty power. Put on all of God's armor so that you will be able to stand firm against all the strategies of the Devil" (Eph. 6:10-11).

The enemy's lies are always overcome by the truth. If you stand firm in Christ, the thief cannot rob you. Use the sword of the Spirit: the Word of God. If you live close to Christ and persist in prayer and faith, Satan cannot oppress you. You have the godly authority to defeat the devil. You can gain the victory through faith.

I worship You as the triumphant Christ who was victorious for my sake. Stand by me in the battle against evil and help me gain the victory through faith. Amen.

Prayer Faith

"You can pray for anything, and if you have faith, you will receive it" (Matt. 21:22).

Reason cannot argue away Christ's above-mentioned statement: every believer's prayer will be answered by God if they only believe, and persevere. It is of the utmost importance to learn to use God's Word in your prayers. The Word is the truth and will never fail you. God keeps watch over His Word to confirm it. Thus, when you pray according to God's Word, you pray according to His will.

You need to be careful, however, that you don't lay claim to promises in the Bible without taking note of the conditions that often accompany the promises. It is pointless to stand on God's promises if you are not willing to meet the conditions involved: "You didn't choose Me. I chose you. I appointed you to go and produce lasting fruit, so that the Father will give you whatever you ask for, using My name" (John 15:16).

Our prayers are answered not when we are given what we ask but when we are challenged to be what we can be.
~ Morris Adler ~

Faith comes from hearing the Word of God. Study the Word and learn to pray according to it. Take a portion from Scripture and make it yours. Accept that God is speaking directly to you. Pray over each phrase, and ask the Hoy Spirit to let your heart absorb that passage and influence your life. In this way, you can develop a new and effective prayer method. Then the Word of God will come to you as a personal revelation *because you believe*. "Ask, using My name, and you will receive, and you will have abundant joy" (John 16:24).

Lord Jesus, strengthen my faith by the vital work of the Holy Spirit. Amen.

Praying in Faith

"I tell you, pray for anything, and if you believe that you've received it, it will be yours (Mark 11:24).

Jesus taught His disciples to pray in faith: He tells His disciples to have faith in God, not in their feelings, reason or problems! Literally, it means praying with the faith that is from God.

He commands His disciples to address the problem: "I tell you the truth, you can say to this mountain, 'May you be lifted up and thrown into the sea,' and it will happen. But you must really believe it will happen and have no doubt in your heart. I tell you, you can pray for anything, and if you believe that you've received it, it will be yours," (Mark 11:22-24).

> The reason why we obtain no more in prayer is because we expect no more. God usually answers us according to our own hearts.
> ~ Richard Alleine ~

Jesus emphasizes that when the disciples pray like this, there must be no doubt in their hearts. They *must* believe it will happen. Then it *will* happen. Christians are not called to move mountains – just to pray in faith and believe that God will answer their prayers.

Hope says: It will happen! Faith says: It has happened! Even if we see nothing concrete, we must still believe that He has answered our prayers: "Faith is the confidence that what we hope for will actually happen; it gives us the assurance about things we cannot see" (Heb. 11:1).

When you pray, it is important to forgive those who have wronged you. If you don't forgive, God will not forgive you and then it is unlikely that He will give you what you ask for. He expects you to show grace to others as well.

Lord Jesus, I thank You that I may learn to pray in faith in Your prayer school. Amen.

In Jesus' Name

Whatever you do or say, do it as a representative of the Lord Jesus, giving thanks through Him to God the Father (Col. 3:17).

To pray in the name of Jesus is to pray in the Person of Christ; to pray like He would have prayed in your circumstances, with the authority He would have exercised. Ask yourself the following questions: If Jesus were in my place, what would He have prayed? What would He have believed? How would He have addressed the problem? Through the Holy Spirit you can act in Jesus' name.

If the prayer is not in line with what Jesus would have prayed, you are not really praying in His name. You can only pray in faith if you know what God's will is. That is why it is so important to listen to what God says to you through His Word and His Spirit: "May Your kingdom come soon. May Your will be done on earth, as it is in heaven" (Matt. 6:10). There is no sin and sickness in heaven. So, it is God's will that there won't be sin and sickness on earth either. This is His wish for the earth and all its people.

A man's heart is right when he wills what God wills.
~ Thomas Aquinas ~

Jesus prayed in Gethsemane, "Yet I want Your will to be done, not Mine" (Matt. 26:39). He knew what His Father's will was, but He had to handle conflict in the flesh. He submitted to His Father's will and obediently faced up to the cross. If you know what God's will is and find it hard to accept, then it is right to pray in unconditional surrender, "Yet I want Your will to be done, not mine."

Thank You, Lord Jesus, that I may go to the Father in Your name and submit to His will in faith. Amen.

Faith that Works through Love

What is important is faith expressing itself in love (Gal. 5:6).

Paul makes it very clear in 1 Corinthians 13:2 that even if we had faith to move mountains but we don't love others, we are nothing. There is no contradiction between a life of faith and a life of love. Faith without love is just as pointless as love without faith. God intended faith to work through love, and love to express itself in faith.

Faith is a gift of the Holy Spirit. The first fruit of the Holy Spirit is love (see Gal. 5:22). When you live in faith and walk close to Jesus, you live in love, and His love will be increasingly revealed in your life. The faith life is sometimes perceived as cold and even heartless. Nothing could be further from the truth. You can please the God of love only by a life of faith. God wants to bring these two principles together in your life. You can walk in faith and live in love.

That thou art happy, owe to God; that thou continuest such, owe to thyself, that is, to thy obedience.
~ John Milton ~

God is love! Whatever He does in His children's lives, He does in love. Our faith depends on our understanding of who God is. He wants to take care of us, provide for us, protect us, heal us and fill us with Himself. He is love and He commands us to love each other like He loves us: "Dear friends, let us continue to love one another, for love comes from God. Anyone who loves is a child of God and knows God. But anyone who does not love does not know God, for God is love" (1 John 4:7-8).

Faith is obedience to God's revealed will: that we will not only know His will and agree with it, but also *do* it.

Heavenly Father, help me to get to know Your will through Your Word, to agree with it and obey it. Amen.

The Star, the Word, the Child

They entered the house and saw the child with His mother, Mary, and they bowed down and worshiped Him (Matt. 2:11).

The wise men followed the star, but then they discovered the light of the Word, and the Word led them to Bethlehem, to the King who was born, to Jesus, the Light of the World. And the wise men fell down before the Child and worshiped Him.

They understood for the first time the mystery of God who became human. The enchantment of the stars was gone. The Light of God triumphantly broke through into their hearts. Now the Child was the star, the bright Morning Star.

We must also go from the star to the Word – or, as Paul puts it, from milk to solid food (see Heb. 5:12) of worship in the Spirit and in truth.

Every Christmas we look up to the heavens: After all, the stars are around us. But they must bring us to the Word, and the Word must bring us to the manger where we surrender ourselves unconditionally: the gold of our love; the frankincense of our prayers; the myrrh of our offerings.

Christ chargeth me to believe His daylight at midnight.
~ Samuel Rutherford ~

And there we will learn that when the stars die one day, God's eternal day will dawn. Then God will no longer speak to us through the stars ... neither through the Word ... but forever and ever through the Word Incarnate, Jesus Christ, Immanuel!

Great and holy God, lead me past the stars, to the Child in the manger, so that I can worship the Word Incarnate. Amen.

Faith and Assumption

By faith we understand that the entire universe was formed at God's command, that what we now see did not come from anything that can be seen (Heb. 11:3).

There is a big difference between faith and assumption. The foundation of our faith must always be in God, in what He says to us through His Word. It becomes an "assumption" when people try to believe in God without founding their belief on what God Himself says in a given situation.

Prayer is an answer to God's initiative. Assumption takes the initiative away from God so that the believer acts on his own initiative. Consequently, the result of assumption is always disappointment.

> The purpose of all prayer is to find God's will and to make that will our prayer.
> ~ Catherine Marshall ~

Assumption acts according to the instructions of the heart and mind, while faith is obediently listening for God's will. With assumption you achieve at best a supposition. Faith gives you certainty about God's will: "But I have pleaded in prayer for you ... that your faith should not fail" (Luke 22:32).

Faith sometimes includes exercising authority. Sometimes we need to address a situation and also speak to God. Joshua did this when he ordered the sun to stand still over the valley of Aijalon. Christians sometimes fail in exercising the authority that God gave them over the forces of evil. Often it only becomes clear later that God's wisdom was greater. You will be thankful later that your prayers weren't answered in the way you thought was right at the time. God had a better plan and purpose for you. Remember, even in your disappointment, that you are safe and secure in God's love.

I am totally dependent on You, O God, and cling to You in faith. Keep me from wrong assumptions that lead me astray. Amen.

To Give and to Receive

"Give and you will receive. Your gift will return to you in full – pressed down, shaken together to make room for more, running over, and poured into your lap. The amount you give will determine the amount you get back" (Luke 6:38).

Fear and worry are enemies of faith. Jesus says you must not worry about tomorrow and other details of life. You can't trust Him and be anxious at the same time. He calls you to seek the kingdom of God and His righteousness first – then you will get all the other things as well.

Whatever you give God, He will give you much more in return. But the principle of His kingdom is that you must first give. When you were born again, God gave you His rich inheritance in Christ. If you give Him your life, He gives you His. Praise the Lord!

> You can give without loving, but you cannot love without giving.
> ~ Amy Carmichael ~

The measure in which you give is the measure in which you receive: "A farmer who plants only a few seeds will get a small crop. But the one who plants generously will get a generous crop" (2 Cor. 9:6). What is God's purpose with this? "God will generously provide all you need. Then you will always have everything you need and plenty left over to share with others" (2 Cor. 9:8).

God wants to give you abundant grace so that you have all you need and can contribute to every good work. What you receive must be made available for His kingdom. So the cycle of the believer's life is as follows: You give to God and God gives you more in return; you give even more to God and God gives you even more in return. You will never suffer loss if you give according to God's instructions.

Loving Master, You sacrificed everything for my sake. Make me willing to give Your riches to others through faith. Amen.

The Spirit of Faith

We continue to preach because we have the same kind of faith the psalmist had when he said, "I believed in God, so I spoke" (2 Cor. 4:13).

You became a Christian because God spoke His word of light over your life. Paul says, "For God, who said, 'Let there be light in the darkness,' has made this light shine in our hearts so that we could know the glory of God that is seen in the face of Jesus Christ" (2 Cor. 4:6). You were in spiritual darkness at first, but God commanded that you receive light and that light would shine from your darkness. That is His purpose for your life. Jesus said, "Let your good deeds shine out for all to see, so that everyone will praise your heavenly Father" (Matt. 5:16).

A living faith is not something you have to carry, but something that carries you.
~ J. H. Oldham ~

Scripture says, "I believed and so I spoke." His words of creation were spoken and He believed what He said would happen. In Jesus' earthly ministry, He believed that all He had to do was speak the word and the blind would see, the deaf would hear, the crippled would walk, and yes, the dead would be raised. The astounding thing that God tells us in His Word is that the same Spirit works in us. We do have the ability to change circumstances in our lives by speaking the word of the Spirit of faith.

Jesus made it quite clear that He never acted independently of His Father. If we speak His words of faith without first learning His will, we will be disappointed. If, however, we listen to the voice of the Holy Spirit who speaks to us through Scripture, we can speak things into being.

Help me, Savior and Redeemer, to speak words of life in every situation. Strengthen my faith through the working of the Holy Spirit. Amen.

The Gift of Faith

"I tell you the truth, anyone who believes in Me will do the same works I have done, and even greater works, because I am going to be with the Father. You can ask for anything in My name, and I will do it, so that the Son can bring glory to the Father" (John 14:12-14).

Whether it is defined as a gift of faith or a spirit of faith, there is no doubt that it is possible for a person to have a definite experience that brings about a number of dynamic results in their lives. This is God's grace at work in the heart and life of the believer.

In the first place, the Christian must have an intense yearning for a more intimate walk with Christ. Only then can today's Scripture come to fulfillment in a person's life. Where there is a sincere desire, God will answer the cry from the heart. Naturally, there will be testing, because it is the only way the believer can learn perseverance and hold on to God's Word. The advantages of this experience are manifold: a fresh revelation of God's Word that inspires our faith; greater submission to the authority of the Bible; determination to hold fast to the Word; a more intimate walk with the Master; a life of increasing victory; no fear of condemnation; dependence on God's grace; a vibrant prayer life; and authority over darkness.

> Faith is God's work in us, that changes us and gives us new birth from God.
> ~ Martin Luther ~

Consequently, it is vital that the gift of faith be at work in your life every day. God wants you to live in the Spirit. Plead with God and reach out for the gift of faith. Only then you will experience your prayers being answered. Take control of negative circumstances in your life and rule with Christ as His child.

Lord Jesus, strengthen the spirit of faith in me, so that Your gift of faith will be used to Your glory. Amen.

The Confession of Faith (1)

Let all that I am praise the LORD; with my whole heart, I will praise His holy name. Let all that I am praise the LORD; may I never forget the good things He does for me (Ps. 103:1-2).

David looks away from himself and fixes his eyes on God. He gives five good reasons why He should praise God: All his sins are forgiven; he is in good health; he has been saved from the grave; he has been crowned with love and compassion; and he enjoys good things in abundance. David's praise of the Lord magnifies as he thinks about God's goodness. We can only explain God's goodness if we know God's Word. God speaks directly to us, and the Holy Spirit confirms it in our hearts. Are you afraid? Read 2 Timothy 1:7: "For God has not given me a spirit of fear and timidity, but of power, love, and self-discipline." Confess the Word in a personal way, because God always stands by it.

> The Bible easily qualifies as the only Book in which is God's revelation.
> ~ Billy Graham ~

Speak the Word with God. Pray according to the Word. If you pray according to God's Word, you can rest assured that you are praying in line with God's will: "And this same God who takes care of me will supply all your needs from His glorious riches, which have been given to us in Christ Jesus" (Phil. 4:19). These riches are your inheritance because you are co-heirs with Christ. It is His will to meet all your needs. Every promise in God's Word is for *you*. Firmly believe that He will fulfill His promises.

Speak the Word of God when evil threatens to overwhelm you. Jesus did this often during His temptation in the wilderness: "'Get out of here, Satan,' Jesus told him" (Matt. 4:10). You can do this only if you know the Word of God thoroughly.

Thank You, God, for the precious gift of Your Word. Amen.

The Confession of Faith (2)

"So now I am giving you a new commandment: Love each other. Your love for one another will prove to the world that you are My disciples" (John 13:34-35).

Speak the Word of God with other believers. God wants you to be an encourager. He expects you to break free from your isolation and reach out to others, love them, forgive them and pray for them. If you love God, you must also love your brother (see 1 John 4:20).

"Teach and counsel each other with all the wisdom He gives" (Col. 3:16). You must be happy with those who are glad, and cry with those who are sad. In this way, God's kingdom and the fellowship of believers is built up by the Word. God does not want His body on earth to be divided. God wants you to be one in His Spirit; at peace with God and at peace with each other. Encourage one another with the Word of God.

> Nothing is really lost by a life of sacrifice; everything is lost by failure to obey God's call.
> ~ Henry P. Liddon ~

Speak the Word of God to the world. You are surrounded by people who don't know the Lord. They urgently need the Word of God. Ask God frequently for the right words in every situation: "When you are arrested, don't worry about how to respond or what to say. God will give you the right words at the right time" (Matt. 10:19-20).

Allow Him to lead you through His Spirit and to put the right words in your mouth. God calls you to a life of faith and obedience. If you answer the call, you will experience life in all its fullness (see John 10:10).

Holy and Loving Father God, here I am; send me! Amen.